Donna's book takes us on a personal journey through her time with Medusa, the band she was a part of in the 70s. It's a book that truly revives that rocker spirit, and introduces you to their music which began all that time ago, but is still relevant today.
— **Thomas Neil, Owner of Off The Record Promotional Group**

When it comes to getting 15 minutes of fame, or in the case of Medusa a whirlwind year and a half of touring and playing to ecstatic fans, there is often a price to pay; shattered dreams, disappointments and the realisation that there is more to life than the illusion. Finding Medusa is a heartwarming story of a rocker's life full of the ups and downs that can go with it. Concerts, albums being recorded band members falling out and how to live a normal life in between it all. If you want an insight into the life of a Rock Star, that should have been even bigger, then this is for you.
— **Darren Walker, Author of several books including his most recent, "Closing Shop"**

I've known Donna Brown for decades. And in all that time, she has never changed. She's always been focused, active, kind, and most of all driven to live each day to the max. Nothing — not severe tinnitus, not a colossal mountain, not knee surgery — has ever stopped her from achieving a goal. Which goal? Any goal, including writing a book about her incredible life. I don't know what Donna has planned next. But whatever it is, it's bound to be spectacular.
— **Barb Garber, Co-Author of Tinnitus: Questions and Answers, Editor, and former Director of Education and Communication for American Tinnitus Association**

Donna has led an extraordinary life. Her stories hold inspiration for musicians, mountaineers and everyone in between.
— **April Green, Former Advertising and Promotions Manager, Bart's CD Cellar**

Reading "Finding Medusa" inspired me to follow my dreams also! Every page made me feel as though I was on this personal and amazing journey with Gary and Donna, Which is what a successful writer like Donna accomplished!
— **Shauna Marrone, Former guitarist and vocalist of christian band, Reignbow 1970s**

Donna has written a wonderful book to read, ranging from her childhood to present day. Donna has had a life full of sadness and happiness but this gave her the steely determination to help people which then in turn aided Donna to follow her dream of playing the music she always had the greatest passion for.

Donna is an accomplished musician in her own right which led her to meet, learn and play with fellow like minded musicians. This only increased Donna's strength to continue with her life's musical dream. During her incredible journey she met a musician who became her one true love and rock, Gary. Without Gary in her life this inspiring book may not have been written.

A truly wonderful book to read!
— **Brian Mclean, Music lover and reviewer, Oswaldtwistle, England, United Kingdom**

Having read the life story of this author, I find that it is an inspiring story of the highs and lows and many trials and errors of the author's interesting life. The book takes one on an emotional trip of ups and downs in the life of the author, Donna Brown. The author's determination shines through. I highly recommend this book. It is a good read.
— **Jan Townsend, lifelong friend**

Finding Medusa is a whirlwind of a book, a definite trip! Donna Brown unfolds the events in her life and the reader is constantly thinking, "What will she delve into next?" You will be entertained.
— **Cyndi Skillings, M.A., retired teacher**

Donna's book, "Finding Medusa", is a page turner from beginning to end. There were adventures in her life from rocking with heavy metal bands to climbing the highest heights of mountains to training with renown mime artist Marcel Marceau. Donna faced numerous challenges in her life but she always got back up and forged ahead. Her book is a promise for an exciting read.
— **Georgia Rothbard, retired reading teacher and second grade teacher**

What a blessing it has been to have Donna's wisdom and patience teaching me all the basics of yoga. It is a gift I have continued to use throughout my yoga practice. My husband and I also love their music. I enjoy telling my friends about my yoga instructor gone rock star.
— **Tami Rash, Tax Director at Experis US**

Author's Note

This book represents my life story to the best of my knowledge and ability and is written solely in my own words. Some characters names have been changed or abbreviated to protect their privacy. It is not my intention to degrade or insult any of the people mentioned in my book, rather to give an honest account of all the events as they occurred throughout my life.

As I have led a diverse life with many different detours, I have tried to keep the events in some semblance of chronologic order, yet there is a considerable amount of overlapping of events as they occurred. The reason for the overlapping is due to the significance of a particular event and, more importantly, how that event changed my life. An example of this is during my high school years (1965-1969), a number of events occurred that were significant enough to be given their own chapter. The chapter on the Democratic National Convention is explained in more detail rather than listed as part and parcel of the high school years. It is my hope this will enhance and clarify the flow of the story.

Finding Medusa

The Making of an Unlikely Rock Star

Donna F. Brown

A3D Impressions™

Tucson / Minneapolis

First A3D Impressions Edition March 2019

Publisher's Cataloging-in-Publication Data

Names: Brown, Donna F., author.
Title: Finding Medusa: the making of an unlikely rock star / by Donna F. Brown.
Description: Includes bibliographical references. | Tucson, AZ; Minneapolis, MN:
  A3D Impressions, 2019.
Identifiers: LCCN 2018915298 | ISBN 9781732728561 (pbk.) | 9781732728578
  (ebook)
Subjects: LCSH Brown, Donna F.--Biography. | Musicians--Biography. | Medusa
  (Musical group) | Rock music--1971-1980. | BISAC BIOGRAPHY &
  AUTOBIOGRAPHY / Music | BIOGRAPHY & AUTOBIOGRAPHY / Personal
  Memoirs
Classification: LCC ML420 .B8175 B81 2019 | DDC 782.42166/092/2--dc23

ISBN Paperback 978-1-7327285-6-1
ISBN eBook 978-1-7327285-7-8
LCCN 2018915298

Dedications

This book is dedicated to my beloved husband, Gary, for living the story. Without his unwavering love and support, this book would not have been written.

Also to Ma and Dad for being the role models I thought I never had.

And in memoriam to Gloria Hansen, whose grace and presence is deeply missed and shall never be forgotten, and to Cindy Davis, my dear friend and hut buddy, whose passion for life and love of the outdoors lives on forever in the hearts of family and friends.

Contents

FOREWARD

I first met Donna on July 7, 1973, when she was 21. She seemed like an ordinary girl with ordinary dreams and aspirations, but when you get to know Donna, it goes much deeper than what you see on the surface.

As long as I have known Donna, she has always remarked that she wanted to write a book. Of course, I never took her seriously because we all say we need to do something, but just never find the time to do it. On February 1, 2012, she got a call from Numero Group records in Chicago about the possibility of releasing an album of songs we had recorded back in 1975. After that phone call, Donna took her book writing seriously.

What to write about? Remember what I said in the beginning, she seemed like an ordinary girl. She decided to write about her life, which was far from ordinary. I knew a lot about her, having been a part of her life going on 46 years, but when you read it, it becomes bigger than the life you know of this person.

Finding Medusa, takes you on a historical journey through the turbulent sixties in Chicago, with the music, and the drugs, as well as a personal journey through her darkest and brightest moments. Through the first Medusa and the 40 year wait it took for First Step Beyond to finally see the light of day, Medusa was secured a place in musical history. The second incarnation of Medusa1975 produced the new album Rising From The Ashes, and led to the tours from hell. Donna struggled with sickness and constant pain, but as the saying goes, "The show must go on."

She will make you laugh and she will make you cry, as she fights to get her identity back from the dark hole she called home. She muscled her way through therapy and painful flashbacks that haunted her through the years. Struggling through her nursing career, she never felt acceptance when she became an RN. The difficulty she faced with authority figures, after watching first hand, the 1968 National Democratic riots in Lincoln Park in Chicago and seeing the people she knew, and didn't know, lying beaten and bloody. Her struggles with endometriosis, the hysterectomy and the tinnitus she was left with after surgery. Fighting against the medical profession in an effort to survive and live a normal life.

Finding Medusa is a testament to anyone who wanted to give up, that there is more to life than being beaten and broken.

Finding Medusa is an inspirational book that leaves you cheering that it is never too late to follow your dreams.

Gary Brown – Lead Guitarist from Medusa, Medusa1975, best friend and husband.
Tucson, Arizona
February 12, 2019

PREFACE

We have all heard stories of how phone calls can change lives and though we want to believe this can happen to us, we may feel this is meant for someone else. I didn't think this would ever happen to me, until one day it did!

The phone rang while I was working in my home office. I was anticipating having surgery on my wrist for a torn cartilage and was focusing on that. The male voice at the other end of the line was someone from my hometown of Chicago, yet was no one I ever knew when I lived there. By the end of the conversation, the realization of what had been discussed, hit me like a ton of bricks and I knew that as of that moment, my life would be forever changed!

The phone call initiated a turn of events that transformed into a journey of self-discovery, enabling me to shed layers of past traumas and pain and emerge, as a butterfly breaking free of its cocoon, with a clearer sense of identity. I was also able to embrace my true purpose in life. Along this journey, I met some incredible people and they inspired me to not only write about the journey itself, but also to write the actual story.

The process of writing this book was also an arduous journey that took five years to come to fruition. At the onset, I felt the satisfaction of someone who has finally committed to completing the daunting, yet necessary task of sharing their life story. Throughout the writing process, what compelled me to press onward was the drive to connect with others and shine light on some difficult topics. If in my writing, I have connected with you, my readers, and given you hope in overcoming your own hardships, then my purpose is fulfilled.

A heartfelt thanks goes out to all the people who helped make this book a reality, including, yet not limited to, my husband, Gary, the members of the original Medusa: Pete, Lee, and to Kim, who is no longer alive, your memory lives on. You guys were the greatest and this journey never would be possible without you! Thanks also to the 2nd reincarnation of Medusa1975, Randy, Phoenix, and Dean for helping us get our music back out there after almost 40 years.

Thanks also to my editors, Donna Fazio DiBenedetto and Barbara Garber, who gave me the correct phrasing and grammar to tell my story, and Darren Walker, Author, for his proofreading expertise.

PROLOGUE

The door slammed hard behind me as I stood outside on a cold winter afternoon, alone with my suitcase and mom's bitter and angry words lashing out at me just moments before. "Get out! You'll never come back here as long as I'm alive!" That went well, I thought, and despite being cheered by feelings of relief for my newly found freedom, I was fearful of the realization of finally flying the coop without a safety net. I envisioned a baby bird first learning how to fly without the reassuring presence of its mother nearby. "What's wrong with you?" I said aloud. "You've waited 18 long and hellacious years for this moment, and now that it's here, you're freaking out?"

Memories were flooding my mind like slide show images in perfect staccato rhythm, recent episodes of slices of life from a typical American middle class, dysfunctional family replaying over and over again… constant arguments with Ma, Dad sitting in his chair aloof and distant hiding behind his newspaper, Ma lying on the couch with her arm over her eyes hiding from her loveless marriage, Dad getting up and walking out the door and not returning for hours. NO WAIT, DON'T LEAVE US ALONE WITH MOM, too late… he's gone… the endless screaming arguments, physical and verbal abuse, uncontrollable sobbing and pleading for Dad to return, the bleak realization of being helpless and all alone… Suddenly I was back to the present standing and shivering outside in the cold, tears streaming down my face, yet laughing at the irony of the situation.

Remembering the events of just a few weeks before with more angry, hostile words from Ma calling me a bad seed, more beatings, and belittling. Enough was ENOUGH. I could no longer stay in a chaotic and abusive home situation and needed to leave for my own wellbeing and sanity. A fortuitous job proposal afforded me an opportunity to escape and a place to live.

Now standing on the back porch, I found myself wanting to go back inside and tell her how I really felt about living in a hellish home environment for the past 18 years and just pour myself out to her, yet to what avail? Would she understand or even care? She was always in her own world of misery and depression. How could she possibly understand my teenage world, much less what I was feeling? Little did I know the events of the next few months would make me regret walking away from the house leaving a very painful past behind. Endless visions of the motherless baby bird would haunt me for years to come.

CHAPTER 1
ALL IN THE FAMILY (1956-'61)

"Family problems come in all shapes and sizes; some are short-lived and easily managed, while others are more chronic and difficult to handle."
— Author unknown

My earliest musical influence at home was my Ma. She played the piano without ever reading a note of music, and played extremely well. I recall her playing practically daily and me, age five, sitting on the floor next to her listening, absolutely transfixed. I watched her hands move gracefully over the keys and her foot rhythmically pushing the pedals beneath the piano bench, curious as to why she did that with her foot, yet afraid to ask her for fear of breaking her rhythm with my question. Every day she would play some kind of music for my younger sister, Morine, and me, either on the radio or more often on the old Victrola record player. We listened to everything from children's songs to big band music. My favorite record was "Train to the Zoo," and I listened to that song so often I sang it in my sleep. Ma's favorite music was that of Glenn Miller, a famous band leader whose music was popular long before I was born. Even though I didn't know who Glenn Miller was, I enjoyed listening to his music nonetheless. I started taking piano lessons at the tender age of five on Ma's insistence. "You'll thank me for this one day," was a favorite expression of hers, and she was right in that instance. I would play marching songs and duets during school assemblies and later on in life write a song about her, "Lady June," praising her musical expertise.

When music was playing, that meant that Ma was in a good mood, a good thing, yet she had a darker side as well. Her moods would often change in a heart-

beat, and you didn't want to be on the receiving end! One minute she was smiling
and holding me in her arms, then her mood would change and she would push
me off her lap onto the floor.

She got quite upset with me one day when she called me for dinner as I played
in the back yard and didn't want to come in the house. Let's just say I wasn't too
thrilled about her interrupting my playtime. I gave her a run for her money when
I tried running away from her, forcing her to run after me. Of course, I was faster
than her, yet she was wiser. And as I stood talking with a friend, Ma was right
around the corner and I got the beating of a lifetime for it.

One day, not wanting to eat the bowl of ice cream Ma had served, I tried hiding
in the bathroom, yet she found me and I got to eat it anyway in an unusual fashion. Suddenly the bowl of ice cream was on my head and although it was quite
the mess, I discovered a new taste sensation that day pulling gobs of cold, gooey
cream out of my hair and licking the remains off my fingers.

On another occasion, Ma was on one of her tirades. I had just taken a phone
message for Dad and was heading down to the basement to tell him about the
call. Ma stopped and questioned me about the phone call. Telling her it was someone for Dad, she insisted I tell her who it was. Sensing her rising anger, I tried
walking away from her. She followed me and grabbed my hair from behind, dragging me toward the brick fireplace in our apartment. She slammed my head into
the wall full force. All I recall after that moment was hearing myself screaming
and bellowing in anger and pain like some wounded animal and falling to the
floor, the world spinning and turning to black.

Some hours later, I awoke lying on the couch in the front room looking up
at the concerned faces of Dad and Dr. Wien peering down at me. Dad asked
me what happened and just as I started to speak, I saw Ma staring at me some
distance behind them. My head was throbbing, I felt dizzy and disoriented
and really wanted to tell them about what Ma did, yet was afraid to tell them
for fear of the consequences. When I told them I didn't know, Dad was patting
my arm trying to console me, and I noticed Dr. Wien had walked over to talk
with Ma. I overheard Ma telling him that I had tripped on the leg of the coffee
table, hitting my head on the edge of the table as I fell. I wanted to scream
out and call her a liar!

In my later teen years, I would learn that Ma was also a victim of child abuse
and in undergoing numerous years of therapy in adulthood, would eventually
come to realize that the source of her anger mainly stemmed from her rough
childhood. I would also learn as in Ma's situation, the abused person often becomes the abuser. One therapist even obtained the records of my early childhood family counseling sessions and in reviewing these documents, I learned

that foster care was recommended by the counselors but vetoed by Ma. This information helped me come to terms with the devastating effects of enduring years of physical and verbal abuse, during my lengthy therapeutic process of healing and reconciliation.

Needless to say, I was not a happy camper at home, so Ma sent Mo and me off to day camp every summer. She thought she was getting back at us for aggravating her, yet going to camp was my saving grace. Mo, two and a half years younger than me, was not a happy camper at camp and missed being at home with Ma.

The hill that lead down into the camp was beckoning to me. Climbing quickly out of the bus that transported us to Shalom Summer Camp, and with the agility of a monkey swinging effortlessly through the trees, I raced toward the hill. With gleeful abandon in the company of my fellow monkey campers, we rolled our bodies like pieces of lumber down the hill yelling and screaming like wild banshees, repeating this process over and over again. This experience brings back fond memories of roasting marshmallows and telling scary stories around campfires, and learning about poison ivy and chiggers. All this rich tapestry with deep interwoven threads running through my veins, carved deep and lasting impressions that are with me to this very day.

The counselors met us at the bottom of the hill to guide us through a plethora of activities scheduled for the day. They taught us how to make lanyards, woven cords worn around the neck or wrist for holding keys and whistles, creative flowerpots, decorative trays and myriads of other interesting art projects. We learned how to swim, to hold our breath underwater, to distinguish poison ivy from poison oak and sumac and to certainly avoid running through patches of same, which we, of course, ignored! They led us on numerous hikes and taught us how to determine different types of rocks and I gathered quite a collection of same, much to Ma's chagrin. I especially enjoyed the midnight hikes and camp-outs. We learned how to fashion sleeping bags out of sheets and blankets and I couldn't wait to try mine out.

The night was ink jet black as I ambled along on one midnight hike. Of course, it wasn't midnight, rather more like 8 p.m., yet it was fun imagining I was staying up late which was forbidden at home. Our counselors seemed to know that their seven-and eight-year-old happy campers needed their beauty rest!

Following some distance behind my fellow campers and counselors leading the hike, I gazed up at the starlit sky above me and turned off my flashlight for a few moments absorbed in the moment. Awestruck at the twinkling starlight show directly above, something awakened in me akin to a wildness I had never before experienced. At that moment, I felt totally at peace within myself and with the world. Even at that young age, I knew it was life-changing. The seed was therein planted that more wilderness experiences were crucial in my life.

Later that evening, we reached our campsite and started setting up tents and loading them with our bedrolls. The temperature had dropped, making us shiver in the cold night air. As we were settling down for the evening, a fellow camper regaled us with raccoon stories, warning us to watch out for raccoons that would find their way into our tents and steal our toothpaste. Hearing the stories gave me more goosebumps than the frigid, chilly air outside which permeated the inside of our tent. The thought of seeing a raccoon up close and personal aroused in me a combination of fear and curiosity. Unable to sleep, I fetched a small tube of toothpaste I carried in my daypack, planted it right by the entrance to the tent and promptly crawled back into the security of my cocoon. *No raccoon would pass by our tent unnoticed, I thought,* trying to stay awake with my gaze focused on the tent entrance until sleep finally overcame me.

Hearing a noise outside the tent, I awoke sometime during the wee morning hours and noticed the toothpaste was still in the same position I left it in hours earlier. Lying prone with an extremely distended bladder and fearful of being confronted by the ferocious raccoon that was waiting to attack me right outside the tent, I peed my bedroll. Wondering how my campmates were soundly dozing right next to me and how I would manage to clean my soiled cocoon, I fell back into a fitful sleep and dreamt about a raccoon peeking its furry head into the tent. Or was it a dream?

One day at camp, I noticed my whole body covered with very itchy, red bumps that I thought was just a rash. Deciding to head over to the camp infirmary, the nurse called me into the exam room, took one look at my rash and informed me I had chiggers. Having no idea what chiggers even were, she explained they are tiny spiders, similar to ticks that bury themselves into your skin and cause inflammation and possibly even spread Typhus, an infectious disease similar to Rocky Mountain Spotted Fever. I was only nine years old, so of course I panicked. But the nurse calmed me down and put a sticky paste-like substance all over me, explaining the paste would suffocate the chiggers and they would just dissolve and pass out of my body within a few days. Luckily, she was right and the itchy red bumps disappeared, yet I never did see those buggers actually abandoning ship.

I enjoyed being away from home and loved the camp activities and learning experiences, all of which played a crucial role in my life shaping me into the avid athlete and entertainer I am today. Ma must have been disappointed that her plans for spending quality time alone were rudely and regularly interrupted. Mo was very content spending time at home with Ma and they spent a lot of time together.

I preferred to spend my time with my dad rather than with Ma for obvious reasons and inherited more of his personality. Dad was easier going, soft-spoken, and somewhat reserved in his mannerisms. He was not one to show his emotions physically, yet I knew he loved me by his actions. Having asthma in my childhood, with a chaotic home environment as a contributing factor, I would have frequent coughing fits, most often when awakening in the morning. Dad often sat by my bed with cough syrup ready to soothe the savage airway spasms. Just his presence would calm and help me fall back asleep. In those days, it was thought that exercise would provoke an asthma attack, and kids with this ailment were encouraged to avoid all physical activity. I vividly recall sitting on the sidelines watching my classmates running, jumping, and playing the sports I longed to play. Ma was convinced that if I participated in any sports, I would actually choke to death.

A sign painter by trade, he worked at Walgreens and wasn't bringing in much money, yet he managed to provide for our family. He also had a second job creating signs for neighborhood small businesses and worked on them every night in the basement of our apartment complex. He fashioned his worktable from wood and had the board attached to the basement wall. Dad spent hours working on signs for his customers with me right by his side watching with fascination every artistic movement of his paintbrush or lettering pen he used. He practiced artistic lettering on white paper or gold leafing for professional door displays, the smell of the turpentine ever permeating the air. He never invited me to watch his work, nor did he chase me away. Dad's artistic impact on me led to my own expressive forays, dabbling in oil, watercolor, and acrylic paint projects in later years.

Dad also introduced me to sports, more specifically running, as he ran track in his youth. He was also a fast walker and I ran at his side trying to keep up with him. Sometimes he swooped me up in his arms and ran with me on his shoulders to the joyous squeals of laughter echoing from my mouth. Bouncing around on Dad's sturdy shoulders felt like sitting on top of the world. His influence on me considerable, he bolstered a lagging self-confidence that hindered me throughout childhood and adolescence, and facilitated a rebirth of intense athleticism in later years.

CHAPTER 2

HIGH SCHOOL YEARS AND BEATLEMANIA (1965-'69)

"Music is like a psychiatrist. You can tell your guitar things that you can't tell people. And it will answer you with things people can't tell you."

— **Paul McCartney, Rolling Stone**

Ma was always demanding that I talk to her. I was often afraid to say anything to her for fear of getting her angry. It seemed that whatever I said or did offended her for whatever reason. Ma and I just did not see eye to eye, and had many arguments over everything from my taste in music, to my future occupation. We argued over her wanting me to go to Roosevelt High School, when I tried in vain to convince her that I should go to Schurz High School.

"All my friends are going to Schurz, Ma!"

"That's too bad! You're going to marry a nice Jewish boy if I have anything to say about it!" (Wouldn't she have been surprised to learn that I ended up marrying a nice Catholic boy who was the lead guitar player of a heavy metal psych rock band called Medusa!)

My biggest musical influences were The Beatles, Hendrix, Led Zeppelin, Cream, and Jefferson Airplane. I also enjoyed listening to folk artists such as Judy Collins, Cat Stevens, Neil Young, and Arlo Guthrie. I saw these great bands in concert back in the day and feel lucky to have had that opportunity.

My very first concert was also the ultimate: I saw The Beatles at the International Amphitheatre in Chicago, during their last American tour in 1966. At age 15, I was a Beatlemaniac, and had every album, 45, photo, article of clothing, and paraphernalia that even mentioned their names on it!

So, there I was, sitting in 35th row, which might as well have been row 3,500. That's how far removed from them I felt. They looked like ants on stage, as I could barely see them throughout the throngs of humanity, much less hear them amidst the relentless screams of adoration all around me. In my hands was a photo of Paul, my favorite, taped to a piece of cardboard. The photo soon turned into the consistency of putty from all the tears I cried over it!

To me, and millions of fans worldwide, The Beatles represented a welcome change from a mostly blues saturated music scene to a refreshing new British style of rock. Their music also brought a sorely needed distraction from the overwhelming and pervasive shock, grief, and sadness over the senseless assassination of President Kennedy.

At that time, no one had ever seen or heard anything quite like them ever before, and most likely never will again. Their music spanned all generations, and their lyrics spoke volumes within every song they wrote. I, like most teens, was looking for a way to rebel against my parents, society, and anyone who looked or acted even remotely grown-up, and The Beatles afforded me that privilege nicely. Their music also helped me cope with an unbearable home life and gave me the desire to learn to play guitar. Dad was none too pleased to have to relinquish the yardstick he used for his sign painting when discovering I was using it as the neck of my makeshift cardboard guitar.

I taught myself how to play a real acoustic guitar during summer break when attending Harand Theatre Camp at the age of 17. Learning simple songs like, "If I Had a Hammer," and Row, Row, Row Your Boat" was certainly nothing even remotely similar to the hard metal-edge music I'd eventually play, but it was a start. From these early guitar beginnings, I branched out to playing folk and protest songs for hours on end in Lincoln Park during the 60s.

The Beatles looked and sounded quite different with their long hair and thick Liverpudlian accents, and they became role models big time! I vividly recall going into grocery stores and asking people where the Campbell's Soup was with a fake, yet well-rehearsed English accent. People actually thought I was from England, and strangely enough, I almost believed it as well! I felt accepted in this persona, as I never was in my own family. It was all part of "Beatlemania," the craze that swept the nation when they invaded America in 1964. None of us who were caught up in it would ever be the same.

The insanity eventually hit my high school, introducing me to people who would play key roles in my life. One day when I was sitting in the lunchroom, I saw a girl named Sue at my table talking about The Beatles, mostly John, and wearing her John Lennon hat. *"Hey, she's a Beatle freak like me," I thought.* I decided to approach her even though she was a sophomore and I was just a lowly freshie, proudly exclaiming, "Paul is my favorite!"

Sue laughed. "Oh yeah? He's pretty cool, yet not as cool as John!" She was short of stature, yet full of personality. Whenever she laughed, her whole body shook and I felt an instant likeability about her.

"Paul is better looking than John!"

"John is HOT!" The banter went back and forth. It was in that moment that we connected and were fast friends thereafter.

Whenever we met passing each other in the halls between classes, she would always pass me notes and expect me to return a note to her by the next class period. That was how we communicated in those days, through notes. It was as though something earthshaking would be occurring in the hour or so that we didn't see each other that just had to be recorded, and it was of course, all about The Beatles. Every Tuesday, rain or shine, we would walk to the Lawrence Avenue train station a few blocks from Roosevelt, and pick up at least a dozen Beatle magazines between us. My bedroom walls at home were plastered with these and more Beatle photos, as were Sue's. We also went to the local record store weekly to pick up any new Beatle 45s and albums, and I had every 45 and album they ever released in my collection. Every night without fail, I would listen to my transistor radio tucked next to my pillow with station WLS playing the top three most requested songs which were frequently all Beatle songs. To say we were "Beatlemaniacs" was an understatement. We could barely listen to their new songs without crying our eyes out or going bonkers.

In my junior year, Sue and I were hanging out in front of the school, when we saw a friend of Sue's named Jan heading toward us. "Hey, you wanna meet this friend of mine?"

I shrugged. "Sure. Does she dig the Beatles?"

"Nope, she's a Stones fan, yet, she's pretty cool." She then introduced me to Jan, a bit taller and a few years older than me. She had long brown hair, as long as mine. Jan smiled at me and we exchanged greetings.

"So you're a Stones fan, huh?"

Jan grinned. "Yeah!

"Who is your fave?"

"Mick, of course!" Jan had a habit of rolling her eyes when thinking something she was implying should be obvious.

"Cool!" Although not into the Stones as much as the Beatles, I still liked their music.

"Do you dig the Stones?"

"I wouldn't say I'm that into them. Am more of a Beatle nut, yet the Stones are pretty cool, especially Mick." Before long we were laughing and talking up a streak for hours about music and our favorite musicians. The more we talked, the more comfortable I felt being around her, and I knew I wanted to get to know her better. She had a very laid-back manner about her and seemed almost shy.

Over the next few years, Jan and I became good friends, and spent a lot of time together at her house listening to music, getting high, and going to concerts practically every weekend. We attended concerts at Lincoln Park known as sit-ins and/or love-ins (terms used interchangeably), and saw mostly local bands playing there, such as Conqueror Worm, and CTA, (Chicago Transit Authority who eventually became known as Chicago)—famous for their big brassy horn/rock and jazz fusion sound. Conqueror Worm got their start playing in Lincoln Park and landed an opening band spot for Cream at the Chicago Coliseum some years later. We sat in Lincoln Park for hours on end blasting music from our record collections, such as the first Led Zeppelin album, on Jan's portable record player at record high decibel levels. We were just biding our time, priming ourselves for bigger and better concerts than we ever imagined at the time, at some of Chicago's most infamous musical venues.

CHAPTER 3
HIGH ADVENTURES IN LINCOLN PARK (1966)

"On an incredible journey, destination unknown, soaring ever higher, my mind is being blown. Is this all real? It's so hard to tell. Could I be in heaven or could this be hell?"

— **Lyrics from "Chemical Journey," a song written by Donna Brown**

One day Sue asked me to go with her to a Beatles rally in Lincoln Park, which was to turn me on to a whole new experience and another opportunity for growth and learning. We went bedecked in our finest Beatles attire, complete with John Lennon hats, flowered bell bottom pants, pea coats, (whether it was chilly or not), and Nehru shirts, (Indian-style tunic tops that were the rave in those days). There were thousands of other colorful folks in attendance and Beatles music was blasting from every speaker. We walked together for a while looking at all the booths filled with Beatles paraphernalia. Sue met up with a bunch of John folks and they soon were chatting away, so I kept walking in hopes of meeting up with some Paul people.

I soon met up with Carm, short for Carmelita, and Sandy, who said they were Paul people and that was good enough for me. Soon we were chatting away for hours about Paul, of course! We walked over to a nearby pond where people were riding in rowboats, and Carm asked if we wanted to go for a ride. "Sure," Sandy and I said in unison and we found an empty boat, got on board, and paddled out to the middle of the pond. I was enjoying the ride and company, watching all the Beatles folks doing their thing, gazing around me at the surrounding scenery of the park, and wondering where Sue was. A nudge on my arm from Carm interrupted my reverie. "Want one?" she asked handing me a cigarette. I looked at her momentarily, then down at the cigarette and my first impulse was to decline the offer as until that moment, I never smoked a day in my life. *Well, why not, I thought. Ma won't ever find out.* "Sure," I said hoping they wouldn't stare at me as I was choking to death on my first puff. She lit my cigarette and I tried to look as if I'd been smoking all my life. As I drew on the cigarette and was engulfed by the familiar smoke I had avoided through my young years, I heard Ma's voice in my head warning me about the dangers of lung cancer and smoking with asthma. *If she only knew, I thought,* chuckling to myself. And suddenly I had a major coughing fit.

Carm looked at me and smiled. "First time?" she teased. *"Damn, she's good!" I thought hacking away, trying not to laugh.* Tears were streaming uncontrollably down my face.

"I'm OK," I wheezed as Carm's smile turned into an expression of concern. "Are you sure?" Sandy and Carm exchanged glances.

"Yeah, I'm fine." After a few minutes, I finally stopped coughing, and took a few more drags on the cigarette without inhaling this time. Thankfully avoiding more coughing fits, I started getting into the whole scene, feeling "cool" once again. We sat in the middle of the pond chatting about Paul, and smoking away the cares of the world. Suddenly, Carm handed me an even weirder looking cigarette, asking if I wanted some weed? *"Aha," I thought, "so this is the infamous weed that our parents warned us could lead to permanent brain damage!"* Sit-ins, Be-ins, Love-ins and numerous other gatherings and rallies, were as commonplace in the '60s as the mind-altering drugs that were so freely used during these weekly events. A virtual plethora of drugs were only too readily available to those free spirits and searching souls longing to break away from the mundane and see things from a different, more enlightened perspective. Amongst the most prevalent and popular drugs of the time were marijuana, PCP (aka: "angel dust"), uppers or amphetamines (aka: "speed"), downers (barbiturates), and very powerful hallucinogens such as mescaline and LSD (aka: "acid"). These drugs were the vehicles that provided an escape from the day-to-day routine and access to a more interesting heightened state of awareness. They were also a hot topic of discussion, absolutely forbidden by parents, teachers, and other authority figures, and completely illegal to own, thus making them more attractive to us kids.

"Sure," I said feeling more curious than cautious. At the tender age of 15, life was infinite, one big long experiential adventure after another, full of endless possibilities and looming eternal. *Damn the torpedoes and brain damage, I thought* and lit up with Carm's lighter.

I don't recall much about what happened after I smoked my very first joint other than stumbling around Lincoln Park, my head in the clouds, feeling like I didn't have a care in the world and that everyone was my friend. I tried in vain to look for Sue amidst a sea of thousands of faces and bodies surrounding me in the park, yet never did find her. I'm still uncertain how or if I even made it home that night. From that day on, I was hooked on the whole free atmosphere of Lincoln Park and the feeling of being high. Lincoln Park was filled with rows of trees, a duck pond in the middle of the park, and was the perfect place to hang out, tune in, and turn on.

There I stood near the pond the following week, Jimi Hendrix album in hand, waiting to meet up with Carm and Sandy again. When we first met the week before, Carm had asked me if she could borrow my Hendrix album and I hesitantly agreed. Hendrix was one of my favorite musicians, other than The Beatles, and "Are You Experienced" was definitely my all-time favorite album by him. I scanned the crowd and suddenly saw Carm and Sandy in the distance heading toward me. "Hey, man! You have the album, I see," beamed Carm as she warmly greeted me. "Can't wait to hear it!"

"Hendrix at his best for sure!" I replied handing it to her with some hesitation.

"I'll bring it back for you next week. Hey, I've got something for you!" We walked around the park for a short time and suddenly she turned to face me.

"Here, have one of these." She handed me a white capsule the size of a horse pill. I looked at the capsule for a moment then back at Carm and Sandy and saw them smiling.

"What's this?" I knew full well that it was some sort of mind-altering medication and that I was about to embark on the trip of a lifetime!

"You'll dig it, man, it's Mesc."

Carm was referring to mescaline, "a naturally occurring psychedelic alkaloid known for its hallucinogenic effects similar to those of LSD and psilocybin." It is derived from the peyote cactus and is best known for its use in religious ceremonies "…for at least 5700 years by Native Americans in Mexico and throughout South America, from Peru to Ecuador." (1.)

However, at that stage of my life, I was more interested in its mind-blowing effects rather than its historical perspective.

I stared at Carm for a few moments, wondering what my parents would say seeing me staggering in at an ungodly time of the morning stoned out of my mind. "How long does this stuff last?" I queried. Sensing my concern, Carm informed me that I would be down in a few hours. I probably should have asked her exactly how many hours were we talking about, yet at 15 you don't think that far ahead. Walking to a nearby water fountain, I slurped down the capsule without further thought. Carm and Sandy took their capsules, and then we were casually strolling off towards Lake Shore Drive (aka: LSD), a path that runs next to the park and extends for 18-to-20 miles along Lake Michigan.

We chatted while walking for hours until evening was upon us, and I didn't even realize the passing of time. I learned from our conversation that Carm and Sandy were a few years older than I, had jobs, and were sharing an apartment in the Lincoln Park vicinity. I envied them for not having to endure living with parents who weren't very cool, and made life miserable, similar to my home circumstances. "You guys are lucky that you don't have to deal with your parents anymore!"

"Hey, I dig where you're coming from. My old man smoked a lot and constantly bugged me about every little thing I did, and I couldn't stand him. The minute I turned 18, man, I was out of there!" exclaimed Sandy.

Carm chuckled. "Yeah, my old lady wasn't any better than her old man!" *OK, so their parents weren't cool either, I thought* and suddenly didn't feel so alone. Glancing out at the lake as we continued walking on LSD, I noticed the water taking on some very interesting and colorful hues. "Hey, when does this stuff start kicking in?" Carm and Sandy were suddenly laughing hysterically, and I couldn't help joining in. Soon we were all doubled over with laughter, and I wasn't sure what was so damn funny, yet it really didn't matter at that point. Glancing down, I noticed the ground was moving in waves much like the waves lapping up on the shore next to where we stood and I felt as though I were on a boat somewhere at sea. Gazing up at the sky, I saw it was dark and the air felt damp and chilly.

"Where in hell are we?" I gasped between guffaws, pulling the collar of my pea coat closer toward my exposed neck. Carm and Sandy suddenly sobered up, exchanged glances, then Carm suggested we head to Old Town and hang out there. She lit a cigarette and started walking away from the lake with Sandy and me following behind. No sooner had we wiped the tears off our faces from our previous hysterical outburst, we were back into fits of guffawing again.

Regaining our composure, we found ourselves walking down Wells, the busy main street of Old Town, a popular hippie hang-out near the downtown area. We strolled amidst the mass of colorful, beaded and bearded masses of humanity flowing down the street around us. Loud rock music was blaring from just about every store we passed, and the air was ripe with the smell of patchouli oil, the familiar, earthy smell so indicative of the atmosphere of Old Town.

We stopped on the corner of Halsted and Wells and watching the throngs of people rushing by, I felt overwhelmed by all the sights and sounds of my surroundings. Here I was in a place that was both familiar and foreign at the same time, with a sea of unfamiliar faces coming at me from all directions, contorted into weird shapes by the effects of the mescaline. I suddenly felt the impulse to want to move or scream or both, yet could do neither. Carm's voice floated toward me disturbing my trancelike state. "We are going to Piper's Alley. Wanna come?" I turned to Carm and stared at what appeared to be her face, yet it looked nothing like her face. It reminded me of the cover of an album called "The Twelve Dreams of Dr. Sardonicus," by a popular psych rock band from the '60s known as Spirit. The cover shows a picture of the band members with their faces distorted in psychedelic fashion.

Wanting to break away from the crowd, I decided to head for home. Trying to reassure them I would make it home OK, I thought finding the train station (called the "El") would be a snap. Sandy pointed behind where we stood, and wishing them goodnight, I staggered towards the El station, four blocks away. Earlier in the day, I had ridden on the train to get to the park, yet it seemed like another lifetime ago in some distant time warp. Somehow I found the station and made my way home.

Standing in the hall by the front door, I nervously glanced at my watch that flashed 3 a.m. back at me. "Oh God, I'm in for it now!" I searched my pockets for the key, and before I could turn the lock, some weird looking guy with five heads was suddenly opening the door! "D…D… DAD?" I stammered.

"Your mother and I were worried about you, Don!" he firmly replied. It's about time you came home! Where were you?"

"At the park, Pop… it's late, and I'm tired! See you later…" I told him trying to avoid looking at his five heads while making a beeline for my bedroom.

"Your mother wants to talk with you." Dad's voice echoed through space and time from another stratosphere, and I wondered which head spoke the last sentence.

I quickly entered the safe darkness of my bedroom and closed the door behind me. Noticing Mo was fast asleep, I tried not to wake her up. Hoping Dad wouldn't follow me into the bedroom, I glanced at the door and noticing it was still closed, breathed a sigh of relief. My attention was suddenly drawn to the fan blowing in the window next to my bed. The fan was throwing off some pretty incredibly vivid color traces and I couldn't take my eyes off it. *"Wow, check this out! This is cool!" I thought.*

Stumbling around in the dark searching for the light switch, I wanted to see what turning the light on would do to the fan effects. With the light on, the room and fan took on their normal appearance and I breathed a sigh of relief. Noticing my guitar lying on the floor, I picked it up and started quietly strumming some chords. The familiar melody was comforting and grounding. I kept staring at the door, hoping Ma and Dad wouldn't be barging through any minute. When they didn't appear, I was relieved. Mo stirred and mumbled a few words about me rudely awakening her, then fell back into her slumber.

"Yeah!" was all I could say at the moment and turned back to strum my guitar. The clock on the nightstand glared 4 a.m., and I knew I should be getting ready to crash, but I wasn't tired in the least. Tomorrow was already today and yeah, it would be a long day and an even longer night. At least I didn't have to worry about going to school on Sunday. Turning the light switch off brought back the darkness of a sleepless night and total immersion in the multi-colored Kaleidoscope light show emanating from the fan.

The next morning, I was aroused from a deep slumber by someone shaking me. "Get up now, young lady, I need to talk to you!" Ma yelled at me, my groggy, sleep-deprived brain trying to process what she was saying.

"Give me a few minutes, Ma, OK?" I pulled the covers over my head in attempt to shut out the inevitable backlash from yesterday's drug-induced escapade, when the covers were pulled off the bed. "GET UP NOW!!!" Ma yelled, the tone of her voice somewhere off the tolerable decibel chart. Wincing at the thought of having yet another encounter with my enraged mother, I dragged my weary body into a seated position on the bed and returned her angry glare.

"Where the hell were you last night?" she demanded.

"At the park, like I told Dad."

"What were you doing there?"

"I was hanging out with a few friends."

"Who are these so-called friends and what were you doing with them?" her voice cranking up another notch.

"Ma, like I said, I was hanging out with some friends I met at the park, that's all."

"You have to stay out all night with these friends while your father and I are worried sick about you? Do you know what can happen to young girls that stay out all night?" Before I could reply, she added, "You could have at least called to let us know where you were!" I wanted to scream back at her to leave me alone, yet knew in my heart she was right, and resigned myself to whatever fate was in store for me.

"Ma…" I stammered searching for words to express how I was feeling, knowing it was futile to try to get her to understand. "I'm sorry I didn't call, yet I was in the park and not around any phones, and I was really OK and was just having a good time with my friends, OK?"

"Are these your boyfriends?" her tone of voice now accusatory.

"No, Ma, they are girls, Carm and Sandy! Get off my back!"

"Where do these girls live, and why do their parents let them stay out so late?" the endless interrogation continued and I remained silent and sullen throughout.

I was relieved when Dad came into the room bringing Ma's tirade to an end.

"Do you have anything to say to her?" she turned to face him with hands on her hips. Dad glanced at me with a stern expression on his face.

"I think you know why we are angry at you, but enough has been said already. Your mother and I have decided you are not allowed to go to the park for the next few weeks."

"How about for the next week, Pop?" I pleaded.

"You'll not be allowed out of the house for the next two weeks, except for school, is that understood?" Dad was firm with imposing his sentence. I felt disappointed being grounded, yet breathed a sigh of relief when they finally left the room. Ma, Dad, and Mo went out shopping, and I promptly pulled the covers over my head for a few more blissful hours of sleep.

The next day I was up early and after eating the remainder of the fried noodles and just about every food available in the fridge, headed off to school. Sue greeted me in the hall between first and second period class with her usual note and comment, "Hey, man, how was your weekend?"

"Oh, nothing special… Man, I saw some pretty cool stuff!"

"Oh yeah? Like what?"

I pulled her to the side of the hall and whispered in her ear, "Like doing Mesc!" She stared intently at me.

"No way!"

"Way!"

"Where did you get it?"

"At the park." It was only a few days ago, yet seemed like an eternity had passed since then.

"No shit! How was it?"

"Pretty intense, man! Stayed up all night tripping my fucking brains out!"

"Dondi's a hippie!" Her whole body shook with laughter. Whenever she called me by my nickname, I knew she was meaning it. I guess, in her eyes I passed that critical juncture of graduating from flower child to the next level of heightened awareness. To the best of my recollection, Sue hadn't yet been turned on, although she was to take that road soon enough. "What did your parents say?"

"Grounded."

"Bummer, man. For how long?"

"Forever! Two weeks."

"Bummer, yeah that's like forever."

"Yeah, no shit!"

"Well, we better get off to class. Let's talk later. Write me a note, OK?"

I nodded and watched Sue rush off and disappear into the endless stream of students in the hallway. Heading down the hall toward class, I pondered my new experiences of getting high, making new friends and about the phenomenal Beatles. Schoolwork would just have to wait, and there was a plethora of great musical and other distractions ready to serve that purpose.

A few weeks later, after serving Dad's grounding sentence, I headed back to Lincoln Park to find solace from the chaos at home in the forms of playing music, seeing friends, especially Carm and Sandy, and of course, expanding my mind. One sunny summer day, I accepted a hit of acid offered by a friend I had just jammed with moments before. Taking my first LSD trip was a bit frightening with all the hype of it leading to brain and chromosomal damage, and I stood there for a few seconds pondering my dilemma. Keeping true to my insatiable curiosity for drug experimentation, I quickly swallowed the multicolored tablet and continued on my meanderings around the park. Sometime thereafter, feeling mellow and sleepy, I lay down on the ground in the shade of a nearby Elm tree for what I thought would be a quick nap. Before closing my eyes, I gazed up at the brilliant blue, cloudless sky above me and was awestruck by the incredible scenario and presence that suddenly overcame me. It wasn't only the vision of the tree branches appearing above me with crystal clarity outlined against the sky that astounded me. It was more the overwhelming presence I felt and with it a sense of calmness and profound peace I had never previously experienced. The realization of what I saw and felt that day was intense and absolute. In that moment in time, I felt the face of God shining down on me. I was not aware of the passing of time and lie there transfixed and motionless for the better part of the day and night, coming down from my trip in the wee morning hours, sometime before dawn. So intense the incident, I don't recall how or if I made it back home. The memory remained until years later I finally, with a bit of coaxing from Gary, wrote a song about it called "Chemical Journey," to start off this chapter. I look back at those carefree days with fond reflections and a sense of longing for the comradery, the community, the good vibes, drugs, and of course, the music from that era that is unparalleled.

CHAPTER 4
ELECTRIC THEATRE DAYS (1968-'69)

"The things which the child loves remain in the domain of the heart until old age. The most beautiful thing in life is that our souls remain over the places where we once enjoyed ourselves."
— Kahlil Gibran

The Electric Theatre (called simply "the Theater") was one of Chicago's most famous and memorable venues for legendary concerts by truly legendary bands. That's where Jan and I saw Led Zeppelin, Ten Years After, Jethro Tull, Steppenwolf, and the majestic Moody Blues. It used to be called The Rainbo Gardens and was originally a dance hall, ice rink, and even bowling alley depending on the time frame, until Aaron Russo, a music promoter from New York, took it over in April 1968, and turned it into the "Fillmore" of Chicago. In addition to the above-mentioned bands, we saw Jeff Beck, Iron Butterfly, Spirit, Country Joe & The Fish, Procol Harum, Fever Tree, Canned Heat, Blood, Sweat & Tears, Rotary Connection, Spencer Davis, Deep Purple, and Santana there, for only a five dollar admission. Although I couldn't have known it at the time, these concerts would go down in musical history as being some of the best music the world would ever play witness to. Unfortunately, a fire destroyed the Theatre and forced it to close in November 1969.

Jan was 19 and I was a few years behind at 17 by this time. Still not dating much, we decided to spend New Year's Eve at the Theatre in 1968 celebrating the arrival of the New Year in fine fashion. The roster for that evening included some musical heavyweights: The Byrds, a very down and dirty bluesy Fleetwood Mac before the addition of Stevie Nicks and Christine McVie, and Muddy Waters. In those days, it was standard fare to have at least three big name bands play all on the same night, much to the delight of thousands of us avid fans. Before the concert, Jan and I were at her house listening to a Byrds album, "Mr. Tambourine Man" and getting stoned on uppers and downers. By the time we got to the Theatre, we were feeling no pain. The atmosphere was similar to a nightclub, smoky and dimly lit, yet there the similarity ended. The huge room where the bands played was filled with constantly changing multi-colored lights ricocheting off walls and a large screen behind the stage that glowed with dancing bright oil-based amoeba-shaped images. Our senses were bombarded from every direction. I imagine the environment would be chaotic for a person in their natural state of mind, let alone for someone who is high. Yet there was a grounding sense of community when we walked on the smooth hard wooden floor and blended in with the thousands of people dancing, sitting, and grooving on that same floor. The smell of incense and pot permeated the room.

Jan and I spent some time sitting in one of the meditation domes—large cylindrical structures that people could go into to do their thing on the carpeted floor in the middle of the dome. Not surprisingly, folks weren't exactly meditating in the domes. It was more like getting high. I had also heard rumors about kids having sex in the domes, which might be why police raids closed the Theatre on several occasions.

We headed back to the concert area when Fleetwood Mac hit the stage. Sitting on the floor, eagerly awaiting The Byrds, I listened to Fleetwood. I sprang to my feet and started dancing. Just moments before, I was feeling mellow and grooving on the effects of the downers, and then the uppers took over and I was dancing like a wild woman! Jan was sitting on the floor smoking a cigarette, and I wondered how she could be so calm. The Byrds finally came on stage at midnight and played "Mr. Tambourine Man" and "Eight Miles High," both favorite songs of mine. Jan and I were on our feet for the rest of their set, immersed in their timeless music. We grooved the night away well into the next morning's New Year.

Another favorite band, Blue Cheer, played at the Theatre that same year, with a heart pounding, hard driving beat that almost defies description. Watching them play was the easy part. Listening to them play their raw and raucous blend of blues and hard rock blaring away at eardrum shattering volumes was mind-blowing. The first set of chords from Leigh Stephens' guitar felt as if they punched me square in the face with the force of a sledgehammer. Blue Cheer played so intensely loud, the drummer had to nail his drums to the floor so they wouldn't fly right out the door. Their songs have been labeled as predecessors to heavy metal music, and I would agree that their music aptly fits the bill.

Sometime in 1969, I saw Led Zeppelin at the Theatre (by then known as Kinetic Playground), during their first American Tour. Also on the bill for that night were Jethro Tull, Savoy Brown, and The Litter. I was familiar with The Litter, a local psychedelic band, yet not so much with Savoy Brown or Tull. After seeing Tull, I became a lifelong fan. The crowds waiting to get in to see the show were backed up around the block. By the time I finally got in the door, Zeppelin had already started. Frantically pushing and shoving my way through throngs of people standing outside the large concert hall, I barely saw the top of Robert Plant's blonde, curly hair. The place was packed! I had to stand on my toes just to be able to breathe. The volume of the music was even louder than Ma in her worst yelling tirades, yet I was in seventh heaven listening to Plant sing the lyrics to songs that I could sing in my sleep! Their music was ballsy, high powered, in-your-face and unmistakably Zeppelin, with John Bonham pounding out the rock-solid drumbeat, thundering bass lines played by John Paul Jones, and of course, some inventive and lightning fast guitar riffs from the infamous Jimmy Page. The music played on well into the night, yet not nearly long enough for me.

In October of 1969, Sue, Jan and I went to see Santana, Albert King, and BB King at the Kinetic. Sue and Jan had already graduated from Roosevelt and by then Sue had also "turned on" to smoking pot and doing other mind-altering psychedelics. Before the concert, Sue did some acid, and Jan and I did psilocybin (magic mushrooms) instead. Doing some sort of sinful psychedelic became our weekly routine, and we were tripping our brains out by the time we got to the Kinetic. Jan and I watched Santana for a little while but spent most of our time in the bathroom watching Sue retch her guts out -- most likely from strychnine in the acid she took. This was her routine at practically all of the concerts we attended. Jan and I took turns checking on her in the stall.

When Sue started to feel a little better we joined her on a bench in the bathroom and watched all the colorful folks pile in and out. One lady came in, looked around at the green walls and made a classic observation, "Wow, man! This bathroom is GREEN!!!"

"No shit!" I yelled.

We started laughing at this lady's comment, despite dirty looks from her. Soon we were crying from laughing so hard. There was no stopping the laughter. We managed to take breaks every now and then to leave our cocoon and see glimpses of the legendary "Kings" of The Blues, BB and Albert. By the time we made it back to Jan's house, it was well into the wee morning hours. We crashed there with visions of flashing strobe lights and loud musical refrains dancing in our heads.

The Auditorium Theatre was another popular concert venue located in the downtown Chicago area. At one time it housed the Chicago Symphony Orchestra, but was forced to close during the Great Depression. In October 1967, it reopened and eventually became one of Chicago's premier rock venues, hosting many notable rock legends including Jimi Hendrix and the Grateful Dead. (2)

I had a chance to see Jimi Hendrix there on August 10, 1968, and was blown away by the sheer power of his music. Soft Machine were the show openers and set the mood for the evening with their mind-blowing light show and discordant sound effects that penetrated the darkness of the Theatre. When the curtain finally opened, Hendrix did not disappoint. Bathed in a sultry purple light, Hendrix emanated a persona so powerful, you knew you were in the presence of greatness. From the opening chords of his first song, "Are You Experienced," he took everyone in the audience on an incredible trip through time and space.

Transfixed by his onstage theatrics, (e.g., setting his guitar on fire and smashing it to bits into his amp), his mere presence onstage was a sight to behold and a force to be reckoned with—his music bold, yet soulful, emotional, and heartfelt. He came onto the music scene in a blinding flash of "Purple Haze" and suddenly he was gone, leaving behind an incredibly rich legacy and irreplaceable void. If you're lucky, once in a lifetime you get a chance to be part of something so much larger than life itself. That's what seeing Hendrix felt like. And I was luckier yet: I got to see him two more times that same year, once at the Civic Opera House and again at the Coliseum. Many heavy hitting guitarists (e.g., Leigh Stephens of Blue Cheer and Mark Farner of Grand Funk) have tried to model their styles of music after his. If you listen carefully to their music, you will hear frequent Hendrix overtones scattered throughout the songs. Thus, it is obvious to me that Hendrix was the true innovator of an incomparable era of music. Jimi's gritty, bluesy blend of heavy psychedelic music is clearly in a category all its own.

Another highlight was seeing Three Dog Night at the Auditorium in 1969. Jan had tickets and asked me to join her at the concert, but I was hesitant at first having never even heard of them.

"You have to check them out!" She was emphatic.

"Who are they anyway?"

"You'll see," she grinned. I don't recall any other bands that night. I just remember watching them stroll on stage with one of the singers, (Cory), dressed in a white leather fringed jacket.. The minute they started to play and sing one of their most popular songs, "One," everyone in the theatre was dancing on their seats for the rest of the concert!

I saw another "kick-ass" concert in May 1969 when Jefferson Airplane played for free in Grant Park as a tribute to the protesters at the 1968 Democratic National Convention. The concert was held in Grant Park where the year before protesters had gathered for an antiwar rally and supposedly peaceful march. I was (and still am) definitely a fan, and had many of their albums. "Surrealistic Pillow" and "After Bathing at Baxter's" were among my favorites.

There were at least 50,000 people in attendance for the free concert, and they were everywhere: hanging on the PA scaffolds, standing on the roof of the giant band shell above. I was miraculously sitting on the stage along with perhaps a hundred people waiting for Jefferson Airplane to come out. I, like the thousands of other fans there that day, were especially anticipating seeing Grace Slick, the iconic lead singer. She was one of the first females to lead the way onto the rock scene and became, whether or not she intended to, a role model. Grace had a truly electric voice that commanded attention. She also did outrageous things wherever she went, like wearing black face and raising her fist in a Black Panther salute on public television. Grace was a rebel and I felt a kinship with her even though we had never met. She started and named her first band, The Great Society, after Lyndon Johnson's programs that were intended to eliminate poverty, and social and racial injustice. (We fell a bit short of that goal as evidenced by the pervasiveness of those very things that defined the era and just wouldn't go away. A big reason these programs were unsuccessful was that most of the funds Johnson allocated for them went instead towards the war in Vietnam.) (3.)

I idolized the very ground Grace walked on, also wanting to someday be a singer in a world renown rock band, and was looking forward to hearing her sing my all-time favorite songs, "White Rabbit" and "Someone To Love."
Suddenly there she was, Grace Slick, onstage standing not more than ten feet away from where I sat. Gazing at her standing right before me, I wanted to somehow connect with her and called out to her. She grabbed the microphone and glanced in my direction, her cool, icy blue eyes staring right at me. She held my gaze and I could stand it no longer! Reaching my hand out to touch her, I longed to be a part of her incredible aura and presence. Suddenly, I was knocked backwards off the stage and found myself lying face down on the ground gasping for breath and trying to make sense of what had just gone down. It all happened so fast I didn't even see who pushed me off the stage. One moment I was so close to Grace and the next I was spitting dirt out of my mouth. The crowd was so dense, I could barely move for fear of getting stomped to death. After what seemed like an eternity, I somehow regained an upright position and my composure. I decided to stay put and enjoy the rest of the concert from a safe distance. Despite that, it was truly a memorable concert—sharing the stage and a moment in time with an incredible shining star. Filled with enduring memories and leaving only footprints in the sands of time and history, I could only imagine what other musical terrain lay ahead waiting for me to explore.

CHAPTER 5

WELCOME TO CHICAGO (1968)

"The kids, my God, look what they're doing to the kids."
— Walter Cronkite, former CBS TV Anchor

As a child of the '60s, I came of age during tumultuous times. Civil unrest, pro-war vs. anti-war divisions within the Democratic Party, and mass protests against the Vietnam War set the scenario of the decade. I spent much of my time in Lincoln Park in Chicago with flowers in my hair, assorted drugs in my brain, and a six string Ovation guitar in my hands. I sat there for hours playing my guitar amidst an odd and colorfully clad assortment of gentle creatures known as flower children and hippies. I was every bit as colorful as my park companions, wearing flowered bell-bottoms, an old girl scout uniform and at least ten-thousand strands of beads. I often started out playing my guitar alone under a tree, and looked up to see throngs of people wielding every musical instrument imaginable, joining in playing full impromptu concerts. These jam sessions paved the way for future musical adventures. It was during one of these sit-ins that I would experience a life-changing event.

The Democratic National Convention was held in Chicago from August 25-29, 1968, and created quite a stir. Lyndon Johnson, then President, was every bit as unpopular as the war he perpetuated by increasing the number of troops sent to Vietnam. The Democratic Party was divided on its stand on the Vietnam War, and many anti-war activists chose to take part in the presidential campaigns of Senators Robert Kennedy, Eugene McCarthy, and George McGovern, all of whom opposed the war. Johnson was forced to withdraw from the presidential race, and Hubert Humphrey, who supported Johnson's pro-war platform, eventually won the Democratic presidential nomination. Mayor Richard J. Daley was also not very popular with the general public due to his insistence that the Convention be held in Chicago, and his vows to enforce law and order despite massively growing opposition occurring throughout the city. There was even talk of moving the Convention to Miami, yet that idea was quickly vetoed by Daley and Johnson.

A number of other events, such as the assassinations of Senator Robert Kennedy and Martin Luther King, Jr., added to the significant tension in the nation. Outside the Convention, thousands of protestors clashed with almost 12,000 Chicago police, 7,500 army troops, 7,500 Illinois National Guardsmen, and 1,000 Secret Service agents over the five days of the Convention. (4.) The primary cause of the demonstrations and riots during the Convention was the Viet Nam War. I strongly believed, and still believe, we had no business being in Vietnam in the first place. And I was not alone. Groups such as SDS (Students for a Democratic Society), Black Panthers, and Yippies (Youth International Party), coordinated their efforts to stage mass demonstrations with over one hundred other anti-war groups. The stage was set for a catastrophic event that has forever changed the course of Chicago's history and reputation.

The MC5, a favorite punk rock band of mine from Detroit, (aka: Motor City), were invited by members of the Yippies to perform at the "Festival of Life" at which I was in attendance. Abbie Hoffman and Jerry Rubin, leaders of the Yippie Party, apparently wanted to have the MC5 perform on the flatbed of a wagon truck, which was used for their stage, but it was not permitted in the area by the police and prompted the violent confrontation that ensued.

The MC5 were managed by a man named John Sinclair. Sinclair along with his wife, Leni, and another anti-war activist, Lawrence Plamondon, founded a radical leftist organization called the White Panther Party in 1968. The White Panthers originally formed to be in alliance with and support of the Black Panthers' programs, (providing free food, clothing, and health care to its communities, etc.), yet eventually headed in a different direction. The White Panthers' slogan became "total assault on the culture by any means necessary, including rock and roll, dope, and fucking in the streets." (5.)

At 4 p.m. that fateful day, August 25th, the MC5 took the stage as I stood there listening to Rob Tyner, singer and front man belting out, "Kick Out The Jams, Mother Fuckers!" Suddenly, there was no sound coming from the stage, as someone had pulled the plug on the raw and rowdy music. The air was charged with more than just the electrical energy of the wild music being played. At that moment, I looked all around me and saw thousands of police officers surrounding the park, all dressed in black battle regalia, complete with helmets, face guards, and batons held at chest level ready for full out attack! Seconds later, they charged into the crowds with their batons in full swing and spraying the crowd with tear gas. Right before my eyes I saw people running and screaming in terror as one by one they were attacked by the police and fell to the ground bloodied and battered. "The whole world is watching! The whole world is watching!" the protestors who were still on their feet roared repeatedly in unison around me. Their chanting became deafening, adding to the intense electrically charged atmosphere, sending shivers up and down my spine at the realization of what was taking place. The whole world watched their TV's in horror as the police unleashed their fury upon the crowds, and left their mark upon attendees, members of the press, innocent bystanders, and American history forevermore. This event certainly left its mark on me.

Shocked and sickened by all the senseless chaos and violence that shattered a once peaceful gathering, I stood up with guitar in hand and started running toward the area where the police were tossing rioters and peaceniks alike into waiting paddy wagons. Not knowing what to do, I stood in front of one of the vehicles with arms outstretched in feeble attempt to curtail the insanity. Well, you can just about imagine what happened next… I was suddenly amongst the inhabitants of the paddy wagon heading for the nearest police station.

I was interrogated by an officer at the station for what seemed like an eternity. "What were you doing at Lincoln Park?"

"Digging the music, that's all." My whole purpose for being at the wrong place at the right time was to see MC5. At that time, I had no idea of all the events leading up to the riots. It wouldn't be until years later in writing this book that I discovered there was more going on in the world than merely music, peace, and love!

"Are you taking any drugs like LSD or marijuana?"

"No!" I was speeding my ass off, but he didn't have to know that.

"Are you high right now?"

"Yeah, on life," I stared defiantly at him. *Get real, Mr. Man. You bet I am!*

The endless questions continued, and I sat through it all wishing my dad would hurry up and bail me out. I never did find out if charges were actually filed against me, and Dad never said anything to me about what bond he paid if any.

Dad actually took it in stride. When he picked me up at the station he said, "I'm glad you're not hurt. We heard something about riots on the news and were concerned about you…" his voice suddenly trailing off into the distance between us as we walked to the bus stop.

"Dad," I started to say, hoping he would somehow understand what I wanted to tell him. "I'm really sorry about this. I just came down here to hear this band."

"Your mother and I are not very pleased that you go to these places, especially alone."

"Dad, I don't always go alone. Most of the time I'm with friends or meeting them at the park."

"Your mother is not happy about that, nor will she be happy about this excursion."

"Ma doesn't seem to be very happy about anything!" We rode the bus in silence the whole way home, and once again I dreaded the inevitable arguments awaiting me there.

Looking back over the years through adult eyes, I realized that Ma tried to be a role model, yet she was merely an angry, unhappy housewife and that's not what I had in mind for my future. After all, she was a parent, and parents weren't considered cool by their offspring who tried their best to flaunt parental authority in their quest to discover their own identities. As a teenager in the '60s, I was no different. Rather than follow directions, I preferred to do things my own way. The tumultuous relationship I had with my mother surely defined my rebellious nature that has shadowed me throughout my life. To this day, I still struggle with authority figures.

CHAPTER 6

DOWN IN OLD TOWN (1968-'69)

"The most important kind of freedom is to be what you really are."
— Jim Morrison, The Doors

How does one describe Old Town, a small city unto itself within the larger city of Chicago? I remember the streets, North and Wells, that formed the area of the city known as Old Town, bedecked with numerous head shops, record stores, music clubs, coffee and pizza shops, restaurants, and candy stores galore. It was also a gathering place and hangout for peace-loving, colorfully garbed hippies, flower children, beatniks, artists, tourists, and anyone else who was even remotely cool back in the day. It has been compared to Greenwich Village in New York on a smaller scale, yet it had a personality all its own.

Having spent a significant part of my younger years wandering around the streets of Old Town, certain buildings and shops come to mind, such as a won-drous place known as Piper's Alley. Marked by a huge white chandelier lamp hang-ing above the entrance, it was a long cobblestone alleyway leading back to candy, book, trinket, and record stores, and every other store imaginable. Strolling down the alleyway, you were inundated with the potent smells of patchouli oil, your senses overwhelmed with flashing lights in head shops and music blaring from record stores. I spent a considerable amount of time inside one particular head shop (In Sanity) reading buttons with every slogan in creation and staring intently at posters hanging on the walls of Hendrix, Beatles, Janis Joplin, and others that jumped right out at me in the dim black lighting. There were also pipes, hookahs, and enough smoking paraphernalia to satisfy even the most discriminating pot-smoking palate.

Strolling through all the shops to the back of the alley, I ended up at a restau-rant known as La Piazza Pizza, where we were treated to an indescribably delicious pizza, Chicago-style. Another favorite place of mine, The Fudge Pot, when I had the munchies, (those irresistible eat-everything-in-sight cravings you get when you're high). Potheads of the world will surely back me up on this one.

While many memories I have of Old Town are great ones, others are not so great.

One night after an intense knock-down, drag out fight with Ma, I rushed out of the house and headed down to Old Town for some solace and solitude. Ending up at Piper's Alley, as usual, I drifted down to La Piazza and sat at a table sipping a Coke, having a smoke and trying to sort things out in my mind. I glanced at my watch and noticed it was around 9 p.m. As I sat immersed in thoughts and the tantalizing smell of pizza, a man approaching my table interrupted my reverie. He stood next to me and I looked up at him wondering if he would try playing the pick-up card, as was routinely how it went when I was somewhere alone. He flashed something resembling a badge at me too fast to actually see what it was. "Are you here alone?" he asked.

-*Hey, this guy is perceptive, I thought.* "Yeah, for now, but I'm expecting some friends any minute," I lied not really in the mood for any company.

"How old are you?"

"Old enough to let you know I'm not interested!" I was about 18 at the time, yet wasn't about to divulge personal information to someone I didn't know. "Who in hell are you by the way?" Once again, he showed the badge somewhat slower, and this time I was able to see a flash of gold and realized I was being harassed once again by "the man." A bit perturbed, I asked why he was questioning me.

"It's after curfew. Do you have an ID?"

"With all due respect, it's only around 9 p.m. and isn't curfew at 10?"

"It's almost that now. You got an ID?" I glanced at my watch and noticed it was almost 9:30. Looks like he's not going away anytime soon, I thought while fishing around in my purse for my Roosevelt ID and flashed it at him. He took it from me and stared at it for a while.

"Do your parents know where you are?" asked Officer Laurel.

"Yes," I lied wishing he would just go away.

"Ma'am, please come with me!"

"What for officer? I'm 18 and it's not even curfew! What's the problem?"

"We're walking down the hall here…" and suddenly his hand grabbed my arm and along I went for the ride. We walked to a record store, the name of which I can't recall and went over to the counter where a guy with frizzy, Chia Pet hair gave me the once over, nodded at the officer and said, "That's the runaway chick from Indiana."

I stood there in disbelief and glared at him. "What in hell are you saying? I've never met you before and you sure as hell have never met me, and I live right here in Chicago!" Shortly thereafter, Laurel was joined by his partner, Officer Hardy, who promptly approached me, asking to see the contents of my purse.

"You won't find what you're looking for, guaranteed!" Before I could say another word, he dumped my lipstick, comb and Lucky Strikes onto the counter. He started shredding the cigarettes one by one, spilling crumbs of tobacco all over the counter and floor.

I laughed aloud at the irony of the situation. Here I was, a gal born and bred in Chicago, being told I was from Indiana, straight for a change and being busted for dope I didn't have. "Satisfied?" I smirked at him. Officer Hardy was staring blankly at me, his face turning dark red. He casually asked the counter guy where the phone was and Hendrix pointed toward the wall. Turning my attention now to the counter guy, I asked him in a voice barely able to contain composure, "Hey, Hendrix, what makes you think I'm from Indiana anyway? You don't even know me, man, and you're a fucking idiot!" I yelled at him. *What the hell? I thought, there's nothing to lose at this point.* The shit was hitting the fan, so why not push the dial to full speed?

Hendrix turned just about as red as a beet and remained silent, glancing nervously over at Laurel and Hardy. Hardy broke the silence. "Ma'am, what's your phone number?" I casually strolled over to the phone grabbing it out of his hand and dialed with trembling hands hoping Ma would somehow straighten out the mess.

"Hello?" Ma's familiar voice spoke on the other end.

"Hey, Ma, it's me… I paused to weigh out my options of how to explain the circumstances to her.

"Don, where are you? "Are you alright?"

"Yeah, Ma, I'm OK. Hey, I'm at Old Town and am in a situation… could you tell this officer who I am and where I'm from?"

"What kind of trouble are you in now?"

"Ma, please just tell the officer who I am, OK? They're trying to bust me for being a runaway!" I handed the phone over to Hardy. All eyes were on him now and I wished that somehow everything would magically disappear.

"Ma'am, we have your daughter here and were wondering if you knew her whereabouts?" A pause, then a few nods of his balding head.

"OK, ma'am, thank you." He cleared his throat, hung up the phone and walked over to where I stood.

Glancing at Laurel, then at me, he firmly said, "Come with me please, Miss!" "Where are we going now, officer?"

"Down to the station." An explanation would have sufficed, yet nothing of the sort was forthcoming.

"On what charge?" *This is going from the sublime to the ridiculous, I thought.*

"What did my mother say?"

He never told me and instead replied, "Ma'am, just please follow me. We can either make this easy or difficult. Your choice!" Now both officers were surrounding me. I did the only thing I could think of at the time. I ran like hell out of the store and into the alleyway with Laurel and Hardy in fast pursuit. They finally caught up with me as I tried to duck into a candy store, and was soon thereafter dragged down the alleyway kicking and yelling all the way to the waiting squad car. Upon investigation of my background, they discovered their mistake and I was released.

Like most kids growing up in the '50s and early '60s, I was inundated with idealistic TV shows such as "Leave It To Beaver," "Father Knows Best," "Ozzie and Harriet," and "The Brady Bunch" that glamorized and painted an unrealistic picture of what family life was supposedly like. Somehow my family life fell short of this fantasy portrait. Perhaps some people growing up in those times enjoyed having normal upbringings, yet it wasn't in the cards for me.

Fortunately, the people I met in Old Town more than made up for the not-so-great memories. One of my favorite memories was strolling down Wells amidst throngs of groovy people crowding the streets dressed in bell bottoms, beads and bandannas, hanging out talking with friends. Then I heard another sound in the distance–a faintly distinct yet familiar sound of tinkling bells. I smiled and turned in the direction of the bells and there was "Mama" floating down the street towards me. She was older than most of us Old Town folk and larger than life, yet every bit as hip with a shock of long flaming red hair, strands of bells around her neck and penetrating blue eyes partially hidden behind ever-present granny glasses sliding down her nose. She carried a bunch of flowers and handed them out to everyone she met. I didn't quite know what to make of her at first sight, yet when she flashed the peace sign and handed me a flower, I decided right then and there she was very cool! She had that effect on everyone she came in contact with and exuded peace and love, everything the original hippie movement stood for. She was a true flower child in every sense of the word, just well, you know, a bit older.

Suddenly Mama floated by me, her face beaming as usual. "Hey Mama, what's going on, man?" I greeted her with a smile.

"Hey man, how are you?" she cheerily chirped handing me another flower. We hugged as though we had known each other all our lives. This was the first time we had actually met, yet she made me feel like I was her best friend. Interaction and conversation with Mama was usually brief, yet in those few moments, you just knew you were truly touched by a graceful, loving presence. She then floated her way down the street like she was on a mission, bells chiming away.

Then there was Vince—black as night, slight of build and right in your face!

He would wear a well-worn long navy corduroy jacket and black velvet cap hovering over one eye, covering electric Hendrix hair. Whenever I met up with Vince, he would sweep me off the ground with bear hugs and belly laughs, a huge smile on his face. That was just part of his persona, warm-hearted and truly genuine. He would always offer me a hit of something or other that he was smoking or "dropping" at the time, and we always got quite high. Just being around him gave me a contact high, and we shared more than just good drugs—we shared the times of an incredible era and bonded together in those moments in time. I had a bit of a crush on him and no doubt, a relationship would have ensued, yet we were too much alike to commit to each other. We were free and restless spirits passing by like two ships in the night.

These are just a few stories of Old Town, when to me the place was alive and in its prime. I have not been back to that area in many years, but I've learned that it has been encased in a glass bowl in an attempt to preserve its once natural environment, which ironically has falsified rather than preserved it. You just can't replace history with high rises.

CHAPTER 7

ON BECOMING A NURSE (OR WORSE) (1969-'70)

"I have an almost complete disregard of precedent, and a faith in the possibility of something better. It irritates me to be told how things have always been done. I defy the tyranny of precedent. I go for anything new that might improve the past."
> — **Clara Barton, Nurse, Humanitarian, Women's Rights Activist,Founder and President of The American Red Cross**

Ma wanted me to become a nurse, but that was certainly not what I wanted to be. I wanted to become a doctor. When I told her I wanted to go to medical school, she replied, "Women don't become doctors!"

"Why not?" I demanded.

"Because they just don't!" Her face flushed with anger. Period. End of topic. *Better quit while you're ahead, I thought.* I dared not get her angry, and after all, she was my mother and mothers know best, or at least think they do. She bought me books about nursing pioneers (i.e. Clara Barton and Florence Nightingale), and I have to admit I was interested in their stories. Still, my heart was more interested in medical practice.

In my senior year in high school, I started a practical nursing program, thinking I could work my way up the career ladder in the medical field. What was I thinking?

The lady who was recruiting students for the LPN Program certainly sounded convincing when she visited Roosevelt High School that fall of 1968, as she explained that we could graduate from the program after one year, and we only had to attend nursing classes for half a day. Heck, I could get out of school early and still have time to head over to Lincoln Park! Again, what was I thinking?

Nursing school was a lot of work. Not an easy-to-understand concept for a teenager. I had to concentrate very hard to gain knowledge of the workings of the human body, put in countless hours studying anatomy and physiology for weekly tests, and take care of real live patients in hospitals two to three days per week. It didn't leave much time for anything else. I have never been one to follow instructions.

I didn't make many friends at Roosevelt, other than Sue and Jan, mainly keeping to myself. But meeting Sylvie was an exception. She was in my nursing class, and when we started talking one day, she mentioned she was a big fan of The Doors, especially Jim Morrison, the lead singer—we became close friends. Every day during lunch hour when it was time to go to nursing school class at Forkosh Hospital, we walked to her house a few blocks from Roosevelt, and had lunch listening to The Doors albums, chatting the time away about music. Sylvie was short of stature yet large in the breast department, and was quite proud of them. She was also quite enamored with a WGLD radio DJ personality known as "Scorpio" and talked about him incessantly, referring to him as "My Little Scorp." We often got so caught up in our conversation that we'd have to run like hell to catch the bus, barely making it to Forkosh in time for class.

One not-so-fond nursing school memory was when I attempted to transfer a rather obese woman from her bed to a wheelchair. I overlooked a key component for transfers—locking the wheelchair—so it doesn't move when you don't want it to. I was suddenly on the floor with this patient on top of me, and of course, very fortuitously, Mrs. B was walking into the room at the same time. After making sure we were both uninjured and still breathing, Mrs. B assisted her into the wheelchair, and then promptly escorted me outside the room.

"What just happened?" she calmly asked.

I thought honesty would be the best policy under the circumstances and replied, "Well, I guess I should have locked the brakes on the wheelchair before trying to transfer her," hoping she would go easy on me for being so brave and honest.

The expression on her face was one of shock and disbelief as she then asked her landmark next question, "Are you sure you want to be a nurse?" I must have turned every shade of red imaginable, thinking I could tell her about wanting to be a doctor, or worse yet a musician. But I realized that neither of those would go over very well. So I just bit the bullet, apologized for being so stupid, and told her that yes, I did want to be a nurse, and would be more cognizant of patient safety when doing transfers in the future. Nursing school taught me one lesson after another. I had great instructors, like Mrs. B, who were very patient with their students and others who weren't.

Looking back on how unsatisfying my nursing career was, I now realize that perhaps Mrs. B was right in implying that nursing really wasn't what I was supposed to be doing with my life. What I didn't realize at the time was that nursing was merely a means to making a living and one of many detours along the road of life that would lead me inexplicably and inevitably back to my musical roots.

CHAPTER 8
GOODBYE TO MA (1970-1971)

"Play me a tune, Lady June, your music ended way too soon
Little girl sitting there at your feet, listening to your every beat."
— **Donna Brown (lyrics from "Lady June," a song**
written in memoriam to her mother.)

Ma sure picked a great time to leave! On a cold winter day in November of 1970, at the age of 19, I had just graduated from LPN school and received an offer to start my first nursing job at Children's Hospital. I was excited about finding an apartment in the dorm at Children's, affording me the opportunity to break free from Ma's dominant and restrictive influence, live my own life and be my own person. Yet, just when I thought I was finally free of Ma, another life-changing event was lurking around the corner.

I had moved into the dorm at Children's and was working in the cardiac unit enjoying my newly found freedom, yet somewhat let down about not having a close relationship with Ma. It was the first week of the New Year, and wanting to try to resolve our conflict, I decided to stop by the apartment and surprise her. She was lying in bed when I arrived, and was still a bit upset about my leaving incident some weeks before. She greeted me with, "Oh, so you're coming back now, huh?"

"Just wanted to see how things are going."

She scoffed at me. "Well, I'm not feeling very well, for all you could care."

"What's wrong now? Is it the dizziness again?" She nodded. I knew that she was overweight, weighing somewhere around 250 pounds and that she was having frequent bouts of dizziness, and severe leg pain that she called, "Sciatica," amongst numerous other health problems. She was seeing our family doctor at least once a week, yet it didn't seem like he was doing anything for her except giving her more medications that didn't really work. I didn't take her complaints too seriously and apparently neither did our doctor! She was only 49 years old, still relatively young, and I thought she would be around forever.

Suddenly, she sat up and moved herself over to the edge of the bed. "I need to do some shopping. Want to come along?"

"Sure, Ma, are you sure you're feeling up to it?" *Stupid question, I thought, Ma was always up for shopping!*

"I'll be fine," she tried to sound convincing, but I had to help her up and she was a bit wobbly at best. I was concerned seeing her so unsteady, yet walking to the store and being involved in conversation and Ma's favorite activity, shopping, she seemed to be fine. Whenever Ma went shopping she brought along her cart to carry all the stuff she bought.

After shopping, I walked down the street with Ma as she toted the cart laden with groceries behind her. We decided to stop at a favorite neighborhood restaurant for lunch. During lunch, we talked about many different topics, including my job at Children's, and I enjoyed spending some quality time with her without arguing. Engaged in great conversation for hours on end, we didn't agree on everything yet listened to and heard each other. I started to see glimpses of the person hiding behind the guise of mother, a woman who also had a hard life. Seeing her struggles, I felt the beginnings of a kinship with her that I rarely if ever felt before. During those hours of heartfelt conversation, we were starting to finally get to know each other, and had established a truce between us. The hours flew by, and I didn't want that time we were together to end. It seemed like neither one of us wanted to leave that place in time.

"So, maybe we should head back home, as you've probably got things you have to do," Ma's comment broke the moment.

"I don't really have that many things to do, Ma." I still had so much to say to her. I wanted to ask her why we couldn't get along before today. I wanted to know if she ever loved me. I wanted to thank her for pulling my nursing uniform out of the garbage when I was frustrated with school remembering her words, "finish what you start." But the words wouldn't come. "Ma," I stammered, "I'm glad we had this time together."

"I am too, dear." We held each other's gaze. I really wanted to hug her and wanted her to hug me, as I couldn't remember getting many hugs from her during the growing up years.

Ma was first to rise, and I helped her put on her coat. We walked together outside into the cold, Ma holding onto her cart and me holding onto her arm. I was enjoying the intimacy we were sharing and was feeling the rudimentary beginnings of a healing mother-daughter relationship that went missing for too many years. We strolled in silence the few blocks back to the familiar alleyway leading to the apartment building I used to call home. I instinctively reached for the cart, and she gently refused my assistance.

"I can take this. Why don't you go around the front and let me in the back door?" She handed me the key and started walking down the alley toward the back stairway.

I watched her walk away with cart in tow, and was filled with an unexplainable anxiety that took me by surprise. I bolted around the buildings down the street, to the front of the apartment complex, my breath coming in gasps, and I couldn't seem to get to our apartment fast enough, despite breaking all speed records for the half-mile. I opened the front door, rushed to the back door and flung it open just in time to see Ma standing on the porch with cart behind her and a blank stare on her face. Now in panic mode, I yelled at her. "MA! ARE YOU OK? WHAT'S WRONG?" Almost yanking her arm out of its socket, I pulled her into our apartment with strength coming from some unknown source deep within. She started laughing, mumbling unintelligible slurred incoherencies under her breath and stumbling around me, as I tried to get her to her favorite chair in the front room. She collapsed into the chair laughing hysterically.

Trying to remain calm and attempting to tap into some storehouse of nursing knowledge seemed as far as the moon at that moment. Feeling nauseous, I ran to the bathroom then back into the kitchen to call 911. Passing the hallway mirror, I gave it a quick glance looking for reassurance that things would be OK, yet knew that Ma's situation was serious.

"Where's my purse?" Ma screamed at me as I ran back into the front room. I stared at her in disbelief. "Didn't you just have it?" Glancing around the room, I ran into the kitchen looking for her purse and found it lying on the floor.

"Here it is, Ma." She was unable to keep herself upright, slumped over in the chair and kept yelling for her purse. I patted her arm trying to calm her down.

"I have your purse. You're going to be OK, Ma!" I tried to reassure her not believing my own words. My mind was on overload searching for some explanation for her odd behavior, some harmless non-fatal diagnosis, yet the options weren't exactly in her favor. *Maybe she's having a stroke? No, that couldn't be, she's only 49! I thought trying in vain to comfort myself. That's way too young... where's the fucking ambulance???*

After what seemed like hours, there was a knock at the door and a policeman entered assessing the situation with a glance. I glared at him. "Can we move things along here, officer, she's not doing very well!" Before long, two paramedics were rushing in with a litter and bag full of medical supplies. They got her down on the floor, rolled her onto the litter and carried her down the stairs to the ambulance waiting outside.

"DONNA! WHERE'S MY PURSE?"

"Here's your purse!" I yelled to her running down the stairs with purse in hand and little else, jumped into the passenger seat of the ambulance, and away we sped to the nearest hospital. She was taken to ER, undergoing every test imaginable, and eventually admitted to a room. The doctor who admitted her said he would contact me once he got the results of all the tests, and told me to go home and get some rest.

I went into Ma's room instead to see how she was doing. She was rather drowsy, and I sat on the bed next to her holding her left hand that was lying limp and cold in my hand. I lifted her arm up and asked if she could move her arm. She didn't respond and had the same vacant stare on her face, and letting go of her arm, I watched it fall back down on the bed. "Ma," I whispered with tears of concern in my eyes, bending over to kiss her forehead and smooth back her hair.

She suddenly closed her eyes and was soon sound asleep. I stood there feeling alone, miserable and helpless, wondering if she would ever recover. I walked out of her room, down the hospital corridor and into the lobby in a daze, found a payphone and called my dad. Hearing his familiar voice offered little solace.

"Hello? Don?"

"Dad," I sobbed into the phone, "Ma's in the hospital with I don't know what, and she's not doing very well! Please come soon!"

His voice was full of concern. "What's wrong with her?"

"I don't know, I think it might be a stroke, yet the doctors aren't sure at this point. They did a lot of tests. Please come right now, Dad!"

"I'll be right there! Does Morine know?"

"No, I haven't had a chance to call her."

"I'll call and let her know and we'll meet you there shortly," Dad said and hung up.

Dad and Mo arrived within the hour, meeting me in the lobby. We hugged and I noticed Mo had tears streaming down her face. Dad looked somber and thoughtful. "What happened, Don?" Riding together in the elevator up to the third floor to see Ma, I recounted the day's events barely able to hold back tears.

"Today was my day off and I stopped by to see Ma, we went shopping, had lunch and spent a great day together. Ma carried the groceries in the cart up the backstairs while I went around the front to let her in, and there she was standing out on the porch and I knew there was something wrong with her, and she was suddenly not making sense and laughing and mumbling under her breath, and then suddenly she went limp, and I helped her to her chair, and then called 911…"

Then I stopped too full of sadness and despair to continue. We walked in silence down the corridor to Ma's room.

Dad went into her room first, followed by my sister, and I brought up the rear. Dad sat on the bed holding Ma's limp hand, while Ma stared blankly up at him. She suddenly recognized him and started crying.

"Where am I, Harry?" she demanded.

"Honey, you're in the hospital, and you're gonna be alright," he whispered softly leaning in toward her face to kiss her with a tenderness that I hadn't recalled seeing in quite a while.

Ma had a confused expression on her face and looked around the room with her eyes half closed. "Where are the kids?"

"Right here, Mom." Mo stepped closer towards the bed where Ma could see her better. Ma stared at my sister.

"Did you do your homework?"

"I'll do it later."

"Oh, good!" Where am I?"

"Ma, you're in the hospital and need to stay here a while longer until you're feeling better," I patted her arm trying to offer reassurance.

"I'm fine, Donna! Where am I anyway?" Dad, Mo, and I exchanged glances, wondering if she would ever be coming back home. A nurse then walked in to remind us that visiting time was over, and we said our farewells to Ma and made our way back home.

The next day we were sitting around the apartment having a conversation about Ma when the phone rang. Dad answered the phone and it was Dr. Wien, our family doctor calling to give us the results of Ma's tests. Dad listened for several minutes then asked, with great concern, "Are you sure? What can be done for that?" Another pause, and several sighs later he replied, "OK, doctor, thank you," and hung up the phone. Dad briefed me on what Dr. Wien told him.

"Your mom has a blood clot in her brain and it caused her to have a stroke," he sighed heavily and stared down at the floor.

Confirming what I had previously surmised, I reached my hand over to pat Dad's hand. We sat there in silence for a few moments letting this information sink into our rattled brains.

"Is Dr. Wien starting anticoagulants to dissolve the clot?" I asked.

Dad nodded, looking very worried. Walking over to where he sat, I slid my arm around his shoulders.

"Don't worry, Pop, things will all work out." Dad didn't look very convinced.

Mo and I exchanged glances, both of us with tears streaming down our faces. Staring into space for what seemed like hours, she suddenly broke the silence declaring in her most cheerful voice, "OK, I'm sure you guys must be hungry by now, so I'll make us something to eat," and away she walked into the kitchen.

After eating our sandwiches, Mo informed us she would visit Ma tomorrow. Dad and I went to the hospital to see Ma, and he once again sat on the bed holding her limp hand. She seemed more settled and calmer, almost resigned to her fate. I stood holding up the wall some distance away from her bed taking in the whole scene as if somehow detached from the events of the past few days, yet at the same time right in the moment. It was as though I was having an out-of-body experience similar to previous LSD-induced highs I had experienced. Perhaps convincing myself that this was someone else's nightmare story was my way of dealing with Ma's illness, as if denying it would make it go away.

Dad slowly got up from the bed and kissed Ma's forehead. They exchanged words and I realized it was time to go home. Moving away from the wall to her bed, I sat down on the bed where Dad had once sat, gazing intently at her. I didn't want to leave, as I felt the same anxiety as only a few days before when watching her walking down the alley toward our apartment with her cart. Dr. Wien informed us that he was hoping the anticoagulant medication he ordered for Ma would take effect and eventually she would regain function of the left side of her body. We tried to remain hopeful, yet seeing the confusion in her eyes made me feel somewhat doubtful. "Ma, it's time for us to go home and for you to get some rest," I whispered.

She looked up at me and tried to smile. "When will you be back?"

"I have to work for the next few days, but I'll try to get here as soon as I can. I promise." Leaning forward to kiss her forehead, I held her hand one last time before leaving with Dad.

The next day was pretty busy at work giving me some sorely needed income and I didn't get a chance to see Ma. My heart ached for her, and I wanted so much to be with her, yet felt so torn as the sight of her broke my heart.

The following day, Monday, I was once again at work, and it was one of those days. Nothing was going right. I had a sleepless night thinking about Ma and felt so tired, like I was moving in slow motion. I tried to hang an IV bottle for a patient and dropped it on the floor, fluid and broken glass spilling all over. I wanted nothing more than to go back to my room, go back to bed, pull the covers over my head and hide away from the world. My head nurse, Nancy, was suddenly standing next to me in the patient's room, and I held my breath thinking she was going to give me a lecture on the correct procedure for hanging IV's, when she instead motioned for me to come into her office. My heart was now pounding as I had been called into supervisor's offices a few times in my life without good outcome.

I followed her down the hall and turning to face me, she pointed to the phone on her desk, informing me I had a phone call. Slowly picking up the phone, I recognized Dad's voice. "Don, I have some bad news," his voice broken and interspersed with sobs.

"Dad, what's wrong?" I blurted barely able to breathe.

"Your mom has taken a turn for the worse."

"Dad!"

Before I could even finish my sentence, he cried, "Don, she's passed away!"

"NO!!!" I screamed into the phone as if my screams could undo the indescribable horror of that moment. The next few moments I hardly recall, as my whole body shook and I felt faint. Nancy was right there holding me up, and helping me slide into a chair. I somehow managed to hold onto the phone and heard Dad telling me to come home right away, "OK, I'm coming"… was all I could muster. Nancy took the phone from me, replacing it back on her desk and holding me as I heaved gut-wrenching sobs of despair. "Ma… oh God, no…" I sobbed for what seemed like an eternity until there were no more tears left to cry. I looked up at Nancy's sympathetic face and told her I needed to go home. She nodded and asked if I needed a ride, which I turned down. "Will you be alright going home alone?" she asked with concern.

"I'll be fine," I lied. "Thanks, Nancy." She touched my shoulder, expressed her deepest condolences, and handed my coat to me. I did a death march back down the corridor, trying to avoid the sympathetic glances from my co-workers, outside to the nearest bus stop. To this day, I still don't recall how I made it home.

I stood outside the front door for the longest time recalling that just a few weeks before Ma had been alive and was carried by litter and paramedics down the same stairs I had just climbed up. It all seemed surreal, almost dream-like and I wished that it really was just a bad dream that I soon would awaken from. It wasn't. I heard Dad's broken voice through the door, took a deep breath, composing myself, then slowly entered our apartment, walked over to Dad and hugged and lost it with him. My grandma was there and I recall hugging her, hearing her say to my dad, "These kids are orphans!" Hearing her say that made me feel even more alone, and Ma's passing more definitive. We lost our mother at the young ages of 16 and 19, grandma lost her daughter, and Dad lost his wife. Whose loss was greatest, I wondered?

Dad was pretty incapacitated by Ma's passing and spent hours sitting on the couch staring into space and doing little else other than breaking into sobs at any given moment. I tried to comfort him as best I could, yet how could I comfort him when I could not find it within myself? I moved back to the apartment to help take care of Dad and assist with funeral preparations and arrangements. After the funeral, we went back to the apartment with family members and had a ceremonious sit-in of another sort.

It is a customary Jewish tradition to "Sit Shiva", or sit around with family and friends and remember and honor the soul of the dearly departed. Of course, food is an integral part of the ceremony. I wasn't very hungry, but it was comforting to be in the company of my remaining family, aunts, cousins, and grandparents, listen to their stories, share family memories and watch them eat almost everything in sight. I wondered if they were there for the person or the food?

Another traditional part of the Shiva is lighting a ceremonial Yahrzeit candle. I recall Ma used to light these candles religiously when family members passed on. In my childhood, I asked her why she always lit the candles, and she replied, "This is in honor of Aunt Shirley who is no longer with us," or whoever the family member was who had passed on during that period of time. At that young age I didn't really get it, and was hardly familiar with the person she mentioned, as we didn't see much of family other than holiday visits to see my aunt Dolly, where we would all convene for delicious dinners she would cook. Also, when I was a kid, life was infinite, and death was little more than a hard-to-comprehend concept, a nondescript netherworld where all those elderly folks hang out.

One day soon after Ma's death, as I lit a candle in her honor it hit me big time! "Hey, I'm lighting a candle and this one's for you Ma," I sobbed. This familiar ritual was as agonizingly painful as it was comforting. I was connecting with Ma in some small way through the tradition she had set over the years, and in that sense I felt closer to her. The flame of the candle symbolizes the soul of the person who has departed, and gazing at the candle, I pictured her face and imagined she never really left. The candle shined like a beacon in the darkness.

The weeks and months following Ma's funeral were a blur of sitting in silence, staring into space, feeling numb yet in excruciating pain, missing Ma terribly, and not hearing from friends or even family members. For whatever the reason, people seem to feel that people whose loved ones have died "need their space." Well, let me tell you, nothing could be farther from the truth! We had too much space, especially the huge space left by Ma's passing. We sorely missed her, yet she was still with us in many weird ways.

One night a few weeks after Ma's death, Mo and I were in bed sleeping after going through the nightly regimen of making sure all closet and bedroom doors were closed. Sometime in the middle of the night, I was awakened by Mo's voice calling my attention to the bedroom door and suddenly realized it was now WIDE OPEN! We dashed out of the room like we were being chased by the devil himself. It was reminiscent of another time when Ma was still alive and we heard a cat loudly meowing outside the bedroom window. We were extremely fearful of just about everything, and were soon doing the 100 yard dash down the hall, waking dad up from a sound sleep, regaling him with monster stories which never seemed to bother him. We also had a nightly routine of having to pee and calling out for Dad to walk us to the bathroom. He always patiently turned on the bathroom light, fetched us from our beds, escorted us to and from the bathroom and killed all the monsters hiding under our beds.

I returned to work at Children's a few weeks after Ma's passing and although it was difficult to concentrate, it kept me occupied, and it felt better than just sitting at home being depressed.

One day at work I was sitting in the nurse's station writing on a patient's chart and suddenly felt someone lightly touch my shoulder. I turned around to see who it was, expecting to see a doctor trying to get my attention, and there was no one there! I sat staring into space for a few moments trying to figure out what had happened. Was I imagining the whole thing? I tried to shake it off and get back to work, yet the feeling of Ma's presence was with me for the rest of the day.

A few hours later I was standing in the middle of a common area in the hospital where the kids were playing, talking with a patient's mother. I was wearing a colored pantsuit with a belt around the waist, which was common nursing attire in those days. We were engaged in conversation about her child's illness and how the child was progressing, when I suddenly felt someone tug on my belt, and looked down expecting to see a child wanting to grab my attention, and once again saw no one there. I looked all around for a child who might be the culprit, yet there were no kids engaged in playing anywhere near where we were standing. OK, this is too weird, I thought.

"Are you OK?" the mother asked me.

"Yes," I stammered trying to compose myself. *Ma, not now,* I scolded her in my mind as if I were talking to her rather than another parent. After finishing my conversation with the parent, I excused myself and hurried away rather embarrassed at the situation. Ma was having fun making her presence known, and I didn't know what to think of these occurrences. Was she trying to contact me in some way, and if so, what was she trying to tell me? I didn't normally believe in ghosts or spirits, yet these and other events made me a believer.

One evening about a month later, I was home alone reading in the bedroom and realized that I hadn't turned on any lights in the apartment. I got up from my bed, opened the door and stared down the hall into the darkness of the living room. After I started walking down the hall, something that caught my eye stopped me dead in my tracks. A sliver of light from the bedroom shone down the hall eerily outlining a shadowy silhouette of a figure standing in the front room. I let out a gasp as the figure became more apparent to me. The silhouette was of a heavy set woman standing in a familiar pose with one hand resting on her hip, which was Ma's favorite stance whenever she was about to lecture me about something or other. I stood there for an eternity with heart pounding before I could even find the words to speak. "Ma, is that you?" I hoarsely whispered, almost expecting the figure to actually reply.

As a little kid, I saw tons of horror movies featuring just about every fiendish creature imaginable, yet this vision that stood before me had me frozen in fear like nothing I had ever experienced. The figure did not move, nor disappear. I tried to move, yet was afraid to for fear the figure would either make a move toward me or fade away. I stared at the figure transfixed with a combination of terror and weird fascination, wanting to run out the front door at that moment. Another part of me wanted desperately to make contact with it as well, as if hearing its voice would reassure me that everything was OK and I was in no danger.

After another eternity, I finally made my move and ran past the figure in the front room to the safety of the kitchen, and breathed a sigh of relief as when I turned the light on the figure suddenly disappeared. Looking back on these experiences, I decided that Ma was indeed trying to make contact with us and that she was trying to reassure and comfort us with her presence. I found this belief to be very consoling. Strangely enough, the figure has never since reappeared.

CHAPTER 9
ALL POWER TO THE PEOPLE (1971-1972)

"America's health care system is neither healthy, caring, nor a system.
— Walter Cronkite, former TV Anchor for CBS

Needing a break from the traditional hospital environment and ever-present memories of Ma's passing, I left Children's Hospital. Finding out from a co-worker that a nearby Free Clinic was looking for nurses, and seeking an opportunity to somehow make a more direct difference in people's lives, I started volunteering at Fritzi Englestein Free People's Clinic for a few months. I found the idea of providing free quality health care very satisfying and enjoyed the environment and friendly staff. While working at Fritzi, I provided care to patients with every health problem from minor colds to VD and was often the only medical provider there when doctors were not available. I did many different procedures, including pelvic exams, usually done by doctors. I also got a chance to see and experience many things not usually experienced in a hospital setting, such as meeting members of the Black Panther Party! More on this later.

There were a number of other free clinics at that time in Chicago, some more radical than Fritzi Englestein, such as Rising Up Angry, frequented largely by the Hispanic population, and the Spurgeon "Jake" Peoples Free Medical Care Center that was started in Jan. 1970 by the Black Panther Party. These clinics, like Fritzi Englestein, offered first aid care, physical examinations, pre-natal care, and testing for lead poisoning, high blood pressure, and sickle cell anemia. We often visited these clinics and met with staff members to share medical knowledge and to further the purpose of delivering free, high-quality care and health services to people in the community. Things were going along really well with the clinics until the day Mayor Daley decided that he needed to have access to our clients' medical records. We were of course, very angry, as after all, that was a blatant invasion of their privacy, even though it was before HIPAA (Health Insurance Portability and Accountability Act of 1996) days. Daley was holding a meeting on this decision at City Hall that week, and the clinic staff sprang into action, appointing a medical student to represent the clinic and speak on our behalf against his ruling. I was present along with the entire clinic staff that day at the hearing and saw firsthand how Daley conducted politics. He stood in the center of the large meeting room and filibustered for hours about the day-to-day operations of the "City That Works," as Chicago was called back then.

It was finally time for Dr. Smith, our medical student, to give his recitation, and Daley introduced him to the assembly as representing Fritzi Englestein Clinic. He stood up and began regaling the court with facts and figures of how our clients were being served by the free medical care provided by the clinic and how the City really shouldn't be trying to interfere with this process. Although he didn't get very far before Daley interrupted him, he did make his point. "Thanks Dr. Smith, I think we get the picture of what you're saying. You may be seated now." "With all due respect, Mr. Mayor, I have more to report," Dr. Smith still standing, attempted to continue with his presentation. Once again Daley interrupted. We were all now on our feet, shouting at Daley and voicing our displeasure in no uncertain terms. Nonetheless, Daley prevailed and had us all escorted out of the room by the police. I was walking out with a co-worker who was pregnant, followed closely by an officer and were approaching a stairway, when suddenly the officer pushed the woman down the stairs right in front of me, adding insult to injury. I turned to face the officer with my fists clenched and said something to him that was not an exchange of pleasantries. He sternly stared right through me with arms defiantly folded over his chest. I don't think I ever felt angrier than at that moment, and mumbling obscenities under my breath, ran over to help my co-worker get up from the ground and out of the building. This was yet another defining moment that resulted in my distrust of authority figures.

Sometime after the City Hall debacle, Fritzi became even tighter with its circle of clinics.

One day a meeting was called to discuss our next course of action to oppose Daley's open door policy with our clinics, and a few members of the Black Panthers were in attendance. Meeting them that day was truly an unforgettable experience.

Sitting across the table from a few party members, I felt somewhat nervous, yet fascinated by their appearance. Donned in black leather jackets, black berets, and militant history, they shared information about the beneficial services they offered at their clinics, such as providing food, clothing and transportation for people in the community. As we conversed, I began to see them more as human rights advocates who shared a common goal of equality for all, rather than racist, revolutionary militants. Despite numerous articles written about the Black Panthers describing their frequent violent confrontations with law enforcement officers, it is difficult to ascertain who was responsible for the confrontations. The FBI was frequently waging war with the Black Panthers. In 1968, J. Edgar Hoover, then Director of the FBI, deemed them, "…without question…the greatest internal threat to the security of the country." (6.)

Another article I read confirmed my feelings that the Black Panthers were often wrongly accused of constantly inciting riots and rebellions, rather than defending themselves against the constant barrage of attacks from the FBI. The article states, … "J. Edgar Hoover directed the FBI to wage a campaign to eliminate the Black Panther Party altogether, commanding the assistance of local police departments to do so. Indeed, as Hoover declared the Party "threats," he pledged that 1969 would be the last year of their existence. In January of 1969, two Party leaders of the Southern California Chapter, John Huggins and Alprentice "Bunchy" Carter, were murdered at UCLA by FBI-paid assassins, with the cooperation of black nationalist Ron Karenga and his US Organization. By the end of that year, nearly every office and other facility of the Black Panther Party had been violently assaulted by police and/or the FBI, culminating in December, in an FBI-orchestrated five-hour police assault on the office in Los Angeles and FBI-directed Illinois state police assassination of Chicago Party leader Fred Hampton and member Mark Clark. (7.)

For better or worse, the Black Panthers were both controversial and influential in improving the status of racial inequality for black communities. They were described as firm proponents of the black movement organization of the '60s and seen as being more criminal than political. No matter what your perspective, they have taken their place in American history by initiating numerous community social and health programs. Some members of the Party have even held elected office in the U.S. government. There are several groups and movements that developed and were inspired by the Black Panthers, such as White Panthers and Gray Panthers, the former as Caucasian supporters of the movement, and the latter, senior citizen advocates for promoting the rights of seniors. As an impressionable youngster of those times, their influence on my life was affirmed by my wearing the familiar purple button with the White Panther logo on it. More importantly, to this day, I still try to be of service to my community by volunteering at various charitable organizations and helping those who are ill and in need of medical assistance.

CHAPTER 10
MEDUSA RISING
(1973-1974)

"If music be the food of love, play on."
— William Shakespeare

It all started with some strange guy named John Fedak who just happened to be at a garage on a hot summer evening in Chicago in July of 1973. He hung around outside the garage entrance listening to God awful rock music played by three long-haired guys. After the song was over, he approached the band and asked if he could be the band's manager, to which they surprisingly and unanimously agreed. John returned a week later asking if they were interested in having a female guitarist as well as a keyboard player named Joe join the band. Of course, you might have guessed who the guitarist was and I had never even met John, as he was a friend of Joe's. As fate would intervene, they would be key players in determining my destiny and a place in rock history!

I had just left my job working as an LPN at Presbyterian St. Luke's Hospital and was relaxing at the beach, when I heard a voice call out to me. "Hey, do you know what time it is?" Gazing up to see a good looking, curly brown-haired dude smiling down at me, *I thought, "OK, I'll give him the time of day any day!"* Before long he was sitting next to me and we got into some very interesting conversation, chatting about music and the ways of the world for hours on end. "Hey, my roommate, Joe, plays keyboards," Mike exclaimed.

"That's far out, man, I play guitar!"

"Cool! Why don't we head back to my apartment so you can meet Joe?" "Cool!"

Things were a lot different in those days in many ways. Before the advent of computers, life was a lot simpler and there were far fewer numbers of kidnappings, rapes, murders, and shootings so prevalent in today's society. People actually talked with each other and worked out their differences more often than feeling the need to settle scores with guns. Incidents of gun violence rarely, if ever, reached into schools. Anger-related gun violence was in the minority and for the most part, involved mentally unstable persons or economic hardship situations (e.g. a man unable to make a decent living for his family.) On the contrary, this was the "Age of Aquarius," and the message that was conveyed was love thy neighbor. The worst that would happen would be that you would get stoned, have sex, get more stoned, have more sex, and wake up with a case of "the clap," (aka: venereal disease).

We walked over to Mike and Joe's apartment and after meeting and talking more music with Joe, he told me he played keyboards and played a few tunes for me. After playing for a few minutes, he turned from the keyboard and gazing thoughtfully at me, asked if I was interested in joining a band. I stared at him open mouthed.

"What band?"

"Oh, just some band I found out about from my friend John." He stood there smiling his big toothy Joe grin. He was tall, lanky, and had a head of hair that could've given Jimi Hendrix competition, and I usually dug guys with long hair. There was a definite connection, yet I was more attracted to the idea of playing music in a band than to him.

"What kind of music do they play?"

"Let's go check them out!"

"OK, far out."

We hopped into his broken down yellow VW Beetle with barely functional brakes, drove to the garage, and met lead guitarist Gary Brown, Lee, the drummer, and Kim, the bass player. We jammed a few times with Joe over the next few weeks and he seemed to be into it. Once again, the hand of fate intervened and John, our would-be manager, was never seen or heard from again. To this day we have no idea whatever happened to him, yet he served his purpose of bringing us all together. Joe disappeared as well. He must have decided that playing in a band wasn't for him after all.

Soon thereafter, I stood in Gary's garage, guitar in hand, listening to these guys playing this God awful music, waiting for my chance to join in on the insanity. After impatiently waiting for the whole evening, I became a bit miffed and decided these guys weren't worth a spit anyway. Storming out to the alley where my trusty VW was parked, I drove off. Driving home, I felt bitter pangs of disappointment at not being given a chance to display the guitar chops I had practiced so diligently while listening over and over again to all the big time bands I constantly tried to imitate.

The next day I received a phone call from Gary, who apologized for the mix-up the evening before and invited me back to this time "play for real" with his band. He explained that Ed, their current guitarist, wasn't exactly working out, yet they didn't know how to tell him.

The next day I was back in the garage playing and singing my heart out, only to be told by Lee, "Man, we still need a singer!" My heart and jaw dropped to my feet at his discouraging comment. After all, I had feverishly practiced my usual repertoire of folk songs on acoustic guitar in preparation for this audition, yet had somehow failed to impress these rock gods with my vocal renditions of Joni Mitchell and Judy Collins.

I joined the band despite all odds, and stuck to guitar playing. We put an ad for a singer in the Illinois Entertainer, a local musical magazine, which is how we met Pete. He showed up at the garage and eventually become our lead singer, completing our band. We clicked and things moved quickly. We wrote original hard rock music, played a number of gigs in the Chicago and surrounding areas, cut a 45 of our music, and even had our music played on Triad Radio, 106 FM, by the station's DJ, Saul Smaizys. We loved the music we played, yet were only kids at the time, and had no idea if our music could be worth listening to much less appreciated by the general public or even by prominent music producers. Unbeknownst to any of us, the musical adventure of a lifetime was waiting in the wings.

CHAPTER 11
MEDUSA IGNITED
(1973-1976)

*"Those who had heard us before surely knew, they listened
for every mysterious clue.
Our music soared and time magically flew, we brought
them a new feeling to get into."*
— Lyrics from "Into the Night," a songwriting
collaboration of Peter Basaraba, former lead singer of
Medusa and Donna Brown, rhythm guitarist

Gary's two-car garage was dusty, dirty and filled with our Peavey amps, PA system, guitars and drums. But there was still ample room for us to play our music. Gary's mom had to park her car on the street in front of their house, which I'm sure she was not too pleased about. On one particular practice night in Gary's garage in 1973, the band was as hot as that July evening. The atmosphere of the garage might have been that of any garage had it not been that this one was destined to house some of the most talented musicians of the day. We came together to create some of the best music of the early '70s although unaware of it at the time.

And then there was Gary. I remember him that July night—tall and slender with shoulder length dark brown hair matching his eyes. He wore faded coral colored cut-off shorts with a short sleeve dark green t-shirt and his body rocked steadily back and forth to the heavy rock beat of the music pouring from his guitar. His fingers were flying lightning rod fast and furious over the frets. He set an insanely fast pace for his band members to try to keep up with, and yet somehow, we did.

Gary had been in a number of bands before meeting up with Lee and Kim, and was kicked out of one band called Pineapple Cloud. That made him even more determined than ever to make his guitar playing smoking hot. Mission accomplished! He played with an intensity of someone who had fought a hard-won battle and emerged intact, supercharged and ready to take on the world with music as his only weapon.

Gary was the leader of the band and we all knew it. He had years of practice

to prepare him for this role, and was one of the original founding members, con-
ductor and pacesetter of the group. We all looked to him for guidance with the
timing, transitions, beginnings and endings, and I often wondered to whom he
looked for guidance. Sometimes there would seem to be no end to a song, as his
Echoplex echoed on forever. If he started a song at warp speed, we all played at
the same speed. If he bounced up and down three times, we knew we'd either be
starting or ending a certain part of the song immediately thereafter, or get lost in
the shuffle.

When he and I first met, I was wearing a dark navy t-shirt with a cartoon picture of a gumball machine on the front. Smiling, Gary told me he liked the shirt
and gumballs. At first, I was a bit embarrassed by his comment, yet there was
something attractive about his directness and tenacity. The next thing I knew we
had our first date at the International House of Pancakes. We spent hours talking
about music and Medusa, and the time flew by too fast. Before long, we were
spending a lot of time together in his basement, writing songs, playing music and
enjoying each other's company. After rehearsals, we would stand in the alley behind his garage embracing for hours on end as our relationship blossomed. Something about the way he hugged me just felt so right. The fire of his Aries fanned
the flames of my Leo, and we formed an intense bond. He had his own ideas
about how a guitar should be played, and tried to teach me his style of playing,
yet this frustrated rather than motivated me. I felt that his level of proficiency
was so far out of my reach, I got discouraged and gave up trying to play like him
and settled for being best at being myself. I created my own playing style, a unique
up stroking rhythm, to distinguish and establish myself as an integral part of the
band with a distinctive guitar sound, offering a diverse blending into the driving,
hard edged music we played.

Although we enjoyed being together and shared some good times, we often
argued about everything from the normal getting to know each other relational
growing pains to differences about the arrangements of songs we wrote. We had
our break-ups and walked out on each other numerous times, yet always seemed
to find a way to work things out and keep our relationship together.

Lee, our drummer and other founding member, had a head full of frizzed out
hair, a goofy laugh and a flair for playing a solid and steady beat for our impossibly
wild and asynchronous rhythms. He and Gary met in 1968 in their Freshman
year at Foreman High School and were in the same home room, yet it wasn't until
1969 that they really solidified their musical friendship. They had similar musical
tastes, being fans of Grand Funk, MC5, The Stooges and Hawkwind.

When Lee finally got a chance to hear Gary play guitar he was pretty amazed
that Gary's style was similar to that of Hendrix and Jimmy Page of Led Zep-

pelin. Lee knew this was the guy he wanted to team up with and thus, the wheels were set in motion for the eventual formation of Medusa. The first band they formed was called The Edge and lasted for a year. Gary and Lee remained together after The Edge split and it was during this time that Kim joined the band they then formed, known as Poor Yorick. They soon gained a rhythm guitarist, Ed, who made feeble attempts to sing, performed incredible onstage antics and often received credit for the incredible guitar licks played by Gary. They played a number of small gigs at VFW Halls and had been together for a few years when I entered Gary's garage that fateful July day, upsetting the apple cart. Ed was the guitarist who refused to leave that day I was to audition, and whom I eventually replaced. Lee and Gary were quite the team by the time I entered the picture to form Medusa.

All Gary had to do was play a few chaotic riffs and Lee was off and running, and uncannily on target with his backing drum beats. We never followed any particular timing, choosing instead to go to the beat of our own drummer, so to speak.

Kim, our bass player, was in a different category entirely, and was a gentle giant both in height and musical talent. He was soft-spoken, yet extremely passionate about music in general, especially bands with exotic sounding names like Toe Fat, Sacred Mushroom, and Twentieth Century Zoo. Kim and Gary became fast friends and met every Saturday for breakfast, then headed downtown to peruse record stores for European imports they were both into at the time. Whenever they talked music, Kim's head would bob excitedly up and down as his voice would suddenly go up a few notches to utter an agreeable, "Yeah, yeah!" He would smile throughout our conversations that went on for almost as long as Gary's guitar solos! (Not during the solos, mind you...) During rehearsals, I often looked up from playing my guitar and meet Kim's kind, yet intense green eyes, our heads nodding in time with whatever groove we were jamming away on.

Last, but certainly not least, was Pete, our one-of-a kind singer with a voice beyond compare, the only band member not born in Chicago. Born in Australia, he spent some time in Germany before moving to Chicago. Pete played guitar and sang in a band called Kaleidoscope before joining Medusa. He was always full of energy, fun-loving and playful, with vocals matching his upbeat mannerisms. He played a mean flexitone—an instrument that resembled a mousetrap and sounded like some weird flying saucer whirling through space that was ever-present in our songs. The lyrics he wrote for our songs were every bit as weird sounding as his flexitone, yet were written from the heart and a perfect fit for the varying moods and rhythms of our music. One moment he was singing about black wizards and the next of "mosquitoes flying scared." He smiled and laughed a lot about one thing or another, and always joked around with members of the band. Pete's persona was dynamic, charismatic and charming. I laughed every time I was around Pete and enjoyed his carefree, easy-going nature and good humor, in definite contrast with the roller coaster ride of my relationship with Gary. Pete and I dated a few times in between break-ups with Gary, yet my heart would eventually lead me back home to Gary.

We were five totally different people from different backgrounds, five pieces of the puzzle fitting together to complete the whole picture. Our personalities were as different as our musical tastes, yet we blended together and created a uniquely original, hard-edged driving sound quite unlike the horn-driven bands typical of the Chicago music scene of the '70s.

Our music would come at you like a speeding freight train, hitting hard and heavy with the force and ferocity of our combined youthful energies and creativity gone wild. We listened to European Prog (progressive) rock groups such as Epitaph, Amon Duul, Hawkwind, and Can.

These influences can be heard throughout the songs we wrote. Their songs were filled with lengthy and intricate guitar solos and riffs and our music reflected similar patterns.

Pete wrote a song called "Think Harder" and sang part of it in German, which I'm sure was influenced by Epitaph and the time he spent in Germany. Gary and I got together in his basement to write songs, and challenged each other to come up with some fairly complex guitar riffs. One of these riffs can be heard in "Black Wizard," a song I wrote after reading J. R. R. Tolkien's brilliant "The Lord of the Rings," my all-time favorite literary work. I could barely play the notes, yet somehow willed my fingers to move in fast and furious fashion. "The more complex the music, the better" was the motto we lived by. Gary and I wrote a song called "Transient Amplitudes" in which we jammed for at least 11 minutes with an assortment of heavy, spacey guitar riffs and rhythms, thundering bass runs, matched note for note by Lee's wild drumming, amidst Gary's eternal Echoplex space ship landing sound effects.

The band came to be named Medusa from my fondness of mythology and it sounded like a cool name for a band. Soon thereafter, Pete came to rehearsal with a banner he had painted of a pentagram with a goat's head inside surrounded by two flaming claws and Medusa's snake-infested head above the pentagram. When showing the banner to me, I wasn't too impressed by the pentagram as I thought it too satanic and told him so. He countered with, "Hey, it's cool, man! It's just art!" I had to admit the artwork was good, yet still wasn't thrilled about the pentagram and symbolic connotation. Nonetheless, the guys all liked it and I was outnumbered, so the banner became our logo. Although there were a few songs with dark references, such as Black Wizard, Strangulation and Unknown Fear, Medusa music was not created with the intent of worshipping Satan. Rather, we idolized the great rock legends (i.e. Hendrix, Clapton, Joplin, Slick, Sabbath) and many others who influenced and inspired us to create the style of music we played.

Medusa played a number of gigs in and around Chicago and the neighboring suburbs, our first gig played at a place called The Post. Gary worked at a company called Switchcraft, and one of his co-workers, Rex Bundy, played acoustic guitar in a band called Gabriel Bondage. One day, Rex and Gary were talking music as they usually did to pass the work day along. Gary mentioned to Rex that he also played in a band, and Rex extended an invitation to have Medusa back up Bondage when they played at The Post. That was our first time playing out in front of an audience, yet I don't recall any details of that gig other than the fact we were all excited to get out of the garage and play out live.

We played another gig at the Civic Center in Glen Ellyn, Illinois, and had a great audience that was every bit as rowdy as we were. The auditorium we played in was located next to a police station by a strange stroke of luck, and we had a number of interesting events occur that night. We had the volume cranked up pretty loud and apparently the police were none too pleased and let us know about it by calling over to a staff person at the Civic Center. The staff person approached someone in the band and asked us to turn down. Of course, I had to make commentary about this to the audience, rabble-rouser that I was. "Hey folks, the cops across the way are telling us to turn down. What do you guys say about that?" The years had somewhat mellowed me and although still radical in many ways, I kept it polite and at least didn't call them pigs! This only incited the audience to get even rowdier and they responded by yelling back their approval of our current deafening decibel level. We responded by breaking into a rip-roaring 10-minute version of Hootchie-Cootchie Man by Muddy Waters, and luckily heard nothing further from the police!

Another event almost brought down the house in a somewhat different fashion. Many bands of that time had pretty awesome light shows, and ours was definitely a force to be reckoned with. Lee fashioned the lights by mounting them on two by fours and rigging it so they could be changed from a keyboard he rebuilt for that purpose. It was the job of our roadies to run the lights and they had a slight mishap in that department. Fred, and another one of our roadies had a few too many tokes and forgot they had already put some flash powder (similar to gun powder) into the flash pods of our stage lights before they went outside to toke up. When they returned, they added yet more powder to the pods and suddenly, a loud KABOOM could be heard, signaling the end of the show. All of us in the band were pretty shaken up and stone deaf at first, yet still alive and laughed it off.

When the smoke finally cleared, the place was still standing, although Kim was lying sprawled on the ground. We feared he had met his maker, yet his pride was hurt more than he was! He picked himself up, brushed off, and carried on about the process of packing up all our equipment like nothing happened. I'm sure that night will go down in Glen Ellyn history forevermore. But it was just another day for the guys of Medusa who were in the habit of shooting bottle rockets at each other in the alley behind the garage where we practiced.

Medusa was even on the radio a number of times. Triad radio, station 106 FM, was one of many popular stations we listened to. Saul Smaizys was a DJ there who played the music of numerous local rock bands of the day. After hearing our music, he decided to play the song, "Seven Miles From Heaven" on his program. This was a song I wrote about my vagabond lifestyle. Due to radio interference, the song was interrupted halfway through, breaking its flow. Nonetheless, we were psyched to hear our music on the radio in whatever fashion. We must have impressed him. In October 1974, he wrote an article about Medusa and our music, complete with a group picture that was published in Triad's monthly magazine. We were rock stars in our own right, even though the world hadn't realized it at the time, and neither had we!

It wasn't all business for us and we managed to find some time for a few fun getaways and adventures in Wisconsin. Sometime in 1975 Jan, a friend of mine, invited Gary and me to spend a weekend with her and boyfriend, Chris, in a rustic little cabin they rented in the woods. It was a beautiful, private place near a lake, and we pretty much had full run of the place, and run we did! Streaking, or running in the nude, was popular in those days, so Gary and I decided to give it a try. We peeled off our clothes, except for our shoes and took off in a full sprint, dashing through the open meadows, with only Jan and Chris and perhaps a few puzzled deer as our audience. Afterwards, we collapsed on the ground winded and laughed with great gusto about our excursion. Ah, sweet youth… I don't recall if Jan or Chris ever joined us, yet we all had a good chuckle about the event.

On another trip to Wisconsin that same summer, Pete, Fred, Gary and I were on a rowboat on a lake and had rowed about a mile or so from shore. We were out in the boat a good part of the day and were ready to start heading back, when Fred, deciding he wanted to swim rather than row, jumped in the water and began swimming toward the shore. I gazed at him in disbelief for a few moments and thinking he was quite the lunatic, found myself lunging into the icy water after him. We were both swimming like lunatics toward the shore and making steady progress, when I made the mistake of stopping mid-stroke to see if the shore was getting any closer. It wasn't. The boat I vacated moments before was now rowing closer to the shore than I was. I panicked for a moment and wasted energy waving my arms in the air in the direction of the boat hoping Gary and Pete would see me and slow down. They didn't. The water in that moment felt even colder than when I first dove in, and I felt my core temperature and confidence plunge! *OK, kiddo, I scolded myself, you can do this! You're a good swimmer, remember?* In a flash, I was swimming toward the shore, envisioning myself effortlessly slicing through the water like some Olympic athlete. I lost all track of where Fred was and imagined he was already standing on shore, toweling himself off and laughing at my stupidity.

Making slow yet steady progress toward the shore, I noticed they were standing on the shore not 50 feet away, talking and laughing amongst themselves, and casting occasional glances in my direction. Swimming the final strokes to where they stood, I wearily heaved my body up on the shore with aching arms, took a few strides and did a belly flop down on the warm sand face down. I lay there motionless for a few moments basking in the warm sand and welcome rest. Gary was now talking to me. "Hey, are you OK?"

I lifted my head to see the guys towering above me and coughed some sand from my mouth. "Yeah, I'm fine."

"What took you so long?" he teased. I stared at him for a moment.

"Savoring the moment." They started laughing and soon I joined them, the tension of the moment was suddenly a distant memory. This excursion would prove to be invaluable training for more challenging athletic endeavors yet to come.

One day in 1976, Pete came to rehearsal with news that a record label, Pepperhead Records, owned by a local recording engineer named Steven Wilcox, was looking for artists to record their music on 45s. It didn't take us long to decide to take the plunge and record our music on vinyl. We picked two of our best songs at the time: "Strangulation," a hard and heavy rocker showcasing Pete's great upper register vocals and memorable lyrics about a black spider on the wall of your mind; and "Temptress," a softer, more melodic love ballad. We recorded them in Lee's basement on his 4–track, then took the tapes to Pepperhead and Wilcox and made the 45s. We were each given a box of one hundred of the records. While Gary kept a few, I don't recall whatever became of mine. At the time, I had no reason to keep them, not realizing they would one day be of considerable worth.

Around the same time period we received our 45s, our music was gradually changing to accommodate cover tunes, and I felt somewhat conflicted about the shift away from writing original songs. I was still pretty young and often wondered what career to pursue at that point in time. While I would have preferred to be a rock star, I didn't think in my wildest imagination that our music had any future potential.

Working as an LPN at University of Illinois hospital, I was told a number of times by my head nurse that I should pursue getting my RN degree for both status and financial gains. I started considering a two-year RN program at Truman College that would give me credit toward my degree for being an LPN, and even took the ACT test a number of times as a prerequisite for the program. But I didn't think the scores I received were high enough to get into the program, until I had a meeting one day with the director who informed me that my scores were high enough to qualify for entry. Her comment pretty much made my decision and changed the course of Medusa history. I decided to leave the band. It was a difficult decision as I still enjoyed playing music and knew my desire to attend nursing school would not go over very well with the guys in the band.

Gary and I talked at great length about my wanting to leave the band, and of course, he was not pleased about it. He tried to convince me to stay, yet saw how determined I was to make something of myself, and relented. Pete, Kim and Lee took the news in stride and the band went about the business of searching for a new rhythm guitar player. Pete had a friend named Art who played guitar and told him about the band. Soon thereafter, Art entered the garage with guitar in hand and seemed to fit right in with his "fro" giving Lee's hair some stiff competition. Art was shy, soft-spoken and small in stature, and was a decent guitarist in his own right. He was a quick learner and soon the band was taking group mug shots in a cemetery and playing numerous gigs for sororities, fraternities, hotels and clubs in the city and surrounding suburbs. The gigs they played at Northwestern University turned into wild free-for-alls, complete with kids wearing togas, drinking alcohol mixed with grape juice from large garbage cans, and running amok. I have to admit I was envious of the guys getting all the attention and glory of being photographed in the cemetery. But I channeled my energy into the challenge of completing the courses required for admission to the nursing program.

It wasn't long after I left that Medusa's flame began to dwindle, leading to an unfortunate and eventual end. Art stayed with the band for less than a year, and was replaced by another guitarist, Tony, who also made a quick exit. Looking back at that stage of my life with some regret, I wonder what would have become of Medusa had I stayed? There were other factors involved in the band's demise, such as conflicting personalities and opinions, and a different feeling to the music, as evidenced by playing cover tunes rather than the original music we created when I was still in the band. There are those critical junctures in life when you have to toss your fate to the winds of time, forsaking what is known and surrendering to deeper, less discernable meanderings of the unknown. Going with your gut doesn't always turn out as planned. Sometimes life in its cyclical nature will throw you a curve when you least expect it in the guise of unfinished business, offering up a second chance to get it right.

CHAPTER 12

THE NURSING SCHOOL YEARS (1977-1979)

"To do what nobody else will do, in a way that nobody else can do, in spite of all we go through; is to be a nurse."
— Rawsi Williams, J.D., B.S.N., RN

Making the transition from music to medicine required the utmost discipline, mental stamina and fortitude and the patience of a saint, in other words, everything I lacked! In my first semester at Truman College, we were thrown right into the mix of an intense nursing curriculum and prerequisite classes required for the course, such as biology, microbiology, chemistry, and algebra. Many of my classmates also worked at full or part time jobs, and I didn't envy their heavy course load. I was lucky to have finished most of these prerequisite classes the year before entering the actual program. I did have one left over Biology class to deal with while working part time at the hospital as an LPN. Trying to learn nursing theory from some fairly interesting nursing instructors was stressful enough when crammed into a day's work.

The teamwork I had experienced when with Medusa also helped me get through nursing school. My fellow classmates, Joanne and Kathy, were on a mission. Sitting together in one of my classes one day, they approached me during break and were looking for classmates to be part of a study group. The group was the idea of Joanne and Kathy. Joanne introduced me to her friend, Kathy, who was the recently-elected president of our student nurse class. I was drawn to Kathy's outgoing and good-natured manner.

Joanne was more the athletic type and did her fair share of running until she "messed up" her knees and switched to biking. After chatting for a short time about sports, she asked if I was interested in joining the group. There was something about her openness, athleticism and inquisitive mind I instantly liked.

"It would be just the three of us for now, yet we could leave it open for others who might be interested," Kathy explained.

"How often would we meet?"

"Whenever we find some spare time," Joanne jumped in. Most likely in the evenings a few times a week."

I hated to give up my evenings, but they were already taken up with studying. Joining a study group might make studying more fun, I thought.

"OK, I'm in."

"Great!" exclaimed Joanne and Kathy in perfect unison. From that moment on we formed a close, cohesive friendship that lasted for the entire two years of nursing school. We had a true support group in the most meaningful sense of the word, supporting and encouraging one another through some of the toughest times I can ever recall. We met several times a week and compared notes, shared thoughts and experiences we encountered during class and "clinicals" or hospital days when we gave hands-on care to patients.

As the year went on we gathered two new team members, Pat and Gayle, who being the oldest in the group were the most mature. They were both married with kids of their own, in addition to their adopting Kathy, Joanne and me. Pat was large of frame and heart with a great sense of humor, and Gayle was the most serious of the group, yet could roar with appreciative laughter when someone cracked a good joke. Each of us, like the members of Medusa, had our own personalities, yet we worked and got along well together, completing the circle.

The first year flew by in a whirlwind of trying to cram an infinite amount of nursing theory into our pea-sized brains. In our senior year, we had four rotations to complete—Pediatrics, Geriatrics, Orthopedics and Psychiatry—and were expected to do projects for our first two rotations. Each project involved selecting one patient and writing a care plan or complete account of how we cared for that patient, typed out and neatly spaced, for either a pass or fail determination by our instructors. If we didn't pass one rotation's project, we had to do a third project on the third rotation and pass that one before we could graduate. No pressure at all!

My first rotation was Pediatrics, and it was a bit disconcerting as there were no actual children on the floor to care for, the youngest child there being a teenager which limited my choice of patients for our project. I picked this child despite the fact that she didn't have any major health problems and there was not very much to do for her. Needless to say, my project did not pass despite my best efforts and I felt devastated. My next rotation was Ortho, and went without a hitch. When most of my classmates were celebrating our imminent graduation festivities, I was still struggling to get through my third project in the Psych. rotation, the most difficult of all the rotations. Graduation for me seemed as far away as the moon.

The facility in which we did our Psych. rotation was originally known as Dunning, an infamous asylum for the insane. Built in 1851, the facility originally housed hundreds of mentally ill people who were deemed "incurable" by the outside world and who seldom returned to the outside, often dying there. Dunning had a reputation as being an "inadequate, mismanaged, and inefficient public mental health system." (8.) The facility incorporated other buildings such as a poorhouse and an infirmary with a large population of patients with tuberculosis. Despite additions made over the years to the original architectural structure, Dunning was plagued with problems. Overcrowding, insufficient heat, no hot water, and poor ventilation contributed to the high mortality rate amongst patients and inmates. Pictures of the facility displayed an ominous and foreboding exterior, and horror stories of mistreatment of inmates were abundant, adding to its harrowing and horrendous reputation. Anyone hearing the name, "Dunning" was instantly fearful of the place. Use of archaic treatments on the residents were commonplace, including ECT or electro-shock therapy and insulin shock to name a few. People residing in the neighborhood often felt unsafe and feared the possibility of an inmate escaping and breaking into their houses.

Dunning underwent numerous name changes, in 1912 to Chicago State Hospital, and again in 1968 to Reed Center, which was the name of the facility when I trained there in 1979. Despite name and treatment policy revisions to more current and humane pharmaceutical modes of therapy, there still remains an atmosphere of fear and stigma surrounding the facility. This stigma currently prevails in regards to the mentally ill and despite the prevalence of antidepressant therapy, the jury is still out on what treatments are most effective for mental illness.

The first day of my Psych rotation, I entered this facility with tremendous trepidation, and was certain some horrible monstrosity awaited me there. Yet the place looked nothing like the dark, forbidding pictures I saw in books. Both interior and exterior were remodeled and appeared bright and had a modern décor. I was relieved to see my fellow classmates and instructor, whom I will call Miss Winner, standing in the lobby when I arrived. We got a tour of the place and as I became more familiar with the environment and learned the routine, my nervousness decreased.

Winner assigned me to "Patrick," a patient with paranoid schizophrenia, who presented me with one of many supreme challenges throughout my nursing career. When I first met Patrick, he stared holes right through me and every other word he spoke was laced with profanity the likes of which would unnerve a porn star. When I approached Winner afterwards to discuss what had transpired with this patient, I hoped she would be understanding of the situation as a nurse skilled in the area of psychology, yet wasn't prepared for her response.

"If you're expecting sympathy from me, you won't get it," she remarked in a stern voice. She reminded me of a Weimaraner, sleek in build and grey of hair, yet her bark was worse than her bite. OK, so now for Plan B, I thought, yet didn't quite know what Plan B was.

"I don't expect sympathy Miss Winner. I was hoping I could be assigned a different patient, or at least get some direction from you as to how to approach a very intimidating patient."

"Every patient here, Donna, will try to intimidate you in some fashion and I see he accomplished that."

"How do you not get intimidated by someone like him?"

"You allowed him to get to you. What do you think you could do differently?"

OK, so now I'm getting psychoanalyzed. I thought for a few minutes then gave my best gut instinct, "Perhaps try not to react to what he says."

Winner nodded. "He's feeding off your negative reaction and you're meeting his expectations."

"So, are you saying I should agree with him?"

"No, neither agree or disagree. Perhaps you should review your therapeutic techniques in your textbook this evening, OK? We will discuss this more in class." She stood up, turned away from me and started for the door. End of topic, with no further discussion, and stated as though it was beyond her capacity to share any further information at the moment or she would certainly detonate right there on the spot. Obligatory thanks exchanged and exit stage left. I drove back home in a daze, feeling even more confused than when I arrived and questioning my sanity for wanting to be a nurse in the first place.

Over the next few weeks, we discussed the various therapeutic techniques used in counseling clients with various types of mental illness, and I felt somewhat more prepared to deal with Patrick who was putting me through the wringer. During one meeting with him, he started throwing his usual verbal barrage at me, and this time instead of reacting to his tirade, I responded, "You appear very angry today, Patrick," trying to speak in as calm a voice as I could muster. No response, only an intense glare in my direction, and crossed legs swinging back and forth in agitation. I met and held his gaze and my breath. Moments passed in visual gridlock and felt like an eternity.

"I want to get out of here!" Patrick bellowed with the intensity of a steel beam hitting me squarely between the eyes. In my mind, I envisioned myself bolting out of that room, yet couldn't move if my life depended on it.

"I get that," I agreed trying to regain my composure. Patrick contemplated my answer for a few moments, then stood up and stormed out of the room. I watched him rush down the hall back to his room, and felt a sudden wave of relief wash over me. In post conference with Winner, she inquired about how I thought the interaction went with Patrick.

"Well, at least he didn't swear at me this time!"

She nodded, a faint smile on her face, and that was a good enough pat on the back for me.

The next few weeks flew by in a whirlwind of more meetings with a silent and surly Patrick. I was also frazzled preparing my project for review by Winner. A very important component of the project remained, the outcome of my futile intervention attempts, and I struggled to come up with an answer. After a considerable amount of deliberation, I decided to be truthful and stated in my written report that I was uncertain as to whether or not any intervention I tried was helpful to Patrick. I realized in the moment, despite my best efforts, it would take a concerted team approach to help Patrick, and perhaps a person has to want to be well to work toward that goal.

With the same nervous trepidation when first entering the facility, I turned the handle to Winner's office door and walked in to learn the outcome of whether or not I had passed the last project. There was no indication from her blank expression as she greeted me and told me to take a seat.

"How do you feel you did?"

"I feel I did the best I could in a difficult situation," Like a contestant being judged on a reality talent show, Simon Cowell's voice echoed in my head, *"Well, that was absolutely abysmal!"* Winner's voice brought me back to reality.

"I appreciate your efforts in this area and gave you a C." She faintly smiled. I passed! Whoopeeeeeeeeeeee! I almost fell out of my chair with surprise and relief. Not realizing another surprise was awaiting me, I thanked her, and almost tore the door off the wall rushing out into the hall. The sight that met my eyes is one I will never forget. A sea of some two hundred or more faces greeted me outside the office and the echoes of my classmates' jubilant yells and cheers filled the air. Right in front of me were the beaming faces of Joanne, Kathy, Gail and Pat, and with tears of joy I joined them for a group hug. Not since the Lincoln Park days did I ever recall PARTYING SO HEARTY!

With only the Geriatrics rotation to complete, graduation looked like a shoe in, yet the universe had other plans. Around the same time a city-wide teacher's strike threatened to postpone our long-awaited graduation. I learned about this strike one evening while watching TV and sat there staring at the screen in disbelief hoping this strike would only affect other schools. Of course, it didn't. When I got to school the next day, I discovered that our instructors were also involved in the strike and that our May 17 graduation date was now to be extended into June. Of course we were disheartened and sick to our stomachs when hearing this sad news. We discussed the situation in our support group and decided to take action. We invited a few other classmates to attend our meeting, including Bruno, also an LPN. It was suggested by Bruno that we form a student nurse association to establish a cohesive platform to represent the nursing students and convey their concerns to administration. This was agreed upon by everyone in the group and then conveyed in a newsletter to all our nursing classmates. An election was then held to vote for officers of the association. Bruno was elected President, and to my surprise, I was selected as Vice President, and thus, the Truman College Student Nurse Association, or TCSNA was born.

Joanne was elected as Secretary and another student, Sandy, became our Treasurer.

With the Association established, we got to work talking to our classmates and trying to get their feedback about the strike. As expected, they were none too pleased about delaying our graduation date, yet only a few students were willing to attend any of our meetings to discuss options on what we could do as a group to end the strike. Our hectic workload, I'm certain, influenced the sparse attendance at our meetings, especially with the end of the course only a few months away. We, as students, could understand their concerns about getting involved, yet were nonetheless disappointed that we didn't have their support for our attempts to keep on target for graduation.

During one of our meetings, it was decided that our board members would approach the administration and see if anything could be worked out in our favor. Our request was, of course, turned down, as money was and always is a key issue in a capitalistic society. The teachers worked hard for their money yet we, as students, also worked every bit as hard to become the good nurses they were training us to become. We looked forward to graduation, realizing our dreams of becoming nurses and making money to earn a living for ourselves. Our graduation also represented a goal achieved, a significant sense of accomplishment, and of course, yet another great excuse for celebration!

The following week the teachers went on strike as planned and although they didn't come to school, we did! Bruno addressed our rag-tag group of rebels with a serious look of concern on his face, as he informed us of more discouraging news.

"I hear that the teachers could be out for at least another two to three weeks and I'm sure you have heard the same on the news." We sat in silence for a few moments pondering the issue at hand.

"Speaking of news, why don't we go to the TV stations and tell our side of the story?" Kathy's voice broke the silence. We all agreed it was a good idea.

"I think we should stage a protest rally as well. If we could get our classmates to join us, that would make this strike and our plight more newsworthy." I excitedly jumped up from my chair.

"Where would we hold the rally?" Bruno queried.

"How about in Lincoln Park?" I offered. *Ah yes, some fond memories.*

"I think we would get more attendance if we held it somewhere closer. Why not have it right out in front of Truman?" Bruno suggested and we agreed to hold the rally where the strike was occurring.

Over the next few days, Bruno, Kathy, Joanne and I made the rounds of the various TV stations talking to reporters about the strike and our situation, and one station in particular, WGN, agreed to do an interview. The reporter asked us when he could do the interview, and we told him to give us a few days to spread the word about the rally to our classmates. We met with the reporter on a Thursday, and he told us WGN would also cover our rally. That evening watching the news and seeing our faces on TV being interviewed was surreal! The fact that we appeared on the news generated a lot of excitement amongst the members of TCSNA and support group, and we hoped this excitement would rub off on our classmates.

We planned to have the rally that Saturday morning at 9 a.m. and made numerous phone calls to our classmates to inform them of this event and invite them to attend. Although most had seen us being interviewed on the news, few were eager to join the rally. We felt discouraged that there wasn't more team spirit and participation, yet were determined to carry on regardless and do our part to bring an end to the strike.

On Saturday, only eleven students, consisting of TCSNA board and support group members and a few classmates, attended the rally. The day was chilly and rainy, yet our spirits were high despite the low number of attendees. We carried "End the Strike" and "Future Nurses of the World Unite" signs, yelled peaceful anti-strike slogans, and paraded around the school for the better part of the day. News cameras recorded our protest for the world to behold and Truman history was made. The world heard our voices, felt our powerful presence, and the teachers union reached a decision to end the strike. The teachers were back to classes by the next week and we graduated on May 17 as scheduled.

Once again, the power of people united for a common good won over the establishment and demonstrated that it doesn't take an army to affect change. Thinking back on the protest at the Democratic National Convention, it reinforced my beliefs that protest didn't have to be violent to be effective. I reveled in the exuberant triumph of working toward and reaching a goal and understanding the true meaning of cause and effect. Much like a spider weaving its web, these early experiences formed initial slender threads waiting to transform into larger infrastructures of future personal endeavors, as yet unrealized.

After graduation, our support group celebrated in fine fashion at a fancy restaurant and enjoyed the camaraderie we shared. Anticipating starting my RN career, I presumed that the concept of teamwork would apply to each work situation I encountered. Despite my best intentions, my expectations in this regard conflicted with the reality of dealing with other nurses, supervisors, and life and death situations on a daily basis. It is all too easy for someone who is easy going and idealistic to be swallowed whole, spit out and left lying in a tattered heap in the midst of the lion's den known as nursing. I had heard the well-known expression, "Nurses eat their young," one too many times for my liking, yet I must admit from experience, this is true.

Nursing School prepares nurses through education, but an area of obvious deficiency pertains to the topic of bullying. Nurses are expected by other nurses to hit the ground running, always be on top of their game, and not be too needy. If you for a moment fall short of this expectation, you will be disposed of in a heartbeat. There is little teamwork or orientation in nursing. Every person for herself or himself is more the rule. Whereas new grads get at least a week or more of orientation to the workings of a hospital, us seasoned veterans might get a tour of the place and then it's business as usual.

Most of my fondest nursing memories were when I worked as an LPN. I had the respect of my co-workers and even supervisors, yet discovered that in being an RN, I didn't have the same experience. After bouncing around from one unsatisfying job to another as an RN, the gratifying work I so long sought after evaded me time and again. Looking back on my nursing career, my mind is flooded with images of the motherless baby bird attempting a solo flight, yet never taking off.

CHAPTER 13
RUNNING IN PARADISE (1978-1982)

"It is a rough road that leads to the heights of greatness."
— Seneca

What started out of curiosity, initiated by a suggestion from my dad to join the Athlete's Foot Running Club, turned into a full-blown addiction. This time the addiction was positive and healthy. When running with the club, we ran anywhere from three to eight miles per run and it was during these weekly runs I built up a respectable amount of strength, stamina, and endurance. I ran my first marathon in October of 1978, while still in nursing school.

Meeting the running club for the first time one chilly Sunday at Belmont Harbor on Lake Michigan where the group was convening, I was a bit nervous yet chomping at the bit to finally engage in some sort of sport, especially something as freeing as running. I really enjoyed it. With every Sunday run, I released more and more inhibitions, realizing that I was not going to die as Ma would have had me believe. I was soon running in weekly 5K and 10K races, and progressed to running in local and out of state marathons, biathlons and triathlons.

At one Sunday run I met Roz, who became a good friend and running partner if only for a short period of time. Informing me within a few months that she was moving to Alaska, my heart sank, as through running, we had established a rapport. We kept in contact through letters, emails and when she came to Colorado, yet I still missed seeing her at the group runs. Her move to Alaska inspired me to develop an interest in pursuing more challenging running adventures in faraway exotic places!

While thumbing through a running magazine one day, an ad caught my interest. "Run In Paradise at The Honolulu Marathon..." and instantly I imagined myself already there basking in the balmy sun under palm trees. There were trips being led by Roadrunner Tours and I called the number and signed myself up straight away. There was little thought behind the plans other than wanting to break away from the rat race of the city to discover a different part of the world. The year was 1982 and I was working at Loyola University in the Health Service department. I worked with some interesting co-workers to say the least!

After signing up to run the Honolulu Marathon, I set about the challenge of training for this event. It was not an easy task working full time and trying to fit training into a busy workday. I would go out for long eight-to-ten mile runs on my lunch hour to the astonished looks from my fellow nurses as I did my quick change routine in and out of sweats. I was most certainly the topic of their conversations over lunch, as the most exercise they ever did was putting students in rooms to see Dr. Khouri, the medical director of Health Service. Between running at lunch and after work, I logged about 40 or so miles per week. The training would give me the mental toughness and determination for future athletic and outdoor pursuits and increasing my self-esteem, so lacking from an unfulfilling childhood.

I had also started taking classes at Northeastern Illinois University working toward a bachelor's degree in liberal arts. So, needless to say, life was pretty interesting. What I didn't know at the time was that I was soon to meet a very important person who would play a key role in my life. There she was, this older woman with shoulder length grey hair pulled back in a ponytail sitting in the seat next to mine on the airplane heading to Hawaii that December. As I sat in my seat, she smiled at me and despite not having met her before that moment, I felt an instant connection. "Hi there, I'm Gloria," she chirped in her cheery voice. And you are?"

"Donna, and it's nice to meet you," we both clasped hands. She exuded a genuine warmth and sincerity I found compelling.

"I'm going to run the Honolulu Marathon."

"That's where we're heading! My husband, Skip, is also running the marathon!" her face beaming.

"Nice! Are you running as well?"

"Oh, heavens no, I'm his cheering section!" she laughed.

"Good for you to be supportive of his running endeavors! By the way, where is he?"

"Oh, he is flitting around somewhere as always. Let me see if I can find him." She got up and walked down the narrow aisle to the front of the airplane. Moments later, she came back with a tall, wiry sandy haired guy and introduced me to her husband, Skip, who was just as nervous and excited about the marathon as I was. We bantered back and forth for a few minutes about our enthusiasm to be running in paradise and, after shaking hands and wishing each other good luck, he was gone in a flash rushing down the aisle to some unknown destination.

He's a man of few words, I thought. Gloria's voice interrupted my thoughts. "You'll have to excuse him. He likes his exercise." As we talked, I recalled all the training and preparation I had done for this trip. I then thought about how difficult it was leaving Gary. I had never been away from Gary's side much less across the Pacific without him. He was just as nervous about my leaving him as well. When I told him about wanting to run the marathon, he didn't understand what the attraction was.

"Can't you just run the Chicago Marathon or another marathon somewhere closer like Indiana or Wisconsin?"

"I've already run the Chicago Marathon, and besides I've never been to Hawaii and am looking forward to exploring those sunny, sandy beaches!" Despite my excitement, leaving familiar surroundings had always been difficult for me and this time was no different. I knew Gary and I would miss each other tremendously and that he was concerned for my safety as a woman traveling alone.

"I'll be fine and besides, I'll be with other people running the marathon in the Roadrunner's Tour group." I pulled him into my arms and we hugged for quite a long time.

Staring intently at me he whispered, "I'm really going to miss you!"

"I'll miss you too." Gazing into his eyes, mine were soon filled with tears. The same scene went down at the airport saying our farewells to each other.

"Are you running alone?" Gloria's voice interrupted my thoughts once again bringing me back to the moment.

"No, I'm part of a group, Roadrunner Tours, and we're meeting at the airport in Hawaii."

We chatted for the whole nine-hour flight talking about everything under the sun. She told me she and Skip volunteered at numerous running races for a local organization in Chicago known as CARA (Chicago Area Runner's Association), and that she swam for exercise at the YMCA near where she lived in Skokie, a suburb of Chicago. She also told me she did some clowning for various charity events and that especially sparked my interest. I recalled seeing a mime show on the campus of Northwestern University in Evanston, Illinois with Gary a few months prior. I watched the performance with amazement at the skill with which the mimes communicated without even saying a word. I told Gloria about the show, my fascination with mime and that I had even taken a few mime classes. She seemed genuinely interested in whatever I had to say and a deep and lasting bond was solidified in those hours of getting to know each other and sharing our life stories. She eventually became more than just a friend to me.

When we arrived in Honolulu, I said goodbye to Gloria and Skip knowing that I'd see them again within the next few days. I met up with the Roadrunners Tour group led by Hal Higdon, a well-known runner from Chicago and featured writer in *Runner's World*, a magazine I subscribed to and read cover to cover. I got acquainted with the group that consisted of runners from all across the country, including Hal's assistant, Ron, who hailed from Indiana, a few other people from Indiana and a couple from New York. We then went back to our hotel, the Hawaiian Regent, for some dinner, and retired to our rooms. Hal informed us we were going to do a six-mile training run through the Kilauea Iki Volcano the next day and urged us to get some shut eye so we could get an early start.

I shared a room with Kathy, a reporter from *The Runner* magazine, and we developed a decent rapport. She even gave me a red duffle bag with *The Runner* logo on it as a gift. She told me she was a runner but was not running the marathon, as it was her job to write an article about the marathon. By the time the week was over, I would be able to write a few articles about her.

Early the next morning we met the group outside our hotel and drove in a van to the airport for an hour flight to Volcanoes National Park on the Big Island. We spent some time sight-seeing and gazing at the awesome volcanoes surrounding the park. As we hiked up a trail to the Kilauea Iki volcano, I was amazed at the astounding number of trees and greenery surrounding the volcano, and glad of it. Kilauea is the most active of five volcanoes that together form the Big Island of Hawaii. Its last eruption had begun on May 24, 1969, and ended on July 22, 1974. (9.) I was hoping any eruptions it was planning would wait until after our run! We stood for a few minutes on the rim gazing down into heart of the volcano, its ground arid, cracked and as desolate and dry as any desert you can imagine. What an interesting dichotomy with the lush green terrain we had just hiked through.

I found my voice after a few moments and asked Hal if we were running around the rim. He suddenly turned and fled down the hill straight into the volcano, shouting back over his shoulder, "No, down and through it!" Making it down the hill into the volcano was the easiest part of the run, and trying to keep up with Hal was the hardest. After the first five minutes or so, I found my pace near the back of the pack and settled into a rhythm.

The day was hot and the dusty and dry terrain we ran through made it seem even hotter. As I ran, I saw steam escaping from cracks in the ground, and the vision hammered home the reality of the fact we were running through a goddamn volcano! The stark landscape was otherworldly. Feeling a bit nervous, I quickened my pace. *"You're crazy to be doing this, you know,"* the rational side of my brain admonished me. *"Yes, but what a way to go!"* the crazier side shot back a good rebuttal. Settling into my stride, all thoughts about the volcano erupting faded and I started to relax and enjoy the run. Focusing on and fascinated with details of my surroundings, time passed quickly. I imagined hearing a rumbling sound coming from the ground beneath me.

After close to an hour of solid running, I noticed we were now ascending a side of the volcano and realized with relief we were finishing our run. We convened at the top of the dome and found ourselves on another trail filled with lush tropical palm trees and greenery galore. A few runners were bent over holding onto their knees and catching their breaths, and I soon followed suit. There was Hal standing in the middle of our group talking with Ron, looking cool, calm, and collected as though he had just finished a casual walk in the park. As we hiked back to the trailhead, I relished the coolness of whatever shade the forest provided, and drank thirstily from my water bottle. Running through the Kilauea had been an adventure and, in that moment in time, I didn't think life could get any better. I had survived the Kilauea, yet was soon to find out that mark had been missed by the narrowest of margins.

The next day, December 7th, we visited the Pearl Harbor Memorial 41 years to the day after Japan attacked Pearl Harbor. This attack so surprised and outraged Americans that the United States officially declared war on Japan, bringing the U.S. into World War II. As this war occurred before I was born, I was not aware of any details of this historic event until I read some articles on Pearl Harbor and learned why and how this event occurred. I then understood that the Japanese wanted to continue expanding their empire within Asia, which threatened China.

Fearful that Japan would become too powerful a nation, the U.S. imposed a restrictive embargo on Japan. In retaliation Japan planned, and carried out, their air raid with devastating consequences for the U.S. "After just two hours of bombing, more than 2,400 Americans were dead, 21 ships had either been sunk or damaged, and more than 188 U.S. aircraft destroyed." (10.)

Comparing that time with modern times, I'm struck with how war is often referred to as a "necessary evil" by journalists and historians for keeping the world's population and powerful nations under control, maintaining security, and enhancing the reputation of any country. I understand how wars are considered to be necessary in certain situations, yet wonder if any scores are ever really settled through violence?

As I walked through the Memorial reading the names of the crewmen who lost their lives that fateful day, gazing out at the wreckage of what used to be the USS Arizona, I was moved to tears at the sight. Feeling a rush of sadness sweep through me, I bowed my head for some silent prayers. It felt surreal to be standing amidst serene and balmy surroundings on the same day that 41 years earlier was the site of overwhelming death and destruction. Seeing the Memorial up close and personal proved to be a sobering experience.

Later that evening, our group had a dinner feast at the hotel that couldn't be beat, and I ate too much spaghetti in preparation for the marathon the next day. By the time dinner was over, I swore I would never eat another strand of spaghetti for the rest of my life, or at least for the rest of the week.

After talking for a time with Kathy who sat next to me at the dinner table, I glanced at my watch and saw it was almost 9 p.m. Realizing the marathon was to start at 6 a.m. the next day, I told her I was heading upstairs to our room to get some sleep. She wished me a goodnight and said she would stay downstairs for a while and join me later. I said goodnight to everyone and headed for the elevator, feeling quite full and tired. Our room was on the 12th floor, and by the time I reached the room I got quickly undressed and crawled into bed. I soon fell into a deep dreamless slumber by 9:30 p.m. In what seemed like only a matter of minutes, I was soon awakened by the sound of Kathy's voice, muttering something about the lights being off in the hotel. Glancing at the clock on the nightstand, I noticed it was 1:30 a.m.

"Thanks for the update." I muttered. *Today is going to be a long day, I thought,* trying to settle back to sleep listening to Kathy clunking around the room preparing for bed. Little did I realize how long the day would be!

Soon thereafter, I fell into a restless sleep for another few hours, when I was awakened again at 3:30 a.m. with severe stomach cramps, and ran into the bathroom. The first wave of Montezuma's Revenge hit me and I was doubled over sitting on the toilet with shaking chills. "Curses," I muttered fumbling around in the darkness trying to find the Pepto Bismol in my suitcase. After finding it, I polished off at least half the bottle. The rest of the night was spent running back and forth to the bathroom and back to bed. It was now around 4:30 a.m., and I knew I had to be downstairs to catch the bus heading for the marathon starting location at 4:45 a.m. Sleepily donning running shorts and grabbing a light jacket, I hurried for the door.

"Break a leg…" I faintly heard Kathy whisper as I shut the door and tore downstairs to catch the bus.

Almost instantly, a rush of heat and humidity hit me in the face and I gazed out at the circus-like atmosphere of the city. The streets were aglow with multicolored bright lights flashing from every store window giving the impression of nighttime despite it being early in the morning. There were throngs of runners donned in their running shorts and tag along well-wishers rushing by me heading towards Kapiolani Park where the Marathon was to start. Apparently, I had missed the bus, as there was no bus in sight waiting outside the hotel. In a panic, I flung myself into the masses of humanity flowing down the street and joined the march towards the park. The rain started as a light drizzle and soon turned into a torrential downpour. It felt rather refreshing and helped wake me up! As we neared the park, I heard voices booming over loud speakers making announcements welcoming runners, families and friends to the event, interspersed with blaring carnival-like music.

Upon arrival at the park, I took a place amongst thousands of other runners lined up and raring to go. Suddenly, the sound of the starting gun and fireworks exploding in the sky startled me awake, and the crowd was now starting to run like a bunch of wild horses right out of the open gate. The crowds on the side of the course were cheering and the carnival music blaring. Within the next few minutes, the crowds thinned out a bit and I soon fell into stride with my fellow middle of the packers. The steadily falling rain was both cooling and reassuring. It reminded me of running in Chicago's similar hot and humid climate minus the palm trees.

As I ran, my mind was immersed in memories of a training run in a torrential Chicago rain one day. I stood for a few minutes under a bridge waiting for the rain to abate, yet it continued to rain even harder. I had planned a 15-miler for that day and was not about to let the rain keep me from that goal! Taking a deep breath, I ran out from under the bridge and within seconds was soaked to the bone. At first the wetness was shocking to the senses, yet soon thereafter seemed to revive every cell in my body, sweat mixing with the incessant torrents of rain washing over me. I was engulfed by huge belly laughs coming from deep within and in that moment running felt effortless. I splashed through numerous mud puddles with the absolute delight of a child covered in mud from head to toe after a hard day of play. After 15 miles of rain running, I raised my arms to the pouring heavens, yelling exuberantly to the sky, feeling strong and invincible.

Six miles into the marathon, my attention was diverted to ascending a short uphill section of the course known as "Diamond Head," an extinct volcano 760 feet high and one of Hawaii's most famous landmarks. Formed more than a hundred thousand years ago, the crater was used as a strategic military lookout beginning in the early 1900s and was named a National Natural Landmark in 1968. Today, Diamond Head is a popular hiking destination with panoramic views of Waikiki and Oahu's south shore. (11.)

As the marathon course circled the crater to the left, I saw phenomenal views of the Pacific Ocean and coastline despite the steady rain falling from a cloudy and overcast sky. The rain was still offering coolness, yet the air was dense with heat and humidity, and my body felt heavy from the wetness. Onward and upwards I plodded. People along the course were yelling encouragement to the runners practically every step of the way, and their words, for the most part, were a welcome diversion from the intense concentration and physical exertion required to run 26.2 miles. Somewhere around 10 miles, someone from the crowds lining the course yelled at me, "Almost there!" I looked up at her and wondered what she was thinking? I still had 16.2 miles to go! A wave and slight smile was all I could muster.

At sixteen miles, the rain had stopped, and the sun came out full blast raising the temperature to what felt like at least 100 degrees. I now missed the coolness of the rain and stopped at a rest station for a drink of water. After pouring most of it over my head, I gulped the rest and started running again. Feeling refreshed by the dowsing, I sauntered onward to Hanauma Bay, a popular snorkeling spot. Gazing at the crystal clear blue waters along the coastline, I wished I were swimming or snorkeling and even imagined myself splashing around in the cool water playing with porpoises and dancing with dolphins. *"OK, that's just the heat stroke talking, I chided myself. Only 10 more miles to go, almost there!"*

The last few miles went by as a blur of splashing water from the water cup I was handed by some charitable person at the water station, walking for a few blessed moments to soothe savage muscles somehow hanging in there for the long run, and trying to get the body moving again as it screamed at me to stop. Wait a minute... do my eyes see what I think they are seeing? Right up ahead were a few Hawaiian Hula dancers shaking up a storm! There were even a few guys shaking their hips around and were doing a decent job of it! I must admit it was a welcome sight for sore eyes at that stage of the race. I even managed to yell a polite "wahoo" as I hobbled past trying to look full of vim and vigor, yet the short burst of energy faded fast.

At mile 24, I ran up another short, yet steep section of the course, not realizing it was Diamond Head, and what seemed like a mere hill at mile six, now felt like Mount Everest! At that point, the heat, lack of sleep from the previous night and exhaustion was taking its toll. Plodding wearily along, it seemed more like a march through Death Valley. I wondered what idiot thought up the idea of running 26.2 miles and in my research discovered a few different theories, although it is difficult to discern what is myth vs. the real story. Most likely, we'll never know the real story, yet according to legend, "the first marathon commemorated the run of the soldier Pheidippides from a battlefield near the town of Marathon, Greece, to Athens in 490 B.C. Pheidippides ran approximately 25 miles to announce the defeat of the Persians to some anxious Athenians. Not quite in mid-season shape, he delivered the message, "Victory!" then keeled over and died." (12.) Probably the most well-known story as to the reason the extra 1.2 miles was added to the marathon distance is little more than frivolity at its finest. In the same article, it stated, "For the 1908 London Olympics, the course was laid out from Windsor Castle to White City stadium, about 26 miles. However, to locate the finish line in front of the royal family's viewing box, an extra 385 yards was added inside the stadium. Hence the marathon tradition of yelling, "God Save the Queen" in the last mile." (13.) Running those last few miles of the marathon in an exhausted state of mind, I changed the interpretation to, "forget about the Queen, it's every woman for herself!"

The last stretch of the course curved around Diamond Head toward the finish near the Kapiolani Park bandstand, and as I dragged my weary body to the finish, I could see throngs of cheering people lining the finish area as I covered those last eternal 385 yards. Photographers were everywhere snapping pictures of us running zombies trying our best to look like we were in states of euphoria known as "runner's high," as we crossed the finish line. I have one of those photos, by the way, and I fell a bit short of looking high. In fact, my eyes were glued to the ground and the finish line just up ahead.

"Just a few more steps… I thought and those last steps seemed never-ending. The crowds at the finish area were cheering and everything seemed to be moving in slow motion. As I crossed the finish line ready to collapse to the ground, two women race volunteers rushed up to meet me. Both were on either side holding me up. One woman offered me a cup of Coke and I heartily drank it with hands shaking from excitement and exhaustion. The other placed a necklace made of shells around my neck. I can't recall if I was laughing or crying, yet that was one of the most joyous moments in my life! I had finished another marathon and did a PR (personal record) of just over 4 hours, on but a few hours of sleep and a cranky stomach! The Coke was cold and wet and tasted good despite it not being Sprite, my favorite beverage.

The volunteers lead me over to a shady area and I couldn't wait to sit and not move. I was soon sitting on the grass slurping on the Coke, amidst countless thousands of other weary finishers, and thanked the volunteers again for coming to my aid. I scanned the crowd for a few moments hoping to see some familiar faces, especially Gloria and Skip, my friends from the arrival flight, yet didn't find them until later that evening before dinner. I soon noticed two men approaching where I was sitting. One was tall and lean and his friend was short and stout, and I recognized Hal and Ron, and waved at them. Hal, despite having run the marathon, looked his usual dapper self, as though he had just returned from his casual walk in the park, yet Ron's hair was disheveled and his face flushed bright red from apparent exertion. "Great run, eh?" Hal smiled and greeted me. "What was your time?"

"4:14, a PR! What was yours?" I already imagined he would say something like, just broke Alberto Salazar's world record of 2:08:13 at the New York City Marathon in 1981. (14.)

"Just a fun run for me today. Wasn't running for time," he shrugged and I never did find out what his finish time was. We posed for pictures with me flanked by Hal and Ron that years later looked like I was holding them up, when in actuality it was the other way around.

Just before dinner, I bumped into Gloria and Skip walking on the beach outside the hotel and we shared our marathon stories, gave each other quick embraces and parted ways, as they were heading out for a private dinner for two. Skip, as it turned out, had finished the marathon not far behind me with a time of 4:35, and we shared our congratulations, and high fives. Before they rushed off, Gloria and I held hands for a few brief moments and with tears in our eyes promised to connect when back in Chicago. Then they were off in a flash and I didn't find out until later in life why they were always in such a hurry.

Later that evening at dinner, our group reunited, chatted about our marathon experiences, and laughed the evening away. For most of the group this would be our last evening in Hawaii, and others would continue on with Roadrunner's to tour Maui, Kauai, and Molokai for another week. Secretly, I envied them, yet promised myself to return to this beautiful paradise again someday soon, and looked forward to returning home to see Gary. I savored the rest of the evening, enjoying everyone's company and stories, and all too quickly the evening passed, fading into fond memories of tropical sandy beaches, palm trees, and half naked hula men shaking their bodies to hypnotic Hawaiian rhythms.

Early the next morning, I sat in my seat on the plane gazing out the window trying to take in every last detail of paradise, already missing the place and the people I met and got to know over the past week. I especially missed my newfound friend, Gloria, and smiled as her face came floating into my mind's eye. I knew I would have to connect with her when back home again. I also looked forward to seeing Gary again as well as our reunion, as even a matter of days of separation from him seemed like an eternity. During the nine-hour flight from Oahu to Chicago, I busied myself writing in my diary of the events of the past week.

My flight arrived on schedule in Chicago and there was Gary waiting for me as I rushed from the plane into his waiting arms. I always looked forward to our reunions.

"It's great to see you!" he grinned and held me tight. I always looked forward to our reunions. Walking to his car holding hands and suitcases in our other hands we gabbed about my Hawaiian adventures, the marathon, and caught up on being together again back in the chaos of the city.

One month later, Gary and I were watching the 10 o'clock news and I started to doze until a story came on that made me sit up and stare at the TV with shock and disbelief at the incredible scenario unfolding before my weary eyes. The story was about the eruption of a very famous volcano... Kilauea Iki... that very morning.

CHAPTER 14
GETTING HITCHED
(1983-1984)

"Holding hands is a promise to one another that, for just a moment, the two of you don't have to face the world alone."
— Author unknown

Gary and I were inseparable. We lived together long enough to be considered "common law" partners without the formality of a license, played and listened to music for hours on end, traveled around the country from Canada to Yellowstone, and somehow managed to end up in Aspen. "That's the place you really need to visit," advised our friends. So, we took a road trip to check out Aspen to see for ourselves if the place was worth a spit, and soon discovered it was.

We went for some great hikes, stayed at a quaint little bed and breakfast, and took in some pretty spectacular surrounding mountain vistas. As an avid lover of the outdoors, I fell in love with the place and even more so with Gary.

After a long day of hiking, we came back to the B&B around dinnertime. As I gathered my daypack and hiking boots, Gary got out of the car, opened the door and reached for my hand to help me out of the car. I thought it a bit strange after hours of scrambling over rocks and boulders on the hike that he would extend me a hand getting out of the car, yet thanked him nonetheless for being the consummate gentleman. Suddenly, he was down on his knee and still holding my hand he popped the question.

"We've known each other now for ten years and neither one of us has been seeing anyone else, right?" I nodded, surprised at the suddenness of the moment and sense of urgency in his voice. "Will you marry me?" he asked with a heart melting smile on his face. It was hard to believe we had been together for that long and still remained single, and it all seemed fine to me, until that moment. The sincerity of his tone of voice had caught me off guard. In the process of trying to play hard to get, I had fallen in love, as I had never done before. I had hoped the attraction to him was purely musical rather than physical, yet there was no denying the feelings were mutual. At the same time, I felt torn and pictured my parents sitting on opposite sides of the room from each other. Ma had made many attempts to reach out to my dad, yet he remained cool and distant, and soon Ma stopped her efforts. Was this a model marriage? I vowed I wouldn't follow suit and share that same fate, yet here was "the question" being asked to me at that very moment.

When I could find my voice, I answered his question with yet another.

"Right here, right now?"

"What better place?" He had made his point. Gazing at the majestic and rugged snow-capped mountains surrounding us in late June, it was so tempting to throw caution to the wind and embrace the moment.

"Let's do it properly next year and have an actual ceremony. We can throw a party and invite all our family and friends and tell them the good news." Little did I know at the time that I would regret my decision to postpone our wedding in favor of doing it the right way.

Gary and I had our engagement party in July of 1983. We were in our apartment surrounded by all our friends including my high school chum, Sue. Gary handed me a huge square box wrapped in a fancy decorative fashion. I shook the box, puzzled by the size of his gift and wondered what was inside. Nothing rattled to give me a clue. As I peeled back the wrapping paper and opened the box, lo and behold, there was another box, slightly smaller than the previous box, and on and on the process continued of opening one box after another. "OK, folks, we could be here all night," I exclaimed to appreciative chuckles from our pals. Paring down to the final box, I let out a gasp of utter surprise and delight at the realization of the contents of the box. In my hand, I held a beautiful diamond engagement ring and held it up for all to see. Gary's face was beaming as we embraced and I sobbed with glee.

"Here is the ring I should have given to you in Aspen," he whispered in my ear.

"Aunt Jemima, what took you so long?"

"OK, you two love birds, get a room!" jeered Sue from amongst the group, and soon our friends were yelling congratulations and cheering us on. Gary and I stood before them with our faces beet red, mine from crying, and his from sheer embarrassment. It was a moment I will never forget.

We planned our wedding for July 7, 1984, and busied ourselves preparing and making arrangements for our special day. I somehow found the time to make most of the arrangements despite working full time at Loyola as a nurse, and of course, there were a few bumps in the road along the way. What would life be without its challenges? Gary and I wanted to have an outdoor ceremony, and we looked at a beautiful little chapel and garden on the campus of Northwestern

University in Evanston, a northern suburb of Chicago. Knowing at first glance that was where we would have our wedding, we secured Shakespeare Garden, yet still had to decide where to hold the reception. Gary and I had originally planned to have it at a place called The Millionaire's Club in Niles, Illinois. But we found out a few months before the wedding that they were going out of business, a bit of an oxymoron! So, I had to find an alternative in a hurry. My Honolulu Marathon friend, Gloria, came to the rescue and suggested we have our reception at a restaurant called Bones, well known for its delicious rib dinners. Bones also had a reception hall downstairs. Things were now falling into place.

Saturday, July 7, 1984

Our wedding day had finally arrived, and was a gorgeous sunny day with the temperature in the mid-70s. Mo and I arrived at Shakespeare Garden around 1:45 p.m. with plenty of time to get dressed and prepared, as the ceremony was to start at 3 p.m. By 2:30 p.m., I was all dressed and ready to go, but Gary was nowhere in sight. I was a bit worried that something dire had happened to him, as he was for the most part, punctual. I tried calling him, (in those days you had to search for a pay phone), and there was no answer. Having heard numerous horror stories about grooms baling out on their weddings, I was hoping that Gary was not one of those "cowboys!" It seemed like an eternity sitting inside the bride's room alone and anticipating news of his arrival. I passed the time talking with Mo who kept trying to reassure me he would eventually show up. She made several trips outside only to report there was no trace of him.

Another fiasco was occurring at the same time. My bouquet of flowers was delivered to the Northwestern University campus in downtown Chicago instead of uptown where we were. After a few phone calls were made to the downtown campus informing them of the correct location, I remembered a line from a poem by Rudyard Kipling: "If you can keep your head while all around others are losing theirs...," you must be a saint! It helped as I tried to keep calm.

"He's here!" Mo cheered returning from her outside vigil. We looked at each other and breathed sighs of relief. Gazing at the clock on the wall, I noticed it was 3:30 p.m., almost the same time the bouquet arrived. Needless to say, I was relieved to see both!

Mo and I went outside and stood in the garden just out of sight behind some nearby bushes waiting for the ceremony to begin. Shakespeare Garden was incredibly beautiful with flowers of every sort, color and hue in full bloom, forming the perfectly sculptured, freshly cut grass footpath that served as the aisle leading to the front of the garden. Several trees towered over an ornately carved, semicircle stone bench there, forming the perfect awning for our marriage ceremony.

During the previous day's rehearsal Kelly, our organist, came with her organ but no amp. And Tom, our singer, never showed. I wondered if Kelly would get her organ together for our big day and if Tom had arrived, yet somehow it all came together. I peeked out from behind the bushes for a glimpse of Gary, and there he stood in front of the Reverend Sheets wearing a rather dapper looking sky blue suit and sneaking several peeks back in my direction. I could hardly wait to stand next to him and finally see his face up close and personal after waiting for the dude the better part of the afternoon.

Dad approached me with a thoughtful expression on his face and took my arm around his as he planted a peck on my cheek and patted my hand. I don't recall either of us saying one word to each other, yet I felt his love for me with each pat of his hand. Lost in thoughts, I wondered what he was thinking and if he likewise felt nervous. The air was suddenly filled with the sounds of Kelly's organ joyfully playing the processional march signaling the commencement of our ceremony. I flashed back to playing marches in elementary school as kids marched up and down from the stage during assemblies. Dad and I proceeded down the aisle in ceremonious style and he then handed me off to Gary.

My stomach was doing cartwheels as I was finally face to face with my handsome groom, his face beaming. As our eyes met, a curious winged object perched on his forehead grabbed my attention. I stared at the object for a few seconds, then seeing it was a dragonfly, tried to hold back a giggle. His smile turned serious for a few moments as I swatted at the poor creature. (The dragonfly, not Gary!) He stared at me in bewilderment as I pulled him towards me and whispered in his ear that I had aimed at the dragonfly. He whispered back, "That's great! I couldn't find a belt and my pants are falling down!" Before long we were both guffawing! Friends, family and our minister were staring on in astonishment and I'm sure they must have thought us to be quite insane.

After regaining our composure, the Reverend Sheets gave a beautiful recitation about the joy of a man and woman uniting in holy matrimony with a few quotes from Woody Allen's "Love and Death" movie thrown in for good measure. He made reference to a part of the movie in which Woody was talking about his dad who "owned a valuable piece of land, it was a small piece, yet he carried it wherever he went." "What will Donna and Gary carry away from this day?" he asked gazing in our direction and smiling. At that point in time, we could not even imagine what the future held in store for us.

Tom, our singer, also gave a moving performance singing "The Wedding Song" by Peter, Paul and Mary with accompaniment on his guitar. Gazing at my sister standing slightly behind me, I noticed she had tears in her eyes that brought tears to mine. Friends and family were lining both sides of the garden, and I noticed they also shared the moment and were wiping their eyes. When Tom finished singing a silent hush fell upon the garden, as our minister pronounced us man and wife. All too soon the ceremony was over and we walked hand in hand down the aisle as Mr. and Mrs. Gary Brown to appreciative applause and cheers from our family and friends.

Everyone joined us for the reception at Bones where we ate, drank, and were quite merry. When Gary and I first entered the restaurant, we headed downstairs to the Banquet Hall and saw huge color photo framed portraits of us placed in various areas around the room, compliments of Stan our photographer. Gloria and Skip were the first to greet us as we entered the hall, and Gloria and I rushed into each other's arms for a long, heartfelt, embrace. When I looked into her beaming face and saw tears of joy in her eyes, tears welled in mine prompting a contact cry. The relationship we shared was so precious, I considered her my surrogate mom.

Gary had informed me, after dinner, that instead of getting himself dressed and prepared for the wedding, he spent at least three hours putting together a tape of dance music for the reception party. That fact combined with the missing belt made for some good comedy relief from all the stress of the months of preparation leading up to the wedding. Ironically enough, only a few of the 40 to 50 guests actually danced to the music of Gary's labor of love. Carol and Dusty, some good friends of ours, got up and danced for a few tunes, but for the most part, people were content to sit and watch Gary and I make fools of ourselves on the dance floor. Let it be known that part of the reason I was on the dance floor, other than loving to dance, was to get away from my stepmother Ann, who insisted that my wedding ring be worn closer to my heart than the engagement ring. Emily Post would have to wait! Let's DANCE!!!!!

Then came the highlights of the evening, Gary picking the garter off my thigh with his teeth, caveman that he is, and smearing wedding cake all over each other's faces. The ceremony ended fairly early around 11p.m., yet we wanted to party on! Gary and I headed to our hotel room, him wearily carrying me across the threshold, then falling together on the bed enmeshed in wedding dress, falling pants, and newly wedded bliss.

CHAPTER 15
HEADING WEST
(1984-1985)

*"What lies behind us and what lies before us are tiny matters
compared to what lies within us."*
— Ralph Waldo Emerson

The year seemed to fly by as Gary and I were adjusting to the demands of work, school, and getting to know each other in our new roles of husband and wife. I worked full time at Loyola, and attended Northeastern Illinois University, pursuing a bachelor's degree in psychology. I was planning on pursuing a master's degree program in exercise physiology at Northwestern, yet couldn't get our honeymoon vacation in Colorado out of my mind and the mountains out of my heart. We spent a few weeks in Colorado hiking in the mountains to our hearts content and longed to be either in the mountains or close by. As a city slicker all my life, I was tired of city living with all the traffic and crowds of people constantly in your face. I had only two more semesters at Northwestern before completing my degree, and started thinking seriously of moving out to Colorado, yet wasn't sure what my better half would say about it. Discussing the situation, he was rather skeptical, as I thought he would be.

"Why move out there when we're settled here with our jobs and friends?" he protested.

"You seemed to enjoy hiking in the mountains as I recall."

"Yes, I did, yet you know we still have to work for a living!"

"Well, I'm sure I can get work as a nurse, and you will find work in your field of printing."

"You can most likely get work as a nurse easier than I can as a printer. I don't think there are many printing jobs out there," he scoffed digging his feet deeper into the trench of resistance he was building around him. Gary wasn't exactly a risk taker, much preferring the familiarity of status quo. "Besides, you still need to finish school."

I decided to let the topic ride for a while in hopes that the passage of time would somehow change his mind.

Soon the holidays were upon us and we got caught up in the madness of the season and rushing around like hamsters on treadmills in pursuit of last-minute gifts for our loved ones. Sometime into the new year, while leafing through a newspaper one day, I came across an ad in the job section looking for a private duty nurse to care for a patient in Telluride, Colorado, of all places! My heart skipped a beat as I read the ad and thought of endless possibilities. Gary, of course, grounded me with reality. "Again, what I am going to do for work?"

"Hey, maybe I can make enough money for both of us to become independently wealthy!" He wasn't buying it, and to be honest, neither was I. Moving out of state is a big risk and the outcome is always uncertain. What happens if the job doesn't work out for whatever reason? If the client dies, there are no guarantees that you'll get another client to replace the first client. While I hated to admit it, Gary was right. If he wasn't able to find gainful employment in his field, we would both be looking for work and in financial dire straits. At least in Chicago, we both had decent paying jobs and a place to call home, even if it was just the apartment we lived in. I also wanted to finish school and enroll in the master's program, and after rationalizing every other possible reason to not move, reluctantly gave up on the harebrained idea of moving to Colorado. Interestingly enough, a tidal wave of events was waiting in the wings to wash over and leave us on yet another shore gasping for breath, leading us into an adventure we would never forget. Life works in strange ways.

A few weeks later, Gary walked into the front room where I was doing homework and showed me an ad in the newspaper for a company in Colorado called Larimer Press advertising for a printer. We stared at each other in disbelief at the irony of the situation. Gary was the first to speak. "Should I call?" *I thought for a moment, so let's go to the chalkboard. Another opportunity to move to Colorado presents itself, and should I dig my feet in and play devil's advocate? Hell NO!!!* I nodded. Telling him to go for it, my stomach was tied in knots anticipating the what ifs and why nots.

What if we moved and things didn't work out for us and we couldn't make a decent living? What if I couldn't find a nursing job? What was I thinking? I'm a nurse and nurses should always be able to find a job, so why not make the move and toss our fate to the wind?

"Hey, I just talked with this guy, Jim, from Larimer Press," Gary's voice derailed my thoughts. "Guess where I'm going? I guess I'm heading out to Colorado after

all! Jim, the boss of the pre-press department liked my vibes and wants me to
come out for an interview!" Gary studied my face for a moment to see what my
reaction would be.

"Wow, that was fast!"

"Yeah, go figure. He wants me out there as soon as I can book a flight."

The next few weeks flew by in a flurry of preparations for Gary's trip to Colorado and soon we were driving to O'Hare Airport in the wee early morning
hours. We waited for a few hours for his flight to arrive, and chatted with excitement about what the future might hold in store for us. As the time for his departure was suddenly upon us we embraced and I didn't want to let him go.

"I will miss you," he whispered.

"Me too! Good luck with the interview and keep me posted." We held hands for
a few moments longer and he was soon out of sight heading for the "friendly skies."

The next afternoon the phone rang and I ran to answer it. "Hey, I just got
done with the interview," Gary sounded upbeat.

"So, what's the story, morning glory?"

"Well, I got the job!"

"Get the heck out of here!!!"

"We are!!! So, start packing your bags!"

"When do you start?"

"Within the next few weeks, if I can get my butt in gear."

"Where are you going to stay?"

"Jim, my boss, said I can stay at his house."

"That should be interesting living with your boss, yet at least you can save up
some money."

"Yeah, no worries there, right? Gotta go. See you soon."

As I hung up the phone, numerous thoughts flooded my mind. Moving to Colorado was realization of a long-sought goal arising from a longing for a simpler
lifestyle. But weren't we making things more complicated by uprooting our lives?
On one hand, I wanted to be surrounded by mountains rather than skyscrapers,
yet knew I would miss the familiarity of the city, friends and family. I also knew I
would have to give up the master's program I had prepared for and felt a considerable amount of angst in that regard; yet the lure of the outdoors had won out. I felt
inexorably drawn in that direction and had to go with it.

Gary came home a few days later and spent the next few weeks packing
and preparing for his road trip, I wished I could go with him, but I still had
another semester at school to finish, and despite my best efforts found it hard
to concentrate on my studies. It was May of 1985 and I looked forward to
joining him in our new Colorado home in August. After talking with a coun-

selor, at school, she mentioned the option of completing my degree with a correspondence course at Western Illinois University, an affiliated college, and I decided to take that course once settled in Colorado.

The task of packing all our remaining belongings seemed daunting to say the least, yet watching Gary leave in his car was by far the most difficult task of all. Seeing him standing by his car loaded to the max with his stuff was surreal, and I thought a bit ironic that it was my idea to move. But there he was ready to hit the road. We had been married for a mere nine months, and now would be separated for a few months. I felt so lonely at that moment! I ran to him and we held each other so tightly I could barely breathe. As at the airport a few weeks ago, I didn't want to let him go, afraid I might not ever see him again and feeling very vulnerable. We bid each other a fond, yet tearful adieu, and I wished him a safe journey. And I told him for the umpteenth time how much I loved him. He sauntered towards his car and glanced back at me one last time, got in, and headed in a westerly direction. It was a trip that would change our lives in ways too many to name.

CHAPTER 16
BREAKING FREE
(1985)

*"Thousands of tired, nerve-shaken, over-civilized people
are beginning to find out that going to the mountains is
going home; that wildness is a necessity."*
— John Muir, Our National Parks

Gary had spent long hours on his new printing job at Larimer Press for the past few weeks and his boss kept him fairly busy around the house in his off hours as well. In exchange for free rent Jim put him to work doing gardening and digging ditches in his front and back yards. Today was Saturday, his long-awaited day off. Jim had recommended that he check out Rocky Mountain National Park and Gary had decided he would head up to the Park to do some hiking and exploring. Upon recommendation from the park ranger he turned left at the first intersection and drove to the Bear Lake parking area where he picked up the trailhead that lead to Emerald Lake. Despite the busyness of working at his new job, Gary had found time to purchase a new pair of hiking boots at REI and was anxious to try them out. He laced up his boots, shouldered his daypack full of food and water and headed up the 2.5-mile trail to Emerald Lake. Pausing for a few moments to rest at both Nymph and Dream Lakes, the first lakes along the trail, he took in the cool, crisp spring air and majestic surrounding mountain vistas. Gazing with wonderment at the intricate patterns of frozen crystals of ice scattered upon the surface of the lake, he imagined himself in paradise.

After about an hour of steady hiking he reached Emerald Lake where the trail ended, and sat down on a rock overlooking the lake. The day was sunny, yet quite breezy and the sight before him was nothing short of breathtaking. The sharp pyramid-shaped summit of Hallet's Peak, some 13,000 feet in height, towered stately and silent, casting its snow-covered reflection on the frozen lake sprawled below. Gary pulled out his pen and pad of paper and started writing a letter, one of many he would send back home to me, trying to capture the moment and bridge the gap of our separation until I could join him in another month.

Gary wasn't gone but a few weeks and already I missed and longed to be with him. We had only been married nine months and now we were apart. I tried hard to bury my loneliness in schoolwork without much success, and went for long runs with my running buddy, Carol, to pass the time until I could join Gary in Colorado. I planned to visit him in June on my semester break and scribbled big red X's on my calendar on the wall counting the days until we would be together again. I also thought about the mountains every waking moment and longed to be surrounded by them, as I felt true freedom whenever hiking in their shadows.

A few weeks before my trip to Colorado my friend Carol called asking if I wanted to go running with her. In the craziness of preparing for the trip, I hadn't seen much of her and readily agreed to meet her at our usual meeting place around Loyola on Sheridan. In fact, that is where she and I first met a few years before. She was standing on Sheridan across from Loyola waiting for a bus and I walked by after work one day. The first thing to catch my attention were her Nike running shoes, as I also owned a pair. "Hey, cool shoes!" I remarked as she looked in my direction and smiled.

"Thanks," she replied. "Do you have Nikes too?"

"Never leave home without them!"

Carol laughed her unmistakable contagious laugh that I would come to know so well in the coming years of our relationship.

"Maybe we could run sometime," I suggested.

"Yeah, that would be cool." We exchanged phone numbers and didn't call each other for another week or so. I'm not sure who called first, but soon we were running together a few times a week and eventually became inseparable. I enjoyed her easy laugh and great sense of humor. I especially enjoyed our 10-to-15-mile-long runs on the Lakefront Trail, comprised of 18 miles of running and biking trails along the east side of Lake Shore Drive. This well-known freeway extends from Hollywood (5700 North) to Marquette Drive (6800 South), paralleling the shoreline of Lake Michigan.

We had some great times running numerous races, marathons, triathlons and biathlons and sharing laughter over almost everything. One day, while we were running along the Lakefront Trail, it began to rain quite hard. As we ran, we talked about everything under the sun and soon our conversation stopped as we spotted a strange object heading towards us. As the object came closer, we noticed the object was a lady in a wheelchair covered almost completely with a huge orange poncho protecting her from the rain. The poncho was flapping wildly in the gusty winds blanketing the lakefront that day, and was a sight to behold. We were soon overcome with fits of hysterical laughter, not at the lady, rather at the sight of her precarious poncho appearing as though it could become airborne at any given moment with her in tow! We also heard the lady laughing as she blew by and shared a miraculous moment with her.

Carol also had her demons. She, like me, came from a chaotic family situation, and suffered from frequent bouts of depression. After a period of not talking to me, she would suddenly emerge and call me or I would call her and the conflict would be forgotten rather than discussed.

The day she called we had a great run as usual until I told her of my imminent move to Colorado. She was a bit subdued upon hearing the news, yet we hugged and parted ways in our usual laughing fashion, and I didn't think too much more about it at the time. As time passed, I heard from her less frequently until she disappeared.

Along the road of life, people come and go. Some will join you for the long haul and other friendships fall by the wayside. The relationship we shared, unfortunately, fell into the latter category. The only certainties of transitory times are bumpy roads and uncertainty, yet we eventually manage to find our way back home, much like Dorothy in The Wizard of Oz.

Departure day, June 19, 1985, was finally here and as I taxied my way to the airport, thoughts of seeing Gary again were first and foremost on my mind. I couldn't wait to see him and rush into his loving arms once again. There he was at Stapleton Airport, standing by the gate, and as I hurried toward him, he was wearing shorts, a t-shirt and a huge smile. I ran full speed in his direction yelling his name, and then he swept me up into his arms and then the world was right again! It had been only a month since his departure, yet it felt like we had been apart for all eternity! I would have about a week and a half to spend with him before returning to Chicago to pack for my final trip, so we decided to make the most of our time together. We were like gypsies living out of and traveling around in Gary's Ford Escort, and sleeping in cheap motels in the Denver area.

Over the next few days we did some hiking around Boulder and planned on heading up to Rocky Mountain Park on Saturday. I was anxious to see the mountains again and we decided to head to Emerald Lake, where Gary had spent a considerable amount of time when not at work.

We parked at the Bear Lake parking area, laced up our boots and packs and headed up the trail toward Emerald Lake. When reaching the lake, we sat on some rocks gazing across at Hallet's Peak, the mountain we decided to climb. The day was blustery with a bone-chilling wind whipping across the choppy surface of the lake. As we ate our sandwiches, we deliberated for quite a long time whether to climb, despite it being so windy. I recall feeling a mixture of extreme nervousness and excitement at the prospect of pursuing adventure. We felt the call of the wild and thought of ourselves as seasoned hikers, yet were woefully unprepared for the level of technicality and mountainous terrain we were to encounter. We were in good company, as countless thousands of visitors from out of state make the same mistakes by not having the proper equipment (i.e. climbing boots with crampons and an ice axe) for safe climbing and suffer dire consequences as a result.

Making our decision, we continued hiking around the lake, scrambling over boulders and dead tree stumps until reaching the other side of the lake, and started to ascend the scree-filled slope now directly above us. We encountered plenty of snowfields on our ascent and were able to navigate them without incident until about halfway up when we were confronted by one especially steep and slick snowfield that lay directly in front of us. Gary ambled up the snowfield with the ease of a mountain goat and I stared after him in bewilderment and amazement at his athletic prowess. He was not what I would have called athletic in the least as, while living back in Chicago, he chose to immerse himself in watching TV rather than run amok through the streets of the city like his weird wife! Now I was struggling to keep up with my mountain goat husband and feeling pretty frustrated. With every step I took, the more exhausted I felt, and made very little progress up the slope where Gary was waiting above.

Standing on a small ledge comprised of nothing but small footholds dug into the snow by previous climbers, making their way up the snowfield, I noticed a guy coming down towards me wearing crampons and holding an ice axe in his hand. Crampons (metal spikes fixed to a boot to provide better traction while climbing on steep and slick mountainous terrain) and ice axe (a tool used by climbers to cut footholds in ice and snow) are both necessary gear for safely climbing in the mountains, and I had neither. As the guy passed me we exchanged greetings and seeing how spent I was, asked if I was OK. "Yes, I'm fine," I lied.

"Here take this." He handed me a spare axe he carried in his backpack. "It's pretty steep from here on up and you'll need this." Eagerly grabbing the axe, I thanked him and we both continued on our separate journeys.

With axe in hand, I was making some progress ascending the snowfield, and about a third of the way up, I heard Gary calling down to me, "Are you coming up?"

"Yes! I gasped in the thin alpine air. I'm coming!" I dared not look down for fear of falling and continued ascending over huge boulders covered with ice and snow. Eventually I saw Gary standing perhaps only one hundred feet away from me. I made my way towards him and collapsed in exhaustion on some rocks, gasping for breath and unready to proceed any farther. Gary sat down next to me and studied my face for a few moments.

"You doing OK?"

"Yeah, just tired and winded."

"Might as well stop and grab a bite to eat," He rested his hand on my knee mentioning, that at 3 p.m., it was getting a bit late in the afternoon to continue ascending. Gary stared at the axe I had stabbed into a pile of snow next to me.

"Hey, where did you get that thing?"

"This guy I met below where we are now passed it to me. How much farther do you think we have to get to the top?" I asked glancing nervously above me towards the vast expanse of ice and snow-covered granite wall summit that towered above us. From where we sat, Hallet's Peak appeared to be almost a hop, skip and jump away, yet I knew from our previous mountain trips that distances in the mountains were always deceiving.

"I'd say we're still at least another hour or so from the summit."

"Should we chance it?" I asked feeling a bit stronger and braver after woofing down my peanut butter and jelly sandwich.

"I think we should see how we feel after lunch, although I still think it's getting too late to continue." Gary always seemed to err on the side of caution unlike his more adventurous wife who always seemed to throw caution to the wind. We stayed there sitting on the rocks for at least 45 minutes taking in the incredible vistas from about 12,000 feet and marveling at the marvelous mountain majesty surrounding us from our dizzying height. The contrasting colors of the snow crystals gleamed like radiant gems planted beneath the surface shining their brilliance on the stark slate granite world around us. As time passed, we sat in each other's arms, feeling as though we were sitting on top of the world. From where we sat, Emerald Lake appeared to be little more than just a tiny sparkling greenish-brown wading pool below. I felt as minute as the lake appeared, very small and insignificant as compared to the mammoth rock and snow strewn terrain that engulfed us.

"Isn't this incredible?" I glanced over at Gary who was lost in thoughts at the moment.

"Yeah, pretty cool stuff!" Glancing towards the sky I saw a climber precariously hanging by a rope from a sheer cliff above us spinning around with the now more noticeable wind that had suddenly kicked up. Glad it's him and not me, I thought. I could see my breath and feel the bite of the chilly mountain air whipping around us. I started imagining a slick and dangerous descent and soon felt my whole body shivering from the cold and nervous anticipation of the long journey downwards. As if reading my mind, Gary's voice interrupted my thoughts. "Hey, I think we should be heading back down." Nodding, I stood up, donning daypack and retrieving axe from where it was planted in the snow.

We started our descent somewhere around 4 p.m. with Gary in the lead as usual. Slowly descending, we traversing across slick snow and ice mixed with scree, praying we would make it safely back down without incident. Gary was way ahead of me and yelled over his shoulder for me to hurry up. I sensed urgency in his voice that was somewhat alarming as though he were sensing impending danger. I decided that glissading (sliding down a steep slope either on your feet or butt with the support of an axe) would be a much faster way to descend and catch up with him. Sitting on my butt, I slid down the snowfield at warp speed narrowly missing a row of boulders dead ahead, my ice axe flopping uselessly in the snow during the glissade. Finally catching up to Gary, we had a heated discussion about my slowness and continued our descent.

After another hour or so of steady downward progress, we encountered the steep snowfield that I had labored to navigate on ascent. Gary grabbed my hand and we began a cautious sort of side stepping down the slope. At the time, I didn't know that holding onto another person was a very dangerous maneuver when climbing, as one slip could mean disaster for both parties. I vaguely recall him saying something to effect of, "Now the fun begins…" and suddenly he lost his footing and the adventure became a nightmarish reality. In a flash, we were tumbling head over heels out of control down the snowfield, rushing at the speed of sound towards some pretty ominous looking boulders below us. The ice axe went flying out of my hand as I hit the first set of boulders feet first. At that point I lost sight of Gary, who was tumbling out of sight, a swirling circle of multi-colored lights the last thing I saw before losing consciousness and everything turning to black.

I awoke lying on my back in the snow and opened my eyes to see the swirling vortex of lights once again, accompanied by profuse nausea and searing flank pain. Disoriented and in a state of shock, I tried to remember what had happened, yet everything seemed to be moving in slow motion and dreamlike. Looking around to try to get my bearings, I noticed Gary sitting up in the snow, holding his left arm and wincing in pain a few feet away from me. Trying to sit up, I felt a jolt of pain shoot like a lightning bolt up my spine and quickly fell back down on the snow. What the hell happened? My stunned mind tried in vain to put together the puzzle pieces, yet nothing made sense. I tried to access the logical, nursing side of my brain, only to find distress signals being emitted on red alert. Some time elapsed, and from the fog emerged the message that I had to help Gary, yet I couldn't move without feeling another wave of nausea and relentless flank pain. Glancing over at Gary, I noticed him holding his head and that one side of his face was drooping. I reached out my hand to him and finding my voice asked, with chattering teeth, if he was OK, thinking perhaps he had suffered a stroke.

"Shit… shit… we're screwed…" he kept repeating and slurring his words.

He was now holding one hand in the other, rocking back and forth in pain. I reached for his good hand to comfort him.

Realizing our dire situation, I felt helpless, my eyes welling up with hot tears of anger and frustration. Sitting up was futile, yet trying to position my body to look downwards, I discovered we were still high up on the mountain with evening fast approaching and the temperature dropping. Injured and shivering uncontrollably in the throes of hypothermia, I realized we would not survive the night on the mountain. Lying on the snow, I tried again to sit up, yet was immobilized with pain and numbing cold.

Suddenly I heard voices and glancing over to my side saw two figures heading up the mountain towards us. Excitedly grabbing Gary's hand, I informed him, "Hikers are coming!" and breathed a sigh of relief. Seconds later, a man and woman were kneeling over us asking if we were OK. The man said, "We were hiking and saw you guys fall. Do you need some help getting up?"

"I can't sit up, and I think he hurt his head and arm."

"I think I can stand OK," I heard Gary say.

The man tried to help me sit up and another bolt of lightning shot up my spine.

"Let me just lie here for a few more minutes!" The man helped me lie back onto the snow. Gary and our rescuers were hovering over me with concern. Gary held my trembling hand trying to comfort me. The woman instructed us to remain still and in an instant turned and left to descend the remaining distance of the snowfield we were on.

Sensing our urgent situation, the man scooped me up off the ground and, slinging me over his shoulders, told Gary to follow along. As we trudged down the slope, my pain intensified and I yelled at the man to stop! He made no comment and continued descending. He suddenly lost his balance and we were again falling down the slope. Fortunately, we didn't fall very far.

Wincing in agonizing pain, I screamed at him to leave me alone, interspersed with outbursts of profanity similar to the oaths I heard uttered from women giving birth. Picking himself up and brushing off the snow, he walked over to me and apologized, his face flushed from cold and embarrassment. I looked up at him and saw Gary out of the corner of my eye rush over to some nearby boulders for an outhouse moment. Feeling my bladder ready to explode, I wished I could join him.

The man was still deliberating the situation, when another man appeared. They were having a discussion, which I couldn't hear, with occasional glances in my direction. They somehow managed to get me to sit between them as they carried me down to the trail perched on their conjoined hands. It was getting towards dusk as they gingerly laid me down on the ground, and I thanked them, nervously glancing around the area for signs of Gary. "Where's my husband? Is he OK?" Wincing in pain, I eased my aching body back down to the ground.

"He's coming down now and doing fine," one of my rescuers reassured me. Gary's face appeared hovering over me and we held hands and each other's gaze.

"What a way to spend the day, eh? How's your head and arm?"

"My head needs to be examined for doing this kind of shit, and my arm hurts, but hey, we're still alive! Looks like we're not going dancing tonight then, right?" I nodded and we both chuckled appreciatively. Another bolt of pain shot up my spine from the movement.

"So, I'm not laughing again either," I grimaced, trying to squeeze my bladder sphincter against the oncoming flood that was sure to occur at any second.

Appearing over Gary's head were paramedics donned with headlamps and carrying litters. Another face now peered down at me, asking if I could move my legs. Fragments of useless nursing knowledge flooded my addled brain. Yes, of course, why didn't I think of that? See if the legs work... I wiggled my toes for all I was worth and was relieved to discover they still worked!

"Don't move. Lie still," the paramedic ordered as he placed a cervical collar around my neck and slid a board for support under my body.

"Don't worry. I have no intention of moving."

"Are you in a lot of pain?"

"Only when I try to move or laugh."

"I'm going to start an IV and give you some pain meds, OK?"

"Any good stuff like Morphine?" The thought of the drug circulating throughout my battered body was a welcome one.

He chuckled. "Could be similar. Darkness was now upon us as the paramedic searched my arm with the beam from his headlight for decent veins to puncture.

"You have a good one right there and one chance to get it!" I tried to sound brave and authoritative.

"Please try to relax. I'm pretty good at this stuff, OK?" A momentary pinch that felt nothing close to the back agony I was now feeling, despite not moving, followed by a mumbled oath.

"OK, let's try again." My heart sank, yet I relented and let him do his job. Another pinch and the needle found its mark. I felt a flush of fluid rush into my vein, followed by some pain relief.

"Good stuff on board!" he exclaimed. I grabbed his hand and thanked him.

"Hey, you have any spare bedpans lying around?" My bladder was pushing maximum density.

"Nope, sorry. We should be at the ambulance soon and then at the hospital."

As the drugs took effect, I started drifting off into another world, imagining my body was floating, when it was being lifted off the ground by a number of paramedics wearing headlamps. Envisioning Star Trek, I imagined hearing William Shatner saying, "Beam me up, Scotty!" and was suddenly jolted back to reality filled with thoughts of Gary. "Where's my husband?" I asked one paramedic.

"No worries, ma'am, he's right behind you telling bad jokes."

"That's my guy!" I whispered relieved that our journey home was finally underway. To say the journey was long is an understatement. The paramedics were carrying us in our litters, hand over hand, through dense layers of trees, maneuvering over huge boulders and down slick and steep rock-strewn steps, some two or three miles back to the trailhead. To this day, I am still amazed and grateful for the paramedic's efficient efforts to carry us back to safety in the pitch black of night, over some of the most unforgiving terrain Rocky Mountain Park has to offer!

Somewhere after 1 a.m. we reached Estes Park Medical Center and were brought into the ER. Lying on my back on the examination table, I could hold my bladder no longer and begged the nurse for a bedpan at long last! I filled one bedpan after another to the brim and saw the nurse breathe a sigh of relief when I declined her offer for another go around.

After examining the x-rays, the doctor informed me I had a concussion, fractured a rib and two vertebrae in my thoracic spine, as well as torn cartilage in my left knee, and that I would have to stay in the hospital for the next week. He also said I would need surgery which would entail having a rod inserted in my spine. I declined that offer as well. This doctor informed me of the consequences of refusing the surgery that I would most likely never walk again. After pondering his matter-of-fact statement for a few moments, I firmly declared that, despite the possibility of not walking again, I would definitely be back to running again in the near future! Doc stared intently at me for a few minutes and I returned his stare. He must have thought I had lost my mind, yet I never before that moment felt saner. Doc shrugged, told me it was my decision and left the room.

Sometime in the early morning hours, I was wheeled on a gurney to my room. Gary came in and sat on the side of my bed. I noticed he was wearing a splint on his left arm and had a few cuts and bruises on his arms and face.

"How's your arm?"

"My wrist is fractured, but I'm not as bad off as you!" I told him about my fractured spine and rib and earlier discussion with the doctor about having back surgery.

"Well, what do you think about the surgery? You're the nurse."

"I told him I don't want to have to walk around with a rod in my spine."

He held his head with his good hand and sighed. "Yeah, no shit. Well, I guess you made your decision, and you will rest for however long it takes to get back on your feet again. Good thing I took out extra health insurance before coming out here!" We stared at each other in silence for a few moments, knowing it was late, yet neither one wanting to leave the other.

"I'm sorry for this mess. The last thing I wanted to do was spend our time together in a hospital."

"Hey, it's not your fault! He reached for my hand and squeezed it. We'll get through this!" He tried to sound reassuring yet wasn't so convincing. There was so much I wanted to say, but knew we were both exhausted and needed to sleep.

Studying his face, I noticed he wasn't wearing his glasses. "Where are your glasses?"

"Lost them in the fall." Sighing again, he looked down at the floor.

"How will you get back to the hotel?"

"Guess without my glasses somehow."

"Yeah, and with a broken wrist." We exchanged glances.

"Don't worry, I'll make it back alright! Get some sleep now, OK? I'll see you tomorrow." We kissed and then he left. I couldn't keep my eyes open any longer and soon fell into a restless and dreamless sleep.

The nurse awoke me sometime the next morning carrying a breakfast tray. "Are you hungry?" she smiled.

"Not really." Attempting to stretch my arms overhead, I winced in pain. My bladder felt like it was once again about to burst at the seams. Apparently, it was making up for lost time since filling countless bedpans the night before. "I need to use the bedpan, or can I use the restroom?"

"Do you think you feel well enough to get up?"

The thought of moving seemed like a supreme effort, yet I was tired of lying on my back since being carried on a litter by the paramedics for hours the previous night. "I guess it's worth a try."

"Wait until I get some help," she patted my shoulder and left the room. A few minutes later, my friendly nurse arrived with another nurse.

"Where's the Hoyer lift?" I joked, recalling my own attempts to lift heavy patients using the Hoyer when working in the hospital as a nurse.

The nurse glanced at my wiry frame. "Don't think we need that for you."

Sitting on the edge of the bed with the nurses holding onto my arms for support, I felt the room spinning like a top, or was it my head? Another wave of nausea washed over me, and I asked to sit for a few more moments to regain my balance. One nurse stood in front of me with her arms holding mine, the other stood to my right, leaning her body into my side for extra support. Soon I was on my feet walking, or rather limping my way towards the restroom. Passing a mirror on the wall, I caught a glimpse of myself and recoiled in horror at the sight. My face was swollen twice its original size, its color a dark purple. "Oh God!" I whispered, almost fainting right on the spot. My nurses rushed me to the restroom where I collapsed in exhaustion onto the toilet seat. I sat there suddenly engulfed in tears with shaking hands holding my spinning head.

Recalling the events of the past 24 hours, the bone-chilling cold up on the mountain, seeing Gary sitting next to me broken and shaking from the cold and shock of the fall was more than I could grasp at the moment and seemed surreal. It felt like I was having a nightmare that I couldn't wake up from, only to discover that the situation was all too real!

"Are you doing OK in there?" I heard the nurse calling to me from outside the restroom.

"Yeah, I'm done." Sighing heavily, I wiped the tears from my battered face with a corner of my hospital gown. The nurses helped me back to bed, and thanking them, I stared at my breakfast tray sitting on the table next to my bed. One nurse left the room and the nurse who brought the tray moved the table closer to where I lay in bed and suggested I try to eat some food to keep my energy up. Still feeling nauseated, I didn't really feel like eating, yet realized she was right. Remembering I hadn't eaten anything since the previous day, I poured some milk over the glob of oatmeal in the bowl an hesitantly spooned some into my mouth. Suddenly rediscovering my appetite, I polished off the oatmeal, buttered the toast and wolfed both pieces down in record breaking time. Having some food in my gut appeased the nausea, and I noticed with relief that the room had stopped spinning. I lowered the head of my bed and soon drifted off into a well-deserved nap.

Sometime in the afternoon, I was awakened by someone holding my hand and opened my eyes to see Gary's blurry face peering down at me. He sat in a chair next to my bed and I tried smiling, glad to see him once again.

"How are you feeling?"

"Great, if I don't move anything. How about you?"

"Well, I made it back to the motel OK last night and got a few hours of sleep, yet am still pretty wiped."

"How's your arm?"

"Sore, but who's counting?"

I tried to smile, yet my mind was on overload trying to process the events of the past 24 hours. So many questions were firing away: Would I be able to walk on my own or would I be confined to a wheelchair? I had another semester of school to complete and wondered how I would keep up with homework and course requirements for graduation the following May.

"Hey, are you with me?" Gary's voice interrupted my thoughts. I looked at him with tears welling up in my eyes.

"I'm sorry for this whole mess."

"It's not your fault, don't even go there!" he insisted, his hand now smoothing my hair as if it could erase the horrendous fall we had endured.

"We should have been more prepared. I'm glad we're both still alive!" I was now sobbing uncontrollably as Gary hugged me with his good arm.

"It's going to be OK, I promise. We'll get through this!"

I looked up at him and noticed he was looking down at the floor as if he had something else on his mind. Drying my eyes with my palms, I stared at him. "What's going on?"

"Well, my car is kind of messed up. Before I could utter another word, he continued, "On the way up here today, I tried making a left turn to get to the hospital, and this guy slammed into me. Noticing the look of horror on my face he patted my hand.

"You're kidding, right?"

"Nothing to worry about really... the front fender is a bit dented, yet luckily it's still drivable!"

At that point, the doctor walked into the room and greeted us. Gary stood up and shook the doctor's hand. Doc then walked over to my bed and asked how I was feeling. Seeing my face streaked with tears, he apologized and informed me that I would have to stay in the hospital for the rest of the week to rest and recover. I thought about my schoolwork and wondered if I'd be able to attend classes.

"My last semester at school starts next week. Will I be able to leave by then?"

"I'm going to order some physical therapy sessions for the rest of the week, and we'll see how it goes. How does that sound?"

I pictured this little old lady hobbling around with a walker and suddenly felt a lot older than my 33 years.

"Doc, I will walk again I promise you that!

"I don't doubt that, young lady, but right now you need to take it easy, OK? You've been through a pretty traumatic experience and you need to give your body some time to recover!" Doctor's orders. Handshakes all around and then doc exits stage left.

"Well, that was quick," Gary watched him leave the room.

"Yeah, I'd like his job! Here, take two aspirins and call me in the morning!"

We shared some welcome laughter to break up the tension, and chatted about his car, joked about how bad things seem to come in threes, and wondered when the next event would take place.

This occurrence, as we thought, was right around the corner.

The week-long stay in the hospital flew by quickly. It was interspersed with daily visits from Otis, the physical therapist, who kept my spirits up with stories of his horse-riding adventures and welcome encouragement of getting me "back on the horse" someday soon.

Although I didn't think at the time I would ever go back to climbing, his comments inspired and strengthened my determination to resume my active lifestyle. He would work with me on strengthening my legs and I did the exercises every day until I could walk the halls by myself using a walker. Whenever I felt like I couldn't do an exercise, Otis would make me believe I could. He was my guardian angel and helped me break through the barriers of pain, anguish and self-doubt.

Another angel presented herself to me one restless night when I couldn't sleep. When I put on the call light, there was nurse, Pam, bringing me pain medication, and she could very well have turned and left the room, yet sensed I needed some company and stayed. She listened as I tearfully recounted details of the accident and helped me put things into perspective, reminding me that I survived the experience and emerged a much wiser person. She stayed until I fell asleep holding my hand the entire time. In that moment, an indelible impression was formed that remained with me throughout my nursing career, and I understood the true meaning of compassion.

One recollection that came to mind was of a patient, at a hospital where I worked, who was quite fearful of undergoing surgery the next day. I entered her room to review her pre-op checklist to prepare her for surgery. It was then she expressed her anxiety about the surgery and asked if I would be working the next day. I sensed her anticipation and told her I would come in despite it being my day off. She squeezed my hand and thanked me profusely. I stood by her bedside after surgery the next day gazing down at her peacefully sleeping face. When she awoke, our eyes met and a slight smile formed on her lips as she once again whispered her thanks, motioning to her husband standing next to me. He pulled from his coat pocket a small wrapped gift box and handed it to me. Stunned, I opened the box to see a beautiful golden butterfly broach pin that serves as a daily reminder that a bit of kindness goes a long way.

Gary picked me up from the hospital the next day and walked beside me as I slowly hobbled out the front door, leaning on my walker. Of course, the doctor who told me I would never walk again was nowhere in sight. We drove to Estes Park, a small alcove of a town located outside of Rocky Mountain National Park, grabbed a bite to eat and walked down the main street crowded with tourists. At first sight, the town reminded me of Old Town in Chicago with its small shops and cafes high-lighting the main street, and throngs of people coming at you from all directions, minus the patchouli oil scents. The day was warm and bright with sunshine, yet I felt chilled and tired from the exertion of walking and trying to stand erect.

Gary helped me sit on a nearby bench.

"I think you've had enough for today. Let's hit the road and find a hotel or motel." I wasn't going to argue. My flight back to Chicago was due to leave early the next morning and I still needed to pack and get some sleep. As we drove to-wards Denver, we spotted the Valley High Motel off Hwy I -25 and spent the evening relaxing and enjoying each other's company, glad to have time together before my trip back home. I didn't want the evening to end, as I knew it would be a few months before seeing him again when I would make the final move out to Colorado.

The next day Gary drove me to the airport and waited with me until it was time to board the plane back to Chicago. We sat side by side looking out the win-dow and not talking much. Gary sensed my not wanting to leave. Squeezing my hand, he tried to reassure me that our time apart would go by fast. We embraced and I boarded the plane.

As the plane was landing in Chicago, I gazed out the window at the familiar airport surroundings and felt relieved to be back home once again. My body felt stiff and achy from the two-hour plane ride, and I wanted to stop moving. The cab ride home from the airport seemed eternal as the driver pulled up to the faded yellow brick apartment building I called home. As I paid the driver, I imagined walking into a small, dark, and drab apartment filled with boxes now collecting dust in my two-week absence. I was suddenly filled with apprehension of im-pending solitude and wished I could step into a time machine and be instantly transported to Colorado and into Gary's waiting arms. What awaited me was far removed from my fantasies.

I hobbled up the stairs to the top floor and reached in my pack for my keys. Something caught my attention as I approached the door with keys in hand, and I stared as though in a trance at the door that was slightly ajar. Did I forget to lock the door before leaving on my trip? I shook my head in disbelief as I tried to recall weeks before when rushing out the door. *"No, I declared aloud. I surely must have locked that door…"*

With shaking hand, I reached for the doorknob and slowly opened the door, not knowing what to expect. The sight that met my eyes was horrific! Someone had broken into the apartment and trashed it. It was as if a hurricane had landed square on our roof, leaving the roof and little else before blowing away. Boxes were overturned with contents thrown on the floor and, as I peered into the kitchen from out in the hall, I saw our stereo sitting on the table awaiting an eerily thwarted departure. Clothes from my closet were thrown helter-skelter around the bedroom, drawers ripped from our dressers, clothes strewn on the beds and all around the room.

Stumbling into the ransacked remnants of what used to be our apartment, I felt faint and had to hold onto the door to steady myself. I noticed, with a sickening feeling in my stomach, that Gary's cream-colored Les Paul guitar and acoustic Yamaha were nowhere to be found. "Oh God... I stammered with hot tears searing my eyes. Staring into the void of our closet, I noticed Gary's Canon camera and lenses were also missing to the tune of $700. Collapsing on the couch, the only piece of furniture that was still in its original place, I reached for the phone and dialed the police. How was I going to explain this to Gary? So much had happened in the course of one week it was difficult to comprehend it all! The accident and break-in weighed heavily on my mind. I felt like I was in a nightmare and wished I could wake up and find this was only a bad dream. No luck with that one. OK, so bad things come in three's and, so, this had to be the end of our bad luck streak, I hoped.

In a state of shock mixed with exhaustion, I watched the police dusting every remaining piece of furniture for fingerprints and wondered if they would find any that would lead them to the thieves. They never did.

Gary sounded disappointed when I finally broke the news to him about the theft, yet took it all in stride as he always did. "It's just all stuff that can be replaced," he tried his best to sound reassuring, yet I knew how much his guitars meant to him and his voice belied his disappointment. A long period of silence covered the distance between the two phones we both held. I'm sure we were both numb at this stage of the game from all our losses.

"I miss you," I whimpered.

"Yeah, I miss you too. See you in another month." I wondered how I would make it through that very lonely period of time, yet chose to dispose of negative thoughts rather than succumb to despair. The whole month of July was spent doing homework and making daily trips to the neighborhood Y to use their swimming pool, which kept me busy and focused on finishing school and resuming running. My body was weak and flabby from immobility and the long road to recovery lay ahead. The contrary words uttered by the hospital doctor that I would "never walk again" made me more determined to run despite my injuries and all odds.

Otis, the physical therapist, had recommended I use light weights when I returned back home, and I picked up some five-pounders on his advice. I did exercises he showed me, placing the weights on my feet and lifting them up and down several times a day, as well as using the weights for overall strengthening. The weight workouts were interspersed with daily running laps in the pool. At first, I felt self-conscious running in the pool instead of swimming, yet rejoiced in the pure ecstasy of the movement! I was running once again, albeit in a weird fashion, yet running nonetheless! Running against the current of the water, more often than not, felt like running through quicksand, but after each session I noticed my body becoming stronger and less sore. Feeling a bit like Forest Gump, I kept hearing the theme to "Chariots of Fire" playing over and over in my head, and that motivated me to finish each challenging water workout.

One hot and sunny August morning, I got brave and decided to give running a try after a two-month sabbatical. Feeling determined to run a mile, I laced up my New Balance shoes and headed out the door. A few steps into the run, my legs felt like two wiggly, wobbly bowls of Jello®. Yet I persisted for another half mile or so then pulled over to a shady patch of grass and collapsed down on the ground in exhaustion. I chided myself for giving up so soon, but I felt elated that I was proving the good doctor wrong! Over the next few weeks, alternately swimming one day and running the next, I managed to work up to running a mile without pausing or collapsing and felt quite proud of the accomplishment.

Shortly thereafter, I was rushing to the airport to pick Gary up and we busied ourselves packing up last minute belongings and getting things ready to be shipped by moving van out to Colorado. At that stage of the game, life loomed eternal and possibilities were endless. We never could have imagined the extent of musical adventures the future had in store for us.

CHAPTER 17
THE WACKY WORLD OF ENTERTAINMENT (1985-1989)

"All the world's a stage, and all the men and women merely players..."
— William Shakespeare

In August of 1985, with move complete, we began the task of unpacking and settling into our new and very cramped 700 square foot apartment. Prior to me joining Gary, he lived in the tiny apartment with little more than a mattress, a 12-inch black and white TV, and an acoustic guitar—a bachelor's dream. Enter the wife and a moving van full of furniture and household items. All of that was about to change! Our apartment in Chicago, that had been burglarized, was huge by comparison, complete with walk-in closet, and a spacious living room, dining room and bathroom. Having lived there for a number of years, we accumulated a lot of stuff. Despite throwing out a lot of it during the moving process, we still had lots to try to cram into our small new abode. Somehow, it all fit.

Gary was already working at Larimer Press and I set about the task of completing my correspondence college course writing a term paper on Women and Exercise to satisfy the course requirements. Upon receiving notification by mail that I had passed my last course, it was confirmed that my B.A. degree would be finalized as of December 1985.

With schoolwork complete, I tried finding a nursing job which I thought would be easy to do, and, in that assumption, I was right. Soon finding a nursing temp agency job, I worked part time at various hospitals throughout the Denver metro area. As an agency nurse, I worked flexible hours and didn't have to commit to any particular hospital or department. I also felt somehow removed from the alienation I experienced from other nurses when living in Chicago. That belief was short -lived! It wasn't long before I discovered that despite moving to a different state, the nursing field was unchanging in its demands of long hours and having to deal with stressful life-and death-situations and likewise stressed out co-workers on a daily basis.

After working in a number of unsatisfying hospital jobs for the next few years, I burned out big time and quit my last nursing job vowing to leave nursing far behind forevermore. Gary, of course, wasn't too pleased about me leaving a steady nursing income behind as he depended on the extra income to supplement the meager wages he received from Larimer Press. He had his reservations about my exit from nursing, yet knew how unhappy I was in my nursing career. After several discussions about our insecure financial status, we came to an agreement that I would continue hunting for non-nursing jobs and he would continue to support me through this transitory time.

In 1984, prior to our move, Gary and I attended a Mime performance at Northwestern University, the same campus where we were married. During the show, one of the performers did a piece about a washing machine and I watched in utter amazement that someone could portray a common household appliance with such astounding authenticity. I could barely contain my excitement at the realization of what I wanted to do with my life. I had taken a series of mime classes for six months with an incredible teacher, Karen Hoyer, who taught me a bit about the art of mime that I found fascinating. My earliest influences and role models as a child were such great comedians as Jerry Lewis, Red Skelton, Laurel and Hardy, Charlie Chaplin, and Marcel Marceau who set the stage for my future aspirations of becoming an entertainer. I found enjoyment in Karen's weekly classes at the Glenwood Center of Performing Arts in the Rogers Park area of Chicago, yet didn't think anything serious would develop from this experience.

One day while sitting alone in the apartment, I was looking for a particular book to read, couldn't find it and was feeling frustrated. Giving up on finding the book, I noticed another book that caught my attention, picked it up and started reading it. Ironically, it was called *The Mime Book* by Claude Kipnis, that I bought after studying with Karen Hoyer. Not long thereafter, I busied myself with practicing the mime exercises in the book on a daily basis and with steady practice developed a certain fluidity of movements and confidence enough to progress in my new found career. Ready for prime time in January of 1988, I signed up for a mime class at Colorado Free University taught by Dan Horsey. After a few months, Dan invited me to study individually with him in his studio in downtown Denver. Dan was already a mime extraordinaire in his own right, and had been honing his craft at The Goldston-Johnson School of Mime in Columbus, Ohio, for a few years. In the year I spent studying with Dan, I learned volumes about the art of mime and about the school that would take me to a whole new level of adventure in my life.

While studying with Dan, I came across an ad in the Denver Post advertising a company that was looking for mimes to work part time and answered the ad not having a clue about what the work would entail. When I showed up for the interview sometime in the spring of 1988, I was greeted by the owner, John, and his partner, Mike, who did mime in the form of what was termed "deliveries." John explained I would be partnering with Mike and delivering flowers and other gifts to clients for special events such as birthday parties, festivals and even doing some street performing on the Pearl Street Mall in Boulder. The work sounded more interesting to me than nursing, and despite not making much money, I agreed to give it a try hoping to gain more experience in performing.

At first, Mike and I got along great and did our deliveries for numerous events including art shows, street fairs, antique car shows, and passing out flowers on Boulder and Denver Malls rain or shine. Mike and I had even worked out a number of skits to do as part of the deliveries that brought smiles to the faces of adults and children alike almost everywhere we performed. I recall an event in which a woman hired us to perform for the opening of her art gallery in Denver one evening in May. Mike was dressed in a colorful jester outfit and I was in my usual mime attire complete with white face, black overalls and some form of striped shirt. We were doing roving entertainment, or in other words, entertaining people as we met them walking around the studio. The lady who was the owner came up to me at one point during the event, asked for my name, and as I started to reach in the top pocket of my overalls for a business card, she stopped me dead in my tracks. "Oh no, you're not pulling that shit with me!" she yelled. "You need to talk to me!" and away she stormed. I guess I didn't make brownie points with her that time and we weren't invited back to her studio, which made us feel a bit dejected. Reflecting back on the incident, I guess I could have broken character, yet felt at the time I wanted to preserve the true nonverbal essence of mime. For years to come, I would deliberate this very issue of nonverbal vs. verbal in my shows.

For the most part, Mike and I made a good team, that is, when he would show up for a gig. There were a number of gigs he didn't show up for, and that didn't bode well for our partnership or the company. After working for this company for only two or three months, John informed me that the company was disbanding. I was somewhat disappointed, yet took the news in stride. Having the experience of working as a mime, albeit in small fashion, only strengthened my determination to keep on doing what I loved to do.

Having had a taste of what it was like to work doing something I enjoyed, of course, I wanted more. Without a hint of business experience or knowledge of what was required to own my own business, on July 25, 1988, I started my company, Mimeworks, with little more than a telephone book and a dial phone. In the beginning, making numerous cold calls did little to generate gigs, and I was getting a bit discouraged. If I expected the sky to open and gigs to start pouring in, neither one happened right away, but the universe would eventually get the hint.

Starting this business was a scary venture for both Gary and me. Gary was not exactly making stellar wages from his new printing company and he depended on my nursing income to supplement his salary. Nonetheless, he tried to suspend his disapproval of my new career venture.

When starting Mimeworks, I was also working for SNAP, a temp agency in Denver and doing whatever clerical work they could scrounge up for me. The owner, Helene, approached me one day and inquired about what I did as a mime, as I had made mention of starting the business to her earlier that day. When I told her that I provide entertainment for all occasions, she mentioned that her daughter, Barbara, was having a birthday the following week, and she invited me to provide entertainment at her party. I immediately agreed as she said she would even pay me! Imagine getting paid for doing something you enjoy! I thanked her profusely for helping my business get started and assured her the show would be well worth the money she paid. I was super psyched and could hardly wait for the event, although fearful at the same time, as up to that point I had mainly performed "street mime." Opening Mimeworks had motivated me to create actual skits, or pieces as they are formally called, for special events, as well as enhance my ability to be spontaneous during roving events.

Barbara's party was held in a popular upscale restaurant in Thornton called Brittany Hill. At that time, the restaurant had been open for a number of years, but closed in 2007 due to legal issues and costly renovations. (15). That was indeed a sad day for Gary and me, and myriads of other people who enjoyed the delicious food, stunning panoramic vistas of the area, and atmosphere of the restaurant sitting up on a hill. Barbara's family and friends, about 30 people or more, were sitting around one large table and several surrounding tables in a common room when I arrived. I was hard to miss dressed in my usual mime attire. Helene approached me immediately and handed me my first paycheck made out to Mimeworks. She introduced me to Barbara and all the guests, and then the floor was all "mime."

In preparation for the occasion, I had created a special story, choreographed to a Beatles song entitled, "Birthday" and broke into the routine with my CD player blasting the music throughout the restaurant. Every head in the restaurant turned to look in my direction, some with smiles on their faces and others who glared at me like I was some alien from Mars who was rudely interrupting their breakfast, lunch or dinner as the case might be. Worrying that the power source for my CD player might be shut down at any given moment, I turned down the volume to a more tolerable decibel level and proceeded through my birthday routine. By the end of my performance, Barbara and all her guests were on their feet giving me a standing ovation. Some restaurant patrons looked disinterested as they ate their meals, and others were laughing and applauding. Barbara ran up to me, gave me a hug and thanked me as profusely as I had previously thanked her mom for inviting me to perform at the event. Helene greeted me with a smile, huge hug, and numerous expressions of gratitude and commendations. Countless guests came up to me expressing their sentiments of how much they enjoyed the show. I was a bit surprised by all the commotion, as I had never before received such accolades when working as a nurse! The next day at SNAP, I heard more great comments from Helene about how everyone enjoyed the show and her sentiments affirmed that entertainment was the work I should be pursuing!

With the start of every new endeavor, there are always dues to pay and I have paid my fair share. A few of my fondest mime memories include the following:

One of my earliest gigs was at a bar somewhere off Federal in Denver. When I entered the bar carrying a few balloons to deliver to the person celebrating her birthday, a lady accosted me asking if I was the stripper? (That comment needed no further commentary!)

The Russians are coming! I was asked to perform for a group of twenty or so people who only spoke Russian. I was a bit nervous as I didn't speak any form of Russian. Luckily, there was a translator present, so I didn't bring my usual signs, choosing instead to announce the names of my pieces verbally. The only prop I used was my CD player. At first the audience was intimidating to say the least, sitting in their seats with arms folded across their broad chests—at least the men anyway. The women simply wore frowns. The piece I always started with was "The Weight Lifter" that mimics a woman working out with weights that are too heavy for her.

While performing my half hour show including pieces about every topic from circus performers to fireless dragons, I watched their expressions soften from stern glares to broad smiles, and heard chortles that turned into laughter followed by appreciative applause. By shows end, I was surrounded by my broadly-smiling audience speaking fluent Russian all at once, reaching out to touch my arms, back, face and anything they could get their hands on. Despite not understanding a word they said, I knew I had communicated something powerful non-verbally. I discovered that day that there are two universal languages in the world, mime and, of course, music.

I had a gig at Coors, a well-known brewing company in Golden, Colorado, in which I performed for an audience of people who were deaf. Once again, I had to choose what to bring with me, and being used to performing with music, it was difficult to leave my CD player behind. I did a completely non-verbal half hour show, using only my signs to announce the names of the pieces. As I performed, once again I watched the expressions on the faces in the audience, and saw smiles. And instead of applause after each piece, I saw hands waving in the air. Not knowing what to make of the waving, I continued on with the show. After the last piece, I noticed everyone in the audience standing up and furiously waving their arms and hands in the air. Once again, I didn't understand what they were doing and dejectedly walked offstage. The lady who hired me for the event greeted me wearing a huge smile on her face. "They didn't like the show," I sighed with resignation.

"What are you talking about?" she queried. "They're giving you a standing ovation, so you better get back out there!" she pushed me back onstage. I stood onstage taking in the sight of one hundred or so Coors employees waving at me, and so I waved back at them. Little did I know then that years into the future I would bear witness to more waving of arms and hands than one could ever dream possible.

After an early morning show at a Montessori School in Denver, I collapsed into my waiting office chair in exhaustion after carting signs, easel, partition, and container full of costumes into the house. *How am I going to do another show tonight? I wondered.* Feeling better after grabbing a bite to eat, I sat at my desk for a few hours doing some paperwork, when the phone rang. I heard a male voice say at the other end, "Hi, is this Mimeworks?"

"Yes, how can I help you?"

"My name is Arthur and I'm hoping you can meet me at 5 p.m. to do some entertainment on my bus."

"On your bus? OK, so you're a bus driver? Where is your route?"

"Downtown Denver."

I sighed and looked at the clock. It was 2 p.m. and I didn't feel like adding another gig to an already busy day. I knew I had the show that evening at The Children's Museum and wanted to save my energy for that.

"Hey, Arthur, I'm pretty booked for today. Have you tried calling Mime Time?"

"Yes, I have tried calling other companies and no one seems to be available."

"I don't think I can do this gig, Arthur. As I said before, my day is pretty full!"

"Please, Donna, I heard you are a really good mime, and I need a good mime to do this special party I am planning for my faithful bus customers. Won't you please reconsider? I'll even drive you to your next gig!" This time he hit his mark and I took the bait.

"OK, so if I did this for you, what would I have to do?"

"Just be entertaining and the rest is up to you. All you have to do is meet me downtown at 5 p.m. and I will give you door prize tickets and party favors to hand out to my customers. And oh yeah, by the way, my boss will be on the bus." *No pressure there, I thought.* Reluctantly, I agreed and after getting more details of when and where to meet, hurried Arthur off the phone. *I have to be nuts to do this insanity, I thought hanging up the phone.*

A few minutes before 5 p.m., I arrived at the bus stop where Arthur said he'd meet me in the Lodo area of downtown Denver. Five minutes later, a man dressed in an RTD uniform approached and greeted me with hand extended saying, "Hi Donna, I'm Arthur. Thanks for doing this. I really appreciate you taking time from your busy schedule to meet with me." We chatted for the next 15 minutes about details of the gig and he gave me door prize tickets and party favors to hand out to his passengers. The more we talked, the more I got to know and like him. He drove an express route and talked at some length about his customers and what they meant to him.

"These passengers you will meet have been making it a point to get on my bus specifically for the past year, and I just want to do something special for them in return, and of course, play a little joke on my boss as well, you know, get him to lighten up a little," Arthur laughed.

"So, how will I know who your boss is?"

"He's a big guy, kind of short and stout and I will either whistle or start to sing as you are passing him in the aisle. He'll most likely be sitting near the front of the bus."

At that point, a bus pulled up in front of where we stood, and a few passengers and driver filed out. Arthur smiled at me. "OK, you ready to rock n' roll?" Before I could reply, he hopped into the driver's seat, motioning for me to hop on as well. The minute I stepped onto the bus, the doors closed and we were in motion. Arthur turned on the rock music. Party time!

I nervously started walking down the aisle and noticed there were at least twenty or so passengers on board staring holes right through me. I passed a jolly looking fellow sitting on the left side of the bus with a bewildered expression on his face, as though he were deep in thought. At that precise moment, Arthur started singing very loudly along with the music that was blaring and I immediately knew what to do. I did what any insane person might have done in that situation and grabbed both of the jolly fellow's hands and started doing the tango with him down the aisle futilely trying to keep in step with the music. He let out an excited exclamation of some sort that sounded like, "OHHHHHHH my!" At first, he tried to resist my attempts to get him into the dance, yet after figuring out what was going on he started to keep up with me step for step. Now he was getting into it and started pulling me towards him with a gleeful expression on his face. I suddenly paused, mid dance, and abruptly changed direction with boss man in tow. Suddenly, he started guffawing and it seemed that everyone on the bus followed suit. People were laughing so hard they almost fell out of their seats. Once again, pause… then abrupt change of direction, dancing boss man back to his seat and he fell into it still laughing uproariously. Arthur turned around to give him a quick glance and as I proceeded once again down the aisle, I heard boss man say to Arthur between fits of laughter, "Man, you sure know how to pick 'em!"

Strolling casually down the aisle, I remembered the tickets and party favors and started handing them out to the passengers. There were the typical party hats with pointed tops and blowers that sounded more like fog-horns. Everyone started to toot in unison at first, then at random. Someone handed me a phone receiver, and I had a silent conversation with a real person on the other end. The person kept asking, "Who am I speaking to?" Of course, I wasn't about to break character at that point, so I handed the phone to another passenger who continued the conversation.

Heading towards the front of the bus, I noticed passengers were still laughing and blowing on their blowers, in full party mode. Arthur was looking in my direction through the mirror directly above him grinning from ear to ear. He was digging it and apparently others were as well. I glanced out the window of our bus and saw a miraculous occurrence, the memory of which has stayed with me to this very day. I saw a few other buses pass by with a number of passengers holding signs up in their windows that read things like, WISH WE WERE ON YOUR BUS! PARTY ON! Once again, I felt humbled and awed by the tremendous power of mime to speak volumes without saying a word. The smiles on the faces of the people I came in daily contact with affirmed that I was right where I needed to be in that moment.

At the end of the route, Arthur and I stood talking at the front of the bus while the passengers gave us hugs, handshakes and shared positive comments about the "best ride they ever had" as they filed past us off the bus. Arthur was beaming as he thanked me and shook my hand for the hundredth time. I looked at my watch and saw it was almost 6:30 p.m. "Don't think I will make my next show," I sighed, slumping into a seat across from the driver's seat.

"Heck yeah!" he exclaimed. "I'll get you there on time!" It was pedal to the metal and we were cruising at warp speed towards The Children's Museum.

Dashing into the Museum a few minutes before show time, I headed for the auditorium and was met by the lady who had hired me to do the show. "Glad you're here! The kids are already seated and ready to go!" I hurriedly started setting up for my show and prepared to greet one hundred or so young faces that were eagerly waiting to be entertained. Stepping onstage, I commenced to entertain them, exhausted yet exuberant and re-energized with the realization that an ordinary day had turned extraordinary.

There were numerous memorable venues, including performing on location in Boulder at the filming of a movie called, *Double Obsession*, starring Margaux Hemingway and Maryam d'Abo. Earlier that day, I received a phone call from Abbie, a friend and fellow mime, notifying me that "extras" were needed for the movie. I was reluctant to accept the offer having another early afternoon gig that same day, yet went to satisfy my curiosity. The location was at Central Park near Boulder Creek and I didn't think I'd be accepted as an extra much less get a part in the movie.

I stood amongst a crowd of tightrope walkers, clowns, and jugglers, as the stage was set on a walking path in the park and waited for the action to begin. Shortly thereafter, I noticed a director, of sorts, trying to bring some order to the chaos, signaling for the crowd to be quiet and yelling "action" into a megaphone he was holding. I saw a pretty, petite blond woman carrying a bag of groceries, walking down the path holding the hand of a little girl walking next to her and recognized her as Maryam d'Abo, best known as Kara Milovy in the 1987 James Bond film, *The Living Daylights*. Thinking the scene was being rehearsed, I jumped into the mix and started following Maryam and her little charge, pretending to try to steal items from her groceries bag. I had no idea the scene was actually being filmed until I heard the director yell "cut" into the megaphone. Stopping dead in my tracks, I feared he wasn't too happy with my performance and wanted to replace me. Glancing towards him, I noticed the director had an amused expression on his face as he asked for a livelier "take."

The second go around was indeed livelier as my attempts to steal her groceries became more obvious with her turning around on occasion to look at me with a feigned disgusted expression on her face. As she would glance back at me, I would stand motionless in some weird pose mimicking disinterest, glancing away from her. We did the hide and seek interaction for perhaps another three or four takes and filmed another bit in which Maryam stopped to chat with another actress, Blair Brown, who was wearing sunglasses. As they engaged in conversation I stood behind Blair and tossing caution to the wind, I grabbed her sunglasses to the sound of appreciative chuckles from the director and cast. She turned around on a dime, scowled at me for a few seconds and grabbing the sunglasses out of my hand, replaced them back on her face without missing a beat of the conversation with Maryam. The moment was ripe with potential for more tomfoolery, yet the director came over and declared the scene a wrap, and there you have it, my 20 seconds of fame and fortune. This experience gave me a chance to meet and interact with two famous actresses, yet I never did meet Margaux or make any fortune from my fame!

CHAPTER 18
GETTING RE-EDUCATED (1989-'92)

"Treat people as if they were what they ought to be and you help them become what they are capable of becoming."
— Goethe

In addition to running Mimeworks and doing gigs, I managed to fit in studying with Dan in his Downtown studio to keep my performance skills proficient. Sessions with Dan were rigorous, yet productive and kept me eager to learn more about the art of Mime.

One day after a session, Dan and I went out for lunch to Racine's, a restaurant near his studio in downtown Denver. During lunch we, of course, talked about mime and Dan shared many of his performance experiences with me. I respected Dan both as a teacher and performer and valued whatever knowledge and expertise he would impart to me. Especially memorable was our discussion about the art of performance and what constitutes a good performance. He explained the importance of involving the audience in the performance and said, "I believe that I have reached a level of proficiency in mime in which the audience is right where I want them," and pointed to the palm of his hand. "When you get the audience involved, they will feel more connected to and have a better understanding of what's being conveyed to them. People love to see you in the act of being human." Dan smiled glancing up from his cup of java.

"Wow Dan, that's pretty cool. I can't wait to get to that level."

I recalled a recent show of Dan's that I saw and aspired to be a performer of his caliber one day. Reminiscent of the washing machine performance I saw with Gary in Chicago, Dan's show blew my mind. The ease with which he conveyed emotions, truths, and human foibles to the audience without a spoken word was honest, humorous, and inspirational.

"You're coming along nicely," he smiled and I felt sincerity in his reply. I knew he had recently done some studying on his own at a professional mime school in Columbus, Ohio and I was curious to find out about the school.

"Dan, you've taught me a lot, yet I really want to learn more. What are your thoughts about the school you recently studied at in Ohio?"

"Oh yeah, Goldston, he chuckled. They're amazing! They really opened my head and took me to another level of practice. You should give them a try."

A slight gasp escaped from my lips. "Do you think I'm ready for that school?" I was fascinated at the thought of attending a professional mime school, but felt unsure if I had that level of proficiency.

"Why not? I think you're ready. You've been putting up with me for the past year, haven't you?"

This time I chuckled. "Yeah, I guess so!" Part of me wanted to keep studying with Dan. The part that was fearful was venturing into new, unfamiliar territory of moving on. Visions of the motherless baby bird once again flooded my mind's eye. Another part of me was chomping at the bit to explore and break through self-imposed limits. "Are you planning on going back next summer?"

Dan nodded his head. "Oh yeah, for sure. It's a lot of work, yet it's fun stuff! Besides, someone has to keep you in line. You might even get better than me!" he chuckled.

"No worries about that, Dan! Although, I can't guarantee that won't happen!"

Dan looked at his watch and said, "Oops, I'd better get back to the studio. Have another class to teach." He waved for the waitress and gave me the school's number, telling me to call and talk with Gregg, the artistic director of the school. I thanked him for lunch and the info and promised to call Gregg soon. "Keep in touch," he smiled, then hugged me and hurried down the street to his studio.

"Hello, Goldston-Johnson, this is Gregg, how can I help you?" the voice declared at the other end.

"Hi Gregg. This is Donna Brown and I am interested in attending your school." My heart was pounding and I had sweaty palms.

"OK, what kind of training do you have?" asked Gregg, getting right to the point.

After telling him about starting Mimeworks, taking a few classes and private lessons for the past year, and feeling rather proud of these accomplishments, the wind was not so gently let out of my sails by Gregg's response. "Uh huh… you sound rather green to me, Donna." Although feeling a bit miffed at his comment at the time, looking back on our conversation, I realized he was right. At that point in time, I had some business experience and through the business, gained quite a bit of mime knowledge or so I thought.

One thing I've realized over the years is that in every possible way life will present you with continual opportunities for growth and learning if you leave yourself open to them. I was soon to discover how much I didn't know about the complex art form called Pantomime.

Feeling somewhat defeated before I even got started, I declared, "Well, I think you should know, Gregg, I have been studying with a student of yours, Dan Horsey, for the past year, and he recommended I continue my studies at your school, and thus, the reason for my call."

"Oh yeah, Dan, he's a pretty cool guy," Gregg replied sounding a bit lighter. "So, I would recommend you start with the two-week intensive and take it from there, OK?"

Houston, we have contact… guess I'll have to give it a go. "Thanks Gregg. See you in another month." I nervously hung up the phone wondering if I had lost my marbles. *Well, a lot could happen in a month and perhaps I'll decide to opt out and do something saner… like return to nursing where it's more familiar and… wait! What the hell am I thinking?* My decision was made at that moment. Mime school or bust!

The month flew by filled with buying leotards and lots of dance clothing and nervous anticipation of this new endeavor. I was physically in good shape, yet nothing could prepare me for the challenges that lay ahead. In fact, I was so nervous that my sleep went to hell in a handbag and I spent a few nights in the basement tearing up old phone books to allay my anxiety. Probably not the best idea, yet it got rid of a lot of nervous energy. I was bringing in some decent income from Mimeworks and I thought if I improved my mime skills this would boost my income. Gary was still not convinced that I could make a living doing mime, yet he agreed that more mime education would make me a better entertainer and more marketable. He also knew how much I enjoyed doing mime and even created music for several of my mime pieces. I dreaded leaving him again, yet knew we would survive for the two weeks I was away.

The day I was to fly to Columbus, Ohio, I was pretty exhausted, yet unable to nap on the plane, and I almost fell asleep in the airport while waiting for my ride to the school. The Goldston and Johnson School for Mimes was located on the campus of Kenyon College in Gambier, a small and quaint town. Its main attractions were ornate cathedral style school buildings, a few book and grocery stores, and of course the local pub Pirates Cove, more affectionately known to students as The Cove. Kenyon College was noted for its theatre and dance studies. Many student productions took place in Bolton Theatre, a modern 389-seat theatre that shares ample backstage and technical facilities with neighboring Hill Theatre, complete with proscenium stage, itself hosting numerous student productions. The college also had an interesting history of hauntings and ghost sightings I was soon to find out from several classmates who would later share their stories with me during late night discussions.

Waiting for my ride at least an hour, I busied myself thinking about reuniting with Dan, as I knew he would be at the school and I hadn't seen him since our lunch meeting a month earlier.

I glanced up from my seat to see a guy walk by me holding up a sign that read KENYON COLLEGE and I called out to him. "Hey, are you the driver for Kenyon?" He turned to look at me and extended his hand.

"Hi there, I'm Steve Chipps, and you are?"

Introducing myself, I stood up from my seat and shook his hand.

"Oh yeah, here you are," Steve smiled pulling his list of passengers from his pocket.

He checked off my name, informing me we would be picking up several other students. After gathering our crew, we headed to his van, loaded our luggage, and left the airport heading for Kenyon.

After an hour's drive filled with conversation about mime, the school's history, and a bit of history about our teachers, I got to know more about Steve. He was quite an accomplished mime, having spent several years studying at the school and traveling the country performing. When we arrived on campus, Steve drove us to our dorm building. He showed us to our rooms and I studied my room for a few minutes taking in the small, yet comfy décor. The room was simple and contained only a bed, dresser and small closet. Sitting down on the bed, I felt a bit homesick and missed Gary. Glancing out the window next to the bed, I was soon sweating profusely, as it was a very hot and sunny July day. I wondered if the dorms had air conditioning and opened my door to get some air circulating through the small room. Suddenly, Steve's smiling cherubic face appeared at my door. "Hey, we're going tubing! He exclaimed holding up a huge inner tube. Wanna come?" I had never gone tubing before, yet thought it would feel good to get into some cool water and a good way to get to know my fellow roomies, and immediately accepted his invitation.

"Great! We'll be leaving in about a half hour so meet us outside the dorm, and oh yeah, wear some water shoes if you have 'em!" In a flash, he disappeared down the hall. Luckily, I had thrown my water mocs in the suitcase as a last-minute item.

Fifteen minutes later, I nervously stood outside dressed in my swimsuit, mocs and terry bathrobe, with towel in tow. I didn't have to wait too long before eight other students including Steve joined me. This time we managed to fit nine students and tubes into a yellow VW Beetle and I barely had a chance to sit down on some guy's lap when the car took off, heading for the river flowing nearby the campus. As we drove, I looked around me at the diverse assortment of students from the dorm, and recognized a lady named "Dutch" who rode in the van with us from the airport, and Joe, a guy from my dorm. Dutch and I smiled at each other and lurched back and forth as the VW navigated bumps in the road.

After a short ride, we arrived at the river and unloaded the tubes and nine hot and sweaty mime students. As I started walking over to ask Dutch if she would be my tube partner, I noticed she was already pushing her tube into the water. Joe came over to me and said, "Well, I guess it's you and me."

Feeling a bit apprehensive about tubing for the first time with a guy I hardly knew, I helped Joe push our tube into the chilly waters of the Kokosing River. We hopped on the tube and were soon rushing down the river with the fast, flowing current. At first, the shock of the cold river water made me shake and shiver uncontrollably. After ten to fifteen minutes of flowing with the current, the incessant shaking slowed to only occasional chills and I started to enjoy the ride.

Sections of the river were fast and furious, and other sections were mild enough to paddle along with our hands. Joe was seated on top of the tube and I held down the middle in the donut hole. The current was so fast that we quickly lost sight of our fellow classmates.

After about an hour of tubing, Joe and I were floating in a calm section of the river not talking to each other, just taking in the peacefulness and stillness of the area, checking out beautiful lush greenery bordering the shoreline and watching birds flying overhead. My attention was suddenly diverted to a large shadowy object, perhaps a foot or more in length, that unexpectedly leapt straight out of the water a mere matter of inches away from our tube, and dove instantly back into the water, creating a huge splash as it disappeared from sight. Joe and I sat there in shock for a few moments, trying to process what had just happened. We then glanced over at each other, our eyes filled with fear. Finding my voice, I hoarsely whispered, "What in hell was that?" Joe was making whimpering sounds and pointing to his back.

"Whatever it was, I just got thwacked!"

"What are you talking about?"

"Are there any marks on my back? It sure smarts!" Leaning over towards him I inspected his back and sure enough there was a large reddened welt across the middle section right where he was pointing.

"Yep! It's pretty red. What do you think it was that thwacked you? A fish of some sort or bird or what?"

"I have no idea. I'm as much in the dark as you!" We sat in silence floating down the river for what seemed like an eternity before either one of us spoke.

My mind was racing with thoughts of what the object was that hit Joe with a fury. *It had to be a fish, I reasoned. It was too big to be a frog and birds don't usually dive under the water and disappear from sight.* Joe was the first to speak. He turned to face me looking puzzled.

"Hey, do you think it could be the Loch Ness Monster?"

I shuddered at the thought for a moment and frowned at him. "Are you serious? I thought those sightings were in Europe!"

"Just kidding. No, seriously, it was probably some big fish." He sat with head in hand pondering the situation and his comment seemed to allay our fears at least for the moment. I never figured out what had hit Joe and I'm sure he never did either.

We floated for the next several hours and I suddenly started to shiver once again and wanted to finish our tubing adventure. "I think I'm done," I stammered.

"We're almost up to where the rest of the group is gathering." Joe started paddling over to the shore. I hopped out of the tube and splashed my way towards the shore. Reaching solid ground, I looked around and saw a towel lying on the ground and wrapped it around my shaking body, yet still couldn't stop shivering. Joe pulled the tube from the water and ran towards me offering me his jacket. "It's kind of wet, yet it's better than nothing, I guess."

Glad for yet another layer despite the wetness, I thanked him and slung the soggy jacket around my shoulders. The group soon joined us and engaged us in conversation about the wild ride we just finished.

"Pretty cool ride, ey?" Steve exclaimed looking in my direction. "You look pretty cold."

"Yeah, it was and I am!"

Steve sprang into action. "OK, everyone! Group hug for Donna!" In an instant, he flung his arms around me, and everyone in the group joined suit. There all nine of us stood locked in embrace. I found it a bit hard to breathe at first, yet feeling the heat generated from the mass of bodies around me, finally got warm again. *Man, I thought, talk about teamwork! Pretty incredible!* It was in that moment that we all bonded together and set the tone for the next two weeks of intense training still to come.

The next day started bright and early getting up at 7 a.m. although we weren't due to be at the dance studio until 9 a.m. I was eager and nervous to start the training and was anticipating meeting Gregg and Nick, our main teachers. Dutch and I walked the two blocks to the studio and arrived a few minutes early. I saw Dan standing inside talking with some students and it was good to see him again. We both hugged and Dan gave me a heads up about Nick's warm-ups. "Ready to get your butt kicked?' he laughed. I thought he was joking, yet found out he wasn't.

Nick arrived a few minutes before 9 a.m., shook our hands, talked with and got to know everyone in the group and off to work we went! C. Nicholas Johnson, his real name, is an immediately likeable and down-to-earth kind of guy and, despite his short build, was tall as ever in talent and mime and dance performance expertise! He is now an associate professor and Director of Dance at Wichita State University, and was then along with Gregg Goldston, "…a founding member and one of the Artistic Directors for the School for Mime Theatre, a summer residency program at Kenyon College, Gambier, Ohio, where he taught for 28 years. He trained with Polish Mime Director Stefan Niedzialkowski, created choreography for Marcel Marceau, and continues to create both mime and dance choreography, directing, teaching and performing." (17.)

After a few thousand pliés and relevés at the barre, (waist-level bar used for support by ballet dancers), I could barely stand up, yet his warm-ups were far from over. The next few hours flew by filled with push-ups, sit-ups and just about every other grueling exercise you can imagine. Of course, there was no air conditioning, just as in our dorms, and I was as wet as the previous day of tubing, only a lot hotter! After a short mid-morning break, we resumed class with Nick teaching arduous mime technique and endless marches across the floor. Once again, the time flew by, and we savored an hour-long lunch and welcome rest for our weary bones. Dan sat next to me on one of the patio benches outside The Cove smiling broadly. "So, what did you think of Nick?"

"Piece of cake," I attempted to laugh and woof down lunch at the same time, spraying flecks of potato salad at him.

"Wait until you meet Gregg this afternoon. Eat hearty. You'll need the energy," Dan chuckled.

"Good to know. Thanks for the heads up."

After lunch, Dan and I walked back to the studio together. He regaled me with stories about Gregg, the mysterious and marvelous mime director and founder of the school. I both feared and anticipated meeting and studying with him, recalling our phone conversation the previous month.

At the studio, we stood and chatted with other students, and I got a chance to know Dutch a bit better. She was also a nurse, as well as my roomie, and I felt an instant connection with her. We talked for a while about our tubing adventure while waiting for Gregg to arrive. I told her about the puzzling sea creature we saw that day that "thwacked" poor Joe, and we had a good laugh about it, when suddenly a tall, slender, curly-haired figure sauntered into the room. The head master had arrived and the stifling hot atmosphere became even hotter.

Gregg introduced himself to the group and his credentials are quite remarkable. He began his mime training in 1975, studying with some outstanding mimes such as Jerusalem-born Moni Yakim, Polish-born mime and Director Stefan Niedzialkowski, and perhaps the most famous mime of all, Marcel Marceau. In 1980, Gregg established The School for Mimes Summer Intensive, (the name of our seminar), and hosted five seminars with Marcel Marceau. (I studied there with Marceau from 1993-1995). He met Marceau in 1985 and spent the next 21 years studying, teaching, and performing with Marceau and his troupe, Compagnie de Mime. (16.)

After a few more announcements related to our schedule, we got right to work and set about the task of trying to keep up with Gregg. He taught by modeling techniques followed by having the group attempt to recreate the moves. His movements were fluid, precise and comparable to poetry in motion. We spent the afternoon learning isolations, moving one part of the body at a time—a difficult thing to learn for someone who is used to moving every body part at the same time! Gregg made the movements appear effortless, and I silently despaired at not being able to do the same. Dan had taught me some basic isolations, yet Gregg was adding on more difficult ones and I marveled at how profusely I was sweating standing in one place. Gregg moved past me a number of times as he circulated around the room giving adjustments to other students. *Well, I thought, he is either very satisfied with my attempts at isolations, or purposely trying to ignore me. More probably the latter, I mused.*

Hours flew by immersed in learning more mime techniques than I could wrap my head around and, by day's end, I was exhausted. Arriving back at the dorm around 10 p.m., I collapsed on my bed and tried to sleep, yet sleep wouldn't come. All the events of the day played over and over in my mind, beginning with Nick's rigorous warm-ups, endless pliés, relevés and marches across the floor to Gregg's relentless isolations and mime drills. I heard the door close and then the voices of my roomies, Dutch and Joe, engaged in conversation about the happenings of the day. Too tired to sleep, I joined them and we bantered on about mime well into the wee morning hours. This would be our routine for the remainder of the two-week seminar. I particularly enjoyed the showcase at the end of each seminar, as we had a chance to perform for live audiences, and our shows were always well received.

The following year, I attended a month-long workshop at the school and despite immersing myself in mime studies and performing, still felt homesick and missed being with Gary. We chatted almost daily on the phone, and he kept me updated with experiences from his corner of the world that I felt so far removed from. Gary was involved in moving from our tiny apartment into our new house and hearing the familiar drudgery tales he told about the lugging and buying new furniture made me glad I wasn't part of it! Being at the school was consuming enough, and the experience was similar to being on another planet. Immersing yourself intensively in something enables you to achieve a certain level of proficiency in whatever you are studying, yet can be isolating at the same time, as you give up some of your former identity to attain another.

I worked hard at refining ideas for pieces I was creating, as we were expected to show them daily to our instructors, Gregg, Nick, and other members of Gregg's resident mime troupe, "The Invisible People," Pamela Chermansky, Rick Wamer, and Jose Rivera. Some pieces I showed them received favorable reviews, and others, not so much. Trying to come up with ideas for pieces and learning how to take constructive criticism were perhaps my biggest challenges, and I struggled with some unfavorable comments from Gregg the most, yet at least he was honest. I had established a great rapport with Nick, and felt that he was more approachable with his down-to-earth sense of humor and frequent offers for me to hop on his motorcycle as I walked to and from the dance studio where we met bright and early each morning for Nick's warm-ups. Gregg seemed more reserved and aloof until I got to know him better. He had high standards and expectations of his students and expected nothing less than perfection and I learned volumes from his style of teaching. Unknown at the time, I was soon to meet another teacher who would test my resolve.

During the intensive, Gregg began to notice my efforts to get noticed by him. One day in class he called out to me and blew me away in the process. "Nice, Donna! Now you're getting it," he smiled and walked away. His comment affirmed my learning progress and process. Many years later, when I was a teacher, I finally understood and appreciated how difficult it is to be able to inspire and motivate your students to want to learn whatever it is you're trying to teach them. I have taught pantomime to both kids and adults and have tried to connect with each student in some fashion, and certainly appreciated when that was returned to me! I felt in that moment, Gregg was sincerely making an attempt to connect with and encourage me. As the month progressed, I felt a friendship developing between Gregg and myself. He remarked to me both in class and wrote on a poster announcing our end of intensive show, "you remind me in many ways of Buster Keaton," which I considered to be a high compliment from a teacher of his caliber.

The last day of the intensive finally arrived, and I nervously paced around backstage waiting for the show to start and went outside to catch a breath of fresh air. There was Gregg standing by the stage entrance, smoking a cigarette and looking cool, calm, and collected as he always did. We exchanged greetings. "Hey, Donna," Gregg nodded, blowing smoke into the air. "Nervous?"

"Yeah, a bit…"

"Come on, you live for this stuff!" Of course, he was right and reaffirmed what I felt. We connected through our love of performing, establishing a lifelong bond. Our show was one of the best I can remember from those magically magnificent years. I came away from the experience a far stronger performer with a wealth of self-confidence and entertainment savvy to unleash upon the world.

The following year after doing some research on other professional schools of mime and performance arts, I decided to expand my studies at Celebration Barn, in South Paris, Maine. My friend and fellow entertainer, Abbie Lawrence, having studied at Celebration Barn, recommended I study with Tony Montanaro, the founder and head instructor of the school. Tony also had an impressive perform-ance background and history. "Born in Paulsboro, New Jersey on September 10, 1927, Montanaro earned a theatre degree from Columbia University and began performing stock theater with actors such as Jason Robards and Jackie Cooper. After seeing Marcel Marceau's historic 1956 performance at New York's Phoenix Theatre, Montanaro flew to Paris to study under Marceau and his teacher, Etienne Decroux. In his later years, Montanaro continued to teach and direct the Cele-bration Barn… with his third wife, Karen Hurll Montanaro. The couple also toured widely with their two-person show, The Montanaro-Hurll Theatre of Mime and Dance." (18.)

Over the two years I studied there, I learned a great deal from Tony. He also was short in height, yet his movements spoke volumes and he had a great spirit and easy-going nature much like Nick, yet there the similarities ended. He developed his own teaching style focusing on the theory of premise rather than perfection in performance. I can still remember him saying in our work-shop, "If you come to technique in your pieces, that's great, yet be sure you don't sacrifice your premise, or what you are trying to convey to your audi-ence, for technique." Coming from Goldston's School where the majority of what we learned was primarily stylized movement focused, this theory was fairly new to me. There are as many different theories of how Mime should be performed as there are ways it is actually performed. I was a firm believer that mime should be non-verbal and wear white face make-up in the style of Marcel Marceau. Once again, life was to present me with another one of those opportunities for growth and learning.

In his later shows, Tony rarely wore white face and felt that wearing it was op-tional and perhaps even excessive. Tony and I had differing opinions about my preference for wearing white face and stylized training. During the course of the workshops, studying with Tony and seeing him model his premise theory, I once again had to suspend my imagination and take a back seat to the genius of his awesome capacity to communicate and convey universal truths and human foibles with exquisite honesty, humor, and accuracy.

Despite our differences and his tough east coast exterior, I discovered Tony really had a heart of gold. One day, I developed a horrid case of the flu halfway through the first workshop, and stayed in bed with a fever of 102 degrees, too sick to go to class. I had just fallen into a light and welcome doze when, sensing a presence in the room, I opened my eyes to see Tony standing next to my bed. He stared at me with concern in his eyes.

"I'm sorry to see you feeling ill."

Before I could find my voice, he sat down on the bed next to me and reached for my hand.

"Thanks Tony." I was deeply touched by the sincerity of his sentiments.

"Is there something I can do or get for you?"

Not needing anything at the moment, other than sleep, I politely refused his offer.

"You sure?" he persisted, his face and voice still full of concern.

"Thanks, Tony. Your visit means a lot. I think I will try to get some rest and hopefully, I can return to class tomorrow."

"See how you feel tomorrow. If you're still sick, then take as much time as you need to rest. I'm sorry you'll be missing some of the workshop, yet will gladly give you a discount for a workshop next year if you plan to return."

"Thanks again, Tony. I appreciate that," I whispered, smiling at his generosity.

Patting my hand and saying he'd check on me later, Tony got up from my bed and walked out of the room. Closing my eyes, I soon fell into a deep slumber and spent the remainder of the last week of the workshop in bed.

Returning the next year, I found that Tony held to his word and discounted my fee for that workshop. My opinion of Tony changed during the two-week seminar and I started enjoying his freestyle and playful approach to teaching mime. His classes were more like improvisational workshops as compared to the disciplined, technical stylized techniques I learned from Goldston. At first, I felt a bit like I was breaking the rules of mime by learning this more laid-back approach, yet no educational experience is a waste if you keep an open mind. I came away from working with Tony with a renewed sense of playfulness, humor, and sense of being a more proficient entertainer.

CHAPTER 19

MEETING THE MASTER (1993-'95)

"Do not the most moving moments of our lives find us all without words"
— Marcel Marceau

In the summer of 1993, my mime school plans were uncertain until receiving a flyer in the mail from Gregg announcing that Marcel Marceau would be teaching a two-week workshop at the school. I stared at the flyer in disbelief! Marceau, world-renown mime, teaching in the States? Filled with excitement at the prospect of studying with a master and childhood idol, my decision was instantly made in that moment.

"Universally considered the world's greatest contemporary mime artist, Marcel Marceau was a true legend. Throughout a career spanning nearly 60 years, the French-born Marceau achieved notoriety beginning in the late 1940's, and brought the art of mime to audiences worldwide with continuous touring of his stage show and appearances in film and on television. His work had a tremendous influence on the art, and earned him some of the highest honors of his native France and countries abroad. In addition to his work as a mime artist, Marceau was also a teacher, author, and painter." (19.)

I spent the weeks previous to the workshop doing mime shows galore at libraries, festivals and schools and felt stronger in my performances than prior to attending mime school. Also, audiences seemed to be more receptive and appreciative of my entertainment, yet I didn't feel as though I had reached Dan's skill level of having the audience "in the palm of his hand." I looked forward to studying with Marceau to add the finishing touches to the mix.

Finally arriving at Goldston-Johnson that hot and muggy July day, it was good to be back in familiar surroundings with familiar faces of students from previous years. There were also many unfamiliar faces of students from around the country who had previously studied with Marceau either at his school in Paris or at various other mime schools. I felt a bit intimidated when talking with these students, as they knew what to expect from Marceau as a teacher, and I didn't have a clue.

Later that day as I sat at The Cove chatting with Pam, an awesome mime, and one of our teachers, I noticed in my peripheral vision a figure entering the area where we sat. With heart pounding, I gazed in the direction of the figure and held my breath as he approached our table. Pam was still carrying on the conversation and I couldn't even make out what she was saying to me. She had spent a considerable amount of time studying with Marceau and to her it was just another day in the life. The figure had an aura of light around him and it seemed like he floated a few feet above the ground where we sat.

Marcel was smiling as he greeted us and extending his hand towards me asked, in a very soft French accent, "How are you?" Barely breathing and quite dumbfounded, I was meeting face to face with my all-time idol! My face was beet red and with trembling hand managed to shake his hand and not pass out.

"And you are?" he persisted. *OK idiot, this is for real, so you'd better say something!*

Finding my voice, I hoarsely replied, "Donna… nice to meet you!"

"Yes, you as well," he nodded and still smiling floated away towards students sitting at other tables. He chatted amicably with them and I could hear their appreciative laughter in the distance, yet it seemed like the scene was almost as dreamlike as his character appeared to me. He looked like an older and greyer version of Harpo Marx minus the trench coat and harp!

Watching him move around the common gathering area outside The Cove, I couldn't take my eyes off him and marveled at the ease in which he carried his 70-year-old body. Unknown at the time, I would be spending a lot of time watching his movements. There was so much I wanted to ask him, yet thought there would be plenty of time to ask questions and get to know him on a more personal level over the next few weeks. I got to know him very well, yet not in the way I had expected.

In class, I saw some pretty interesting dynamics. Marceau called the students that had previously studied with him the "ancients," an interesting dichotomy, as none were even close to his age. The rest of us were relegated to some distant planet in the stratosphere. The ancients would follow him around the room with glassy stares in their eyes, as if in a trance. Everywhere he went and every movement he made, they surrounded and mimicked him. Every word he so softly, yet eloquently spoke, every ear in the room was straining to hear. The scene was reminiscent of a prophet with his disciples.

Marceau was a strict teacher and ultimate taskmaster. He, like Goldston, demanded nothing less than absolute perfection from his students and modeled it.

From the onset, he devoted the front part of his body to the privileged ancients who worshipped the ground he walked on, and dismissed the rest of the students to the back of the dance studio to study his back side from a distance.

"You watch, you learn," he admonished us.

Once again suspending my disbelief over the two weeks, I discovered that watching the back half of the man was a bit humorous, albeit educational. From my back-row seat, I learned volumes about how the Master, and this magical art form called mime, worked. Perhaps his strategy was based on the technique of reverse psychology in that something seemingly out of reach will make you want to work that much harder to attain it. If so, it worked for me! Working my butt off daily to become the best entertainer I could be, the results of this disciplined training prepared me for numerous other challenges I would face in my life.

A typical day in Marceau's class would include watching him from a distance, teaching what he referred to as "Conventions of Character," or what is actually the mime's emotional vocabulary. When we as humans experience a certain emotion such as anger, for instance, we most often express our anger verbally or other means, (e.g., flipping someone off in traffic), and often make fools of ourselves in the process. When Marceau demonstrates anger, for example, he economically displays one movement and facial expression to capture the emotion and you see and feel the anger without ever hearing him utter a single word. His illusions are so realistic, you feel as though you are living the moment right along with him.

Watching him perform a piece in which he ascends a spiral staircase and walks into a room to find a scrapbook of memories from his life was magical! His reliving those memories through vivid images and scenes inspired me to write a piece called "Memories." My favorite piece of his is called, "The Mask" in which Marceau finds a mask depicting a hideous smile, puts it on and at first you see the hideous smile and laugh at the absurdity of him wearing it. As the piece progresses, you are drawn into the drama of the mask getting stuck on his face and his struggle to remove it. The dichotomy of his struggle of wearing the gleeful expression on his face, despite being miserable underneath it, is incredibly touching and admirably displays his mastery of Mime and the nature of humanity!

There were also classes he instructed in the Bolton Theatre that were pure fun and frolic. He would stand before us, once again his back to us, moving through some of his most memorable pieces, (e.g., The Creation of The World), with his students following suit. To see the master in action and be a part of his genius was an unforgettable journey well worth taking.

I returned to study with Marceau for the next two summers and found him more open and friendly, even welcoming me back. Marceau often spoke at great length about his idol, Charlie Chaplain, whom he emulated with his "Bip" character. As he spoke to the group about his meeting with and admiration of Chaplain, it became apparent how traditions are passed down from one generation to another in the form of gifts. Chaplain's and, thus Marceau's, gifts to the world were their remarkable abilities to engross and delight audiences across the globe without the benefit of verbal communication. Other pearls of wisdom I learned from Marceau, pertained to adding humor to performance. He emphasized, "Don't try to be funny, and you will be funny!" I discovered his wise remark to be true after each performance. When I did a particular action just for the sake of evoking laughter from my audience, the complete opposite reaction would occur and I would be met with silence and puzzled looks from the audience. Other times, I would hear appreciative laughter when honestly portraying how a human being would respond to a situation, such as being chased by a bee, or being late for an appointment. The audience appreciates and relates to similarities inherent in the act of being human.

One day, after showing a piece to the group I called "The Race," based on my experiences running in numerous 10K and 5K races, I stood on the side of the stage nervously anticipating feedback from Marceau. Performing the piece, I was well aware of his presence in the audience and heard his words of not trying to be funny echoing in my head. Without the guise of doing the piece for comedy sake, I was completely in the moment of running the race and exhausted from the effort. My piece was the last to be performed. Observing other students receiving harsh critiques from Marceau, I was worried that I would share the same fate. A few of my female counterparts even broke into tears and as I stood now onstage, felt tears welling up in my eyes.

Marceau jumped onto the stage with the amazing agility of a grasshopper frolicking in the fields and confidence of a seasoned performer well familiar with being Commander in Chief of the theatre. Glancing at me with a stern facial expression, he then stepped up to the front of the stage announcing to the audience, "You know… she made me laugh." After his comment, I felt a tremendous sense of accomplishment and relief, yet was still unable to stop shaking. He went on to say there were "mistakes," and made me do the piece over again under his ever-watchful eye, yet working with him one on one onstage was an incredible learning experience and the only chance I ever got to spend one on one time with him. The day was a memorable one for more than the obvious reason. After we finished working on my piece, I was heading off stage to find a seat in the theatre, when suddenly hearing a familiar song being sung that stopped me dead in my tracks. What a sight for sore eyes to see my fellow students and teachers in the audience standing and singing "Happy Birthday!" Too overcome with emotion to speak, I alternately smiled and cried my eyes out. Perhaps, I was in the moment of birth and rebirth. The ensuing birthday festivities for me at The Cove were filled with food galore, cake, dancing, miming and celebration equivalent to the popular expression, "what happens at (fill in the blanks), stays there!"

Another defining moment, that was right around the corner, was about to steer me in a different direction; back to my musical roots. At the end of the last workshop with Marceau in the summer of 1995, we attended a concert featuring some friends of one of our excellent instructors, Rick Wamer. Linda and John Vining, both musicians, owned some acreage near the school and invited us to attend their concert. Linda played a dulcimer and her husband, John, played electric and acoustic guitar equally well. We spent the evening mesmerized by their combination of mostly original folk and rock songs and warmly applauded their show.

As the concert was ending, John asked if Gregg would join him on stage and we thought he would do one of his famous mime pieces. We were amazed to see Gregg grab one of John's electric guitars and start jamming away with him. Soon, Nick jumped into the mix and all hell broke loose! Sitting with mouth agape, taking in the rock musical spectacle, I realized their greatness spilled over into the music genre! Nick and I had talked some music here and there and I knew Gregg played guitar, yet I had never heard him play until that moment. A few students joined them in jams and I could barely stay in my seat! When the jam session was over, John asked if anyone else was interested in doing an open mic, and I catapulted myself onstage. Gregg and Nick eyed me standing there wondering, OK… so what is this chick in a pink jumpsuit going to do? One of my favorite Hendrix songs called, "Voodoo Child" popped into my head. Asking if Gregg knew the song, he nodded. We were off and rocking. Nervously clutching the mic and wondering if I could even remember any of the words, I started to sing. It felt surreal first of all, to be standing on a stage once again singing with a band behind me just as back in the early '70s with Medusa. It felt like time was standing still and yet everything around me was in electric motion, and I didn't want the song or music to end, and neither did the audience. After the song was over, they yelled their enthusiasm right back at us. I was swarmed by students, teachers and fellow musicians pouring out their praise and was immersed by the tidal wave of emotions washing over me. It reaffirmed that I needed music in my life forevermore.

The miraculous thing about jamming is that it joins everyone together in absolute harmony and bliss. Everyone manages to follow along and bring some semblance of order to chaos channeled through each musician's uniquely individual contribution and talent. With Gregg, Nick and John rocking out on guitars, the song sounded as though Hendrix was onstage playing right along with us. The music gods were smiling down on us that day!

Alone in my dorm room after the concert, I called Gary and shocked the hell out of him by telling him I wanted to play music again. We had all but given it up in favor of trying to make a decent living for ourselves and, in the process, had given up on our passion and reason for making living worthwhile. He had just returned from a one week seminar at the National Guitar Summer Workshop in Connecticut studying with Ronnie Earl, lead guitarist of Roomful of Blues, and three-time Blues Music Award winner as Guitar Player of the Year.

After returning from these experiences, Gary and I were inspired to resume our musical passions, shook the dust from our guitars and keyboards and started playing again as a duet we called "Hearth and Soul." We wrote a few songs and created a CD called "Standing In the Rain," that never went any further than our CD player. The music that Gary and I created was the start of an endeavor that would take us places we never dreamed possible. One of the songs I wrote, "Memories of Mountains," was written about tinnitus, a very challenging health problem I was dealing with in the mid '90s and the song was so difficult to sing it took at least a month or more to be able to sing without crying. After perhaps a year or so, we threw in the musical towel. But unrevealed at the time, the songs we wrote were preparing and directing us towards a more extraordinary future event that was to launch us into the annuls of musical history.

CHAPTER 20
CAN WE PLEASE KEEP IT DOWN TO A LOW ROAR? (1996-'99)

"Character cannot be developed in ease and quiet. Only through experience of trial and suffering can the soul be strengthened, ambition inspired, and success achieved."
— Helen Keller

"You have brain damage," the doctor matter-of-factly stated. There's nothing more I can do for you." Studying my shocked face for a few seconds after imposing his death declaration, he shook my hand, turned and walked out the door. Gary helped me stand and slowly walked with me back out to the car, both of us in a state of grief and shock. My body shaking with gut-wrenching sobs, I used his shirt to dry the waterfall of endless tears.

A few months prior, I was sitting in the bathtub holding my belly and trying to soak away the horrendous cramps that plagued me since the start of menstruation at age 12. Prior to being diagnosed with endometriosis at age 45, I had seen several doctors throughout my life and one mentioned the possibility of me having endometriosis, yet no treatment was offered. I had cramps so severe I could barely get out of bed and menstrual periods lasting up to ten days, painful intercourse and profuse bleeding every month. After enduring this for more than thirty years, I contemplated having a hysterectomy and sought the opinions of three different doctors to confirm that I was doing the right thing.

One woman doctor suspected I had endometriosis and recommended I undergo a laparoscopic D&C to scrape the lining of my uterus which would confirm the diagnosis and curtail the profuse bleeding and cramps. Months after undergoing this procedure, I was still in significant pain and desperate to find some solution to end the suffering. Discussing my situation with this doctor, and considering that I didn't want to have children, she recommended a hysterectomy. Talking with numerous women who had undergone a hysterectomy, and hearing their positive stories of relief of their menstrual woes, I was almost convinced. Up to that point, I had only stood at the other end of the hospital bed as a nurse, and had little idea of what the human body endures going through any surgical procedure. In the mid-nineties, there were only a few treatment options for endometriosis: takes drugs such as Danazol, which induce an artificial menopause, or undergo a hysterectomy. After consulting with two other gynecologists who also recommended a hysterectomy, I did some research and discovered they were considered elective surgeries, meaning they were not always necessary. Nonetheless, I had the surgery in April 1996 deciding this was the best option for my personal situation at the time. After months of enduring the symptoms of a surgically induced menopause such as hot flashes, sleeplessness and depression, I found the right dose of Estrogen and was finally pain and symptom free!

In current times, there are other alternative treatments, depending on a woman's individual health situation, such as taking oral contraceptives, hormones or undergoing minor surgical procedures such as laparoscopy or laparotomy. I believe it's in a woman's best interest to consult with her doctor and, above all, do her own research before undergoing a hysterectomy.

In June of 1996, I finally started feeling like my old self again, and sat at the pool talking with a neighbor friend after a refreshing swim. I was enjoying our conversation as much as feeling like the hellish haze I had been through since the surgery was finally clearing. As time passed, I became aware of a faint ringing sound in the distance and didn't think much about it at first until it started to become more noticeable and annoying. "Angie, do you hear that ringing noise?"

Angie looked at me with surprise. "What noise?"

"You don't hear that ringing sound?" I persisted, my heart sinking in despair at the realization of the moment.

"No, I don't," she stared intently at me. "Are you OK?"

"Yeah, I'm fine. I think there's some water in my ears," I muttered sticking a finger in my ear, hoping that would make the ringing noise go away. It didn't.

"Ready for another swim?" I thought perhaps swimming would distract me from hearing what I was hearing. It didn't.

Later that afternoon, after our swim, I decided to take a nap and lie in bed wide awake for the longest time listening to what now sounded like an intermittent whooshing noise in my ears. I got up and called my gynecologist and was told by the receptionist she was in surgery. I left a message, and sat by the phone waiting for her call, wondering if the whooshing noise I was hearing was related to the effects of anesthesia. *Possibly, I thought, yet why would this appear now more than two months after the surgery?* Scanning my brain's medical memory banks, I wondered if the noise was due to side effects of anesthesia or another drug used during surgery with harmful effects on one's hearing. The ringing of the phone roused me from thoughtful musings and provided a welcome distraction from the whooshing.

"I don't think the noise you're hearing is related to the anesthesia, yet you might want to talk with the anesthesiologist directly," was the doctor's disappointing reply. "You might also want to consult with an ear, nose and throat doctor." *Well, at least I have some options, I thought, thanking her and hanging up the phone.*

Still having a considerable amount of abdominal pain, and now with sudden, ear- splitting, shrill high-pitched ringing, I decided to make an appointment with my gynecologist and discuss my situation with her in person. After doing an exam, she told me that she couldn't understand why I was still having persistent pain and ringing in my ears. She also told me that everyone heals differently and advised me to wait another few weeks and see how I would feel. I left her office feeling pretty dejected and shell-shocked. Still in pain after a few weeks, I saw another gynecologist who told me I had an incisional hernia and underwent more surgery. So much for "healing well," and the quest for wellness continued.

The first ENT (ear, nose and throat) doctor I saw, who looked in my ears and delivered his "brain-damage" report, is not even worthy of being called a doctor! With firsthand knowledge of how the medical system works, both as a medical provider and patient, I realize that doctors are limited in the amount of time they can spend with a patient due to insurance-mandated care that currently dominates our health care system. That being said, throughout my lifetime, I have not found many doctors who are willing to step out of the box and do some research on health problems they know very little about, tinnitus being one of them. I do see doctors referring patients to specialists. But more often than not, patients get caught in the maze of seeing one doctor after another and still come away without answers or even options. A person should at least be given viable treatments options rather than be told to learn to live with it! If the good doc is going to make this thoughtless statement, it would be prudent to follow it up with how to do so!

I saw numerous other ENT doctors who ordered numerous blood tests, CT scans, and MRIs, yet I still got no good answers or treatment options. Tired of not getting any help from doctors, I turned to the Internet. Gary and I spent countless hours searching online for any information we could find. We put together several notebooks full of information and one day, I was leafing through a notebook and an ad for the American Tinnitus Association (ATA) in Portland, Oregon caught my eye. Reading their description of tinnitus made me feel like I wasn't alone with this problem. "Some … fifty million Americans experience some form of tinnitus."

Roughly twenty million people struggle with burdensome chronic tinnitus, while two million have extreme and debilitating cases." (20.) Pretty damn sobering stats, yet there is no cure.

Deciding to spend the $25 per year for membership, I began receiving *Tinitus Today*, a magazine this organization compiles and distributes to its members across the country and around the world. This magazine offers a plethora of information and treatment resources for people with tinnitus and it was through *Tinnitus Today* that I learned about a treatment option that was providing significant relief, called TRT (Tinnitus Retraining Therapy). TRT was created by a leading neuroscientist, Dr. Pawel Jastreboff, in 1990 and is a form of habituation therapy designed to help people with tinnitus, a buzzing, ringing, hissing, or other sound in the ears when no external sound is present. This "sound-based" therapy involves wearing hearing aid like devices, or white noise generators, in your ears at least eight hours per day. Over the course of a few months, or even years, this therapy can help retrain a person's brain to distinguish the tinnitus as non-threatening and even ignore it. Counseling is another critical component of TRT in that it helps you to refocus your perception of tinnitus to accommodate or habituate to the intrusive sounds over a certain period of time.

In numerous articles I read in Tinnitus Today and other hearing-related magazines, it is repeatedly written most likely by people who don't have the problem, that tinnitus can be ignored and is often overreacted to. It was only after undergoing TRT and finally achieving some semblance of normalcy that I found that to be true. Before the treatment, I found it hard to ignore the intrusive noises especially at night when trying to sleep. In fact, I could still hear the noises over the tinnitus music CD playing in my bedroom that added more comforting sounds to the chaotic cacophony playing in my ears. It's natural to overreact when your once-peaceful and quiet world is turned upside down.

I was one of those "extreme and debilitating cases," hearing a sound similar to a high-pitch, shrill, whistling tea-kettle in my ears 24/7. Before I found TRT, I felt so depressed, I didn't even want to get out of bed. Lying in a darkened room in the basement of our house day after day in a fetal position, I just wanted the noise to go away! It didn't. There are times in your life when you have to make some hard choices, either throw in the towel or tie a knot and hang tight, and I chose the latter. That decision wasn't made in an instant. It took years of searching and trying everything from acupuncture and Chinese herbs to gingko biloba, yoga and meditation before I made that choice. Although not cures, each strengthened my belief that, with perseverance, I could somehow cure myself. I found yoga and meditation especially valuable in helping me relax and distracting me from the noise in my ears. This actually led to my taking a teacher training course and receiving certification to teach yoga.

Reading the article in Tinnitus Today about TRT and how people were getting relief made me feel hopeful and I decided to give it a try. Finding knowledgeable practitioners was another story. At that point in time, TRT was available in Maryland, California, and other states, but not yet in Colorado as it was still a relatively new treatment.

Through ATA, I heard about Dr. Steven Nagler who had an established practice in Atlanta, GA who himself has tinnitus and had used the TRT devices with good success. In a phone conversation with him, he suggested I try TRT at his clinic. I was about to make the trip to see him, when a letter arrived in the mail from the local ENT doctor I was seeing at the time that his office was going to offer TRT. Rather than have to travel, I decided to give the program a try and made an appointment to see the audiologist at his office. Once I got fitted for the sound generators, I had to wait a few weeks for them to be sent from out of state. The generators finally arrived and I hurried to the office in eager anticipation of actually wearing them and getting some relief. Putting them on and hearing the soothing white noise emitted by the generators was music to my ringing ears, yet the relief was short-lived. They didn't fit my ears and kept falling out. I was told by the audiologist to give them a try anyway, and I thought, *How could I possibly wear them for eight to ten hours per day if they didn't fit my ears?* She gave me another option of re-ordering the generators that would take another few weeks. Dejectedly walking out of the office, I decided to not go back and do some research on finding the devices on my own.

In my exhaustive online research, I read about the most commonly used generators for TRT called Viennatones and thought about ordering them online, yet wanted to make sure this time the fit was right. Although disappointed with the audiologist that couldn't get the generators to fit my ears, I remembered seeing an audiologist who was sympathetic and helpful when needing it the most, so I made another appointment to see her and discuss the possibility of getting the devices through her. Linda Fudge was familiar with a treatment known as masking, or covering up the sound of tinnitus with white noise. Masking was first initiated in the mid-1970s by a leading research psychologist and co-founder of ATA, Dr. Jack Vernon, when he reported that masking was effective in alleviating tinnitus. "Vernon pioneered the use of sound-generating devices to mask the onslaught of tinnitus…" (21.)

Masking is different from habituation in that your goals are approached differently. With masking, your goal is to completely block out a sound, whereas with habituation you are adding a more tolerable sound to co-exist with your tinnitus to teach your brain to adapt over time to the less intrusive sound.

When meeting with Linda, I asked if she had ever heard of TRT or the Viennatones and she had, yet claimed she was not knowledgeable enough to offer the therapy. She asked if I was interested in trying masking. Preferring to try TRT for longer-lasting relief, I declined her offer. I gave her the information I had researched on the Viennatones and she said she would try to order them for me. Recommending I consult with Marsha Johnson, an audiologist in Oregon, for the requisite counseling component of TRT, she fitted my ears for the devices and said she would contact me when she received them.

While waiting for the devices to arrive, I called Marsha and told her about my situation. Informing me she would be willing to counsel me over the phone while going through the TRT and despite being busy seeing her own clients, she was always available to answer numerous questions I had. Marsha and Linda were my lifelines during the first year of wearing the devices and to them I am eternally grateful!

The phone rang one day a few weeks later and it was Linda informing me the devices had arrived. I ran to see her, tried on the long-awaited devices with trembling hands, and they actually fit this time! It took at least a month before I got used to wearing the devices in my ears and it was kind of a shock to the system at first. They are similar in appearance to hearing aids yet that's where the similarity ends. I had to laugh when first putting them in my ears, as I pictured elderly folks trying to adjust their hearing aids to be able to hear and suddenly felt older than my forty-something years. These devices certainly did not help me hear any better, as my ears were being bombarded by yet another more soothing white noise sound. As instructed by Marsha, I turned up the volume of the devices to the highest level of four to match the level of my Tinnitus and wore them for a solid eight to ten hours per day, removing them at bedtime.

Marcia also informed me that if I noticed a day where the Tinnitus was not as loud, to lower the volume on the devices accordingly.

After wearing the devices for a month, I began noticing subtle fluctuations in the loudness of the tinnitus, and rather than have the noise blaring in my ears 24/7, there would be "good days" when it would recede in volume and intensity. During the first month, the devices were always stationed at four. Soon, I was able to maintain a fairly steady three on the volume. After wearing them for four months, I started to notice a substantial decrease in the loudness of the tinnitus and became more and more hopeful as the days wore on. I shared the good news with Marsha in our weekly phone conversations. She was a wonderful coach always offering words of encouragement to stay with it, even during the bad days. I asked her when I'd be able to remove them for good, yet after getting used to them I secretly didn't want to ever give them up! Her words of advice were, "The longer you wear them the more effective they are," and she was right. I still had bad days, yet they seemed to be getting fewer and farther between. I wore the devices for two years and discovered I could leave them out of my ears for longer periods of time as the noise was much more in the background. Eventually I didn't need to wear them at all.

One of the things that drew me to Colorado was, of course, the mountains. But now that I was feeling better, I once again pursued outdoor activities that had fallen by the wayside when tinnitus shattered my world. Thinking back to 1986, the year after Gary and I moved to Colorado and despite our almost-catastrophic mountain accident, we decided to "get back on the horse" and climb the 14,000-foot Grays Peak, (aka: "14'ers"). The exhilaration of reaching the summit left me with a longing to do more and the 14'ers were plentiful totaling 54 in Colorado.

When on the summit, Gary and I sat munching on some snacks gazing at the weather starting to deteriorate, as it often does after 12 noon, yet the ridge connecting Gray's with neighboring 14'er, Torreys, beckoned to me. The tired expression on Gary's face said it all. Nodding towards the dark grey clouds gathering above our heads, he said, "You're on your own. I think I'm going to head back down." The wind was kicking up and it got colder as a light rain started to fall. The sound of thunder echoed in the distance. Shivering, I glanced once again at the ridge and hesitated a moment. Although still feeling strong and wanting to trek over the ridge to Torreys, I realized with some disappointment that the weather was probably not going to clear anytime soon and that heading back down would be a wise decision. Torreys would have to wait. "OK, let's hit it!" We started descending the same footpath we toiled on ascent hours before. Several hours later, reaching the roadside area where our car was parked and glancing back at Grays, I knew this was only the beginning of a new and exciting chapter I never wanted to end.

I started reading every book even remotely related to mountains I could get my hands on. One book I read called *No Mountain Too High* recounted the story of 17 women breast cancer survivors who organized a climb on Aconcagua, a 22,000 foot peak in Argentina. (23.) The story inspired and gave me hope that despite any adversity the human spirit can and does endure. *I thought, if these brave women fighting cancer can climb a mountain, what is my excuse?* The seed was therein planted.

CHAPTER 21
HEADING FOR THE HILLS (2000)

"We are now in the mountains and they are in us, kindling enthusiasm, making every nerve quiver, filling every pore and cell of us."
— John Muir, My First Summer in the Sierra

It took another two years before the seed was harvested. The previous year, Gary and I did a camping trip to Mount Rainier National Park and hiked to our hearts content through the beautiful state of Washington. Mount Rainier is the highest peak in the Cascade Range at 14,410 feet. On a hike up a neighboring peak one day, I recalled seeing the mountain for the first time as huge as all outdoors and seemingly a stone's throw away from where we sat eating our lunch. I couldn't take my eyes off the sheer massiveness and majesty of the mountain. Something resonated in my heart that day and I knew I had to climb the peak someday soon. When I made the remark, Gary's only response was, "Eat your lunch."

Every time I talked about climbing Rainier, Gary was less than enthused. He either ignored the topic all together or made comments to try to dissuade me. "What am I going to do if you die on that mountain?" I knew he was concerned for my safety pursuing such a risky endeavor, yet whenever I tried to reassure him he would say, "You're on your own." Visions of the baby bird flying solo once again flooded my mind, and I felt disappointed that Gary wasn't supportive of this climb, yet this was my decision and sheer determination and purpose of the mission spurred me on.

I dialed the number with shaking hands waiting for someone to answer the phone, wondering if they would be receptive to my idea.

"Hello, American Tinnitus Association. This is Barbara speaking. How may I help you?"

"Hey Barbara, this is Donna. I'm a member of ATA and I have an idea for a fundraising event. Whom would I talk to about this event?"

"Well, you could certainly speak to me about your idea. We're always interested in ways to better serve and gain more resources for our members," her voice cheery and uplifting. After talking with her for a few minutes, I realized I was having a conversation with Barbara Tabachnik, as she was then known, the Director of Education and editor of *Tinnitus Today*, ATA's quarterly publication. *Tinnitus Today* offers a wealth of treatment options in the articles written by audiologists, doctors, and leading research scientists, as well as the most current research being conducted for this problem. There are also numerous stories in the magazine written by courageous people with Tinnitus relating their heartrending and inspiring stories of how tinnitus has invaded their lives and how they are coping. I could relate to their stories and was encouraged by all the research that was being conducted, yet dismayed that people I talked to about this problem told me about how their tendonitis was a bitch!

"Here's my situation. I have been a member of ATA for the past few years and have read every article on tinnitus in your magazine. Each story I read gave me more information than I could ever have imagined on this hellacious problem and far better news than the same old, worn-out 'Learn to live with it' adage, given by doctors to their patients with tinnitus."

"Thanks for your feedback about our magazine. I'm so happy to hear that it has helped you with this problem. How long have you had tinnitus? And what things have you tried?"

"Since 1996, and I've tried everything from Chinese herbs to chiropractic, and the most effective treatment has been TRT. Just finished wearing the devices and finally feel like I'm alive once again. It's been a long uphill climb… which leads into what I called about in the first place. So, here's my idea." I told her about the story of the women who climbed Aconcagua and how it inspired me to want to do a climb on Mount Rainier to raise funds for ATA. Further explaining how this would be my way of demonstrating how I am choosing to "live with" tinnitus, I paused breathlessly awaiting her reply and heard dead silence on the other end. Remembering the sight of seeing majestic Mount Rainier up close and personal just months before filled my head. After a few seconds, Barb found her voice.

"Have you ever done a climb before?"

"Yes, I've climbed about 16 14'ers here in Colorado. I'm also an avid runner, cross country skier and hiker."

"That's a pretty big mountain. Are you aware it's a technical climb and of all the dangers involved?"

"Yes, I know it's technical. I don't have any technical climbing skills yet, but I plan to take a mountaineering skills course offered here to be more prepared for this climb." Dead silence once again.

"You still there?"

"Yes, and you're giving me the chills," Barb paused, trying to choose her words carefully while—she told me later—her mind was racing about how amazing this would be. "You know, no one has ever attempted anything like what you are proposing for a fundraiser for ATA. We've had a guy do a bike ride, but never any climbs."

"I'm sure it would be an attention grabber!"

"Yes, it sure would," Barb chuckled.

"So, what would ATA do to support this endeavor?" I persisted.

"Well, tell you what. Why don't you send me a proposal for your climb and I will run it past the board and call you back next week."

"OK, thank you. Talk to you soon." I hung up the phone feeling rather disappointed. *Guess I won't hear from her again, I thought.* The only proposal I had ever previously written was when Broomfield Arts Council President suggested I apply for a grant to fund the mime shows I was proposing to do for Denver Public Schools. How do you put a lifelong dream down on paper to convince others you're qualified to make your dream come true? No easy task. But I somehow muddled my way through, sent it off in the mail and, eventually, got the grant.

A week flew by and there was Barb's cheery voice greeting me on the phone. "So, you're sure you really want to do this?"

"Yep."

"Well, good news! It's a go on this side! When are you thinking of doing the climb?"

"How about this July?" My birthday is in July and I couldn't think of a better way to celebrate than eating cake and ice cream on the summit of Mount Rainier.

Pause. "Well, would that give you enough time to train?" I looked at the calendar and realized I would have six months to prepare for the climb. The realization of what I was proposing actually coming to fruition was mindboggling, yet exciting as hell!

"Yes, I know I can do this climb by then, Barb." I tried to sound reassuring, wondering if a flatlander from Chicago could really reach the summit of a 14, 410 foot active volcano!

"Are you doing this solo?"

"Yes, as I don't know anyone else crazy enough to do this crazy stuff! Unless, you can pass this along to ATA staff and see if they might be up for the challenge."

"Donna, I think you had better do this solo! I don't think anyone here would be of that mindset or caliber."

"OK. So, what would ATA's role be in this endeavor?"

"Let me talk to the staff and do some brainstorming and then I will get back to you and let you know. I do know that we can run an article in *Tinnitus Today* on your climb which I'm certain will generate interest and support from our members in the form of donations. Speaking of donations, give some thought as to what percentage of the donations you would like to have allocated to tinnitus research."

Thinking about her comment for a few moments, I then replied, "Of course one hundred percent toward continued research for an eventual cure for this problem."

"Thank you so much, Donna. This is so incredibly generous of you."

"Barb, I just want to see a cure for this horrendous problem some time in my lifetime and am sure there are millions of others who stand with me! This climb is for them and I won't be alone as they will be with me in spirit."

"Well said! Let's talk within the next few weeks."

Hanging up the phone, I felt a combination of elation and uncertainty that I could pull something of this magnitude off, not having any previous technical climbing experience, much less fundraising experience. I had made it through the first obstacle, obtaining support and interest from ATA, yet felt overwhelmed by the monumental task in front of me: training for this climb. Despite not having met Barb, I felt a definite connection with her, and the bond we formed during numerous phone conversations would last for years to come.

Over the next few months, I busied myself looking for outdoor organizations I could join that offered mountaineering courses and became a member of Colorado Mountain Club.

I signed up for a month-long mountaineering course and went on several hikes they offered just to have some company while I trained. During the course, I learned the "ropes" of tying knots and how to use an ice axe to arrest your fall when sliding break neck speed down wicked steep mountain slopes. I climbed everything that went up, including hills, several 14'ers, and every riser in the parks I hiked through. While training, I worked at The North Face, a leading outdoor wear and gear store then located in Boulder and bought every article of mountain attire imaginable, from climbing boots to GORE-TEX® jackets and backpacks. My store manager, George, even gave me a decent discount on a down sleeping bag to take with me on the climb. Every weekend would find me on some sort of cross country ski adventure or at the local gym hoisting weights and spending countless hours training on elliptical machines donned with backpack filled to maximum capacity and weighing the 40 pounds I would be carrying on the climb.

This being my first technical climb prompted me to contact Rainier's guide service, RMI, (Rainier Mountaineering Inc.), and I signed up for their two-day climb. The first day was spent learning self-arrest techniques with ice axe and moving over the heavily glaciated terrain of the mountain as part of a rope team. Day two would be our long summit push from Camp Muir at around 10,500 ft.

and descent back down to our starting point at Paradise. Signing RMI's waiver was a bit sobering reading about all the potential dangers of the climb (i.e. getting buried by avalanches, rock fall, and you falling, amongst other grievous consequences such as loss of life and limb), and I almost reconsidered. Nonetheless, with each outing, I gained more experience and confidence in my mountaineering skills and as the climb drew nearer, I could hardly wait to begin the adventure!

Barb kept in touch with me regularly during the six training months prior to the climb, wrote an article about the climb that was published in Tinnitus Today, sent out letters to all ATA members asking for donations, and kept me updated as to the amount being donated at least once a week. I received letters of encouragement and support from ATA members and staff, as well as a banner with ATA's logo to carry with me and place on the summit. One of ATA's Portland, Oregon, office staff who kept in touch with me was the Executive Director of ATA, Cheryl McGinnis. I developed a great rapport with her as well as with Jessica Allen, Public Relations Director, and Lisa Freeman, Client Services Coordinator. Jessica informed me in a phone conversation that Lisa had designed the beautiful white and blue banner that I received. I was touched by their enormous displays of support for my climb.

A few months prior to the climb, I contacted several TV stations attempting to gain publicity and more awareness of tinnitus and funding for continued research for ATA's mission of an eventual cure. Through the whole process of training for the climb, I had been doing some research of my own on how much government funding was allocated towards tinnitus research and discovered the figures were pretty pathetic. For example, an increasing number of veterans were returning from war with tinnitus. Veterans Administration figures cited some, "... 144,243 veterans with tinnitus-related disabilities in 2000." (22.) There were more disability payments being made by the government rather than money allocated towards research for a cure, which I found to be disconcerting. Several articles were written about my climb by local and out-of-state newspaper reporters, yet I received no replies from the media. This climb would be my chance to make the media and general public stand up and take notice of someone deciding to take control of her life and doing more than just learning to live with it! I decided to call the climb, "Expedition Hopeful Cure," in hopes that it could generate enough donations for ATA to continue their vital research for an eventual cure.

I started the journey bright and early on my birthday, July 29, and met my guide, Liam and other climbers in the parking lot of Paradise Inn, a historic hotel located in Mount Rainier National Park in Washington, where the climb was to begin at 5,400 feet on the south slope of Mount Rainier. After a thorough gear check by the seven guides accompanying our group of 22 climbers, we headed up the Skyline Trail, our packs filled with food, water, and gear. Our nervous anticipation of reaching the summit weighed heavier than the 40 pound packs on our backs. Our first day goal was to reach Camp Muir at 10,500 feet—about a five or six hour trek up the Muir Snowfield, where we would camp overnight and awaken early the next morning to prepare for our summit bid.

The ascent up the Snowfield to Camp Muir was an arduous trek and, despite using trekking poles, I was soon winded and lagging behind my climbing companions. Each step was a supreme effort due to the altitude and relentlessly steep grade of the Snowfield. Liam was keeping his eye on me, trying his best to dissuade me from continuing, yet I persisted on sheer determination and adrenaline. After six hours of almost continuous ascending, I heard Liam yell to me, "We're here!" I gazed up ahead of me and there was the tiny Muir Hut I had only seen in pictures standing a few feet away! I was too tired to cry out the elation I felt at having reached our first destination and, instead, settled on squeezing my sleeping bag into an upper berth of the sleeping areas inside the hut. My companions had arrived about fifteen minutes before me and quickly snatched up the lower berth spaces for themselves.

After a sparse supper of dehydrated soup and tea and a pep talk from our guides, we retired for the evening around 7 p.m. I didn't get much sleep, just like the previous evening, and lay awake in nervous anticipation of what was ahead. It was also difficult to sleep amidst 22 bodies squeezed into tight sleeping spaces like sardines and the snoring from my neighbors that rivaled the wind howling outside the hut. My usual evening dose of Xanax was calming the tinnitus, yet failing miserably in the sleep department. I thought about the Ear Planes® I had used on the flight and berated myself for forgetting to pack those sound-blocking ear plugs in my pack. The next few hours were spent pulling my bag over my head in an attempt to escape the ambient noise assaults inside and out, while praying I wouldn't have to go outside to the smelly latrine to pee! I cheered myself with thoughts of crawling over my slumberous companions and lumbering down the ladder with the grace of a 500-pound polar bear trying to quietly make my way to the latrine. Perhaps a few heads would turn in the process and curtail the cacophony… But wishful thinking! These climbers were dead to the world!

I was soon awakened by the voice of one of our guides giving us a wake-up call at midnight, and groggily realized I must have dozed for a while. Now wide awake in anticipation of the moment I had dreamt about for months, I sprang into action like a whirling dervish, and donned warm outer layers of clothing, headlamp, boots, and crampons. SHOWTIME!!! Feeling the surge of welcome adrenaline rush through my weary body, I reached for my ice axe, pack, and a

Pemmican power bar to munch on and, bracing myself against the onslaught of wind, headed out the hut door. In what seemed like mere minutes an hour had passed and I found myself in a single file line with five other climbers harnessed together on our rope team. We silently started to ascend and it felt like Liam was pulling me up the mountain with his blistering pace. I somehow managed to keep up without getting tangled in the rope while coordinating the dance of rest step, pressure breathe, huff, puff, pant, pant, and trying not to stab myself in the foot with my ice axe. The climber behind me on my team was a strapping young lad of barely 15 and as the terrain got steeper he got HEAVIER!!! I was actually pulling him up the mountain in addition to carrying my 40 pound pack! *He should be pulling me! Not bad for an old lady! I thought,* yet this endeavor would cost me dearly.

Continuing our ascent, we traversed across more snowfields, jumping over huge yawning crevasses, and wearily trudging our way over rocks and loose gravel with crampons scraping and slipping at every step. After two or more hours of steady climbing, we finally took a rest stop and I threw my pack and myself down on the snow-covered slope in a state of utter exhaustion. We had reached 12,000 ft. and I had reached my limit! Just sitting on my pack was a supreme effort. I knew I needed to eat a snack and drink water, yet had no appetite or strength for either task.

Liam came over and, sitting down next to me, asked if I felt I could continue onwards and upwards. I nodded, yet felt like I had been run over by a charging bull, no doubt from the effects of high altitude and little sleep.

The decision on whether to proceed or turn-around is never an easy one to make, yet I needed to make that decision quickly, as my companions were already packing up and heading up the mountain. I could barely stand up. Before I could respond, Liam helped me up and said he was sending me back down with another guide, Brian, who was heading back to Camp Muir with several other exhausted climbers. Too tired to complain, I realized that Liam made a wise decision, as he had to consider the safety of the group as a whole. Such are the advantages and disadvantages of climbing with a group.

Roping into Brian's descent team, I felt so disappointed that I wouldn't have a chance at reaching and placing ATA's banner on the summit. Feeling sick of stomach and heavy of heart, I glanced back over my shoulder taking in the majestic panorama all around me, watching Liam continuing his ascent with the group. Through the darkness I could barely make out the summit's silhouette and realized that I was so close yet so far away. Some consolation then came in the form of an awesomely unforgettable sight that Rainier was providing at that moment. Directly above me were the captivating orange glows reflected from my companion's headlamps winding up the mountain as far as the eye could see.

Wishing I could be with them, I felt the familiar tug of the rope at my harness pulling me back down the mountain. Descending with feelings of despair at 3 a.m., I wanted nothing more than to stop moving, reach Muir and catch some sorely needed shut eye! The wind had died down somewhat, yet my body shook uncontrollably from the bitter cold.

We descended back to Muir in record time. What took us hours to ascend took perhaps 1½ hours to descend. As we approached the camp, the sun was just rising in the sky displaying a breathtaking array of brilliant pinks and peach colors against the stark white jagged contrast of the mountain. What a magnificent sight for sore eyes.

Once back at the hut, I quickly shed outer layers of sweat-soaked outerwear and crawled into my bag hoping for a few blessed hours of sleep. The hut seemed like a ghost town now, devoid of all the bodies stockpiled there just a few hours earlier. I tossed and turned reliving the scenario of the previous night replaying itself over and over in my mind's eye, exhausted yet unable to sleep. *At least I'm resting, I tried to convince myself of that.*

Sunlight was pouring into the Hut and despite having the bag pulled up over my head, I could still feel the penetrating rays warming and illuminating the hut. After a few hours, I wearily crawled out of my bag and stumbled down the ladder from the loft, out the door into the bright daylight. Looking at my watch, I saw it was almost 11a.m. and enviously thought of my companions already making their way back from the summit. I wondered how long it would take them to reach Muir.

Gazing around Camp, I noticed the surroundings looked very different in the morning light than at dusk the previous evening when we first arrived. Heading towards the latrine to pee, I noticed Brian walking ahead of me and caught up with him.

"Hey Brian," I greeted him.

"Hey, how's it going? Get any zzz's?" he asked.

"Not much. I wondered if there might be any chance of giving the summit another try?" It wouldn't hurt to ask.

Shaking his head, he denied my request. "Nope, not a chance, as we're heading back down when the other folks return."

My heart sank. "Do you know when they will be coming back?"

"Probably due within the next few hours," he replied excusing himself and disappearing into the dark abyss of the latrine. I did the same in the women's section. Emerging quickly from the stench of the reeking outhouse, I headed over to sit on some rocks overlooking the footpath descending down from the upper flank of the mountain, imagining I were amongst the group heading back from the summit. Still fairly wasted from the exertion of the previous night's climb, I scrambled up some boulders in the area to get a better view of the area and took in the awesome scenery from my high, rocky perch.

After some time passed, I saw in the far distance a group of people descending on the footpath towards camp. I watched them approaching for a short time and then crawled back down from the rocks where I sat and headed back towards the hut where they would be gathering. Waiting impatiently for them to arrive, I busied myself with thoughts about what I would ask them, regretting not having had the presence of mind to hand ATA's banner to Liam to place on the summit.

Another guide was the first to arrive, followed by his rope team, and Liam's team was right behind them. I ran up to meet the guides and fellow climbers asking if they made summit. Seeing their weary, yet gleeful faces was all the affirmation I needed. I wished them all congratulations, shaking every free hand that was offered. They briefly thanked me and headed for the hut to remove their crampons and reload their packs. Seeing Liam heading for the hut, I approached and congratulated him and heard him reply, "Thanks, Donna. Sorry you weren't along with us."

Tears welled up in my eyes and I tried to wipe them away without being noticed, yet failed in that attempt.

"There's always next year," he consolingly patted my shoulder.

Shaking my head and looking down at the ground, I replied, "Don't think so. This was enough for me."

"Hey, do you still have your banner?" he persisted.

Remembering the banner in my pack, I perked up a bit. "What are you saying?"

"Well, we could perhaps head up somewhere in the area and take a few pictures for the record to at least show you made it to Muir," he graciously offered.

Thinking about the rocky ledge where I had climbed earlier, I pointed in that direction. "How about up there?"

"Yeah, that will work. Let me take off my pack and we'll head up there."

We headed up to the ledge and had a fellow climber take a few shots of Liam and me standing arm in arm with us both holding on to one side of the banner. Descending back down to Camp, I saw a few other climbers I had chatted with earlier who also didn't make summit and took more pictures with them and the banner.

Outside the hut area, my companions were sitting on rocks hungrily munching on snacks and we joined them. Although still not feeling very hungry, I managed to eat some trail mix snacks I found in my pack. Some of the guides offered to whip up more dehydrated, substantial packaged food fare, and we took them up on their offer.

After lunch, I started to head into the hut and was stopped by someone calling out from behind me. Turning around, I walked back over to where the group had gathered and noticed the guides suddenly walking purposefully together and disappear behind some rocks a short distance away from the hut. Sitting down next to a few climbers, they engaged me in conversation and I soon forgot about the guides. Suddenly, I noticed Liam approaching where I sat carrying something in his hands. The other guides were right behind him and glancing over my shoulder, I noticed Liam holding a delicious looking glob of vanilla ice cream with a candle in the middle of it flickering in the brisk breeze blowing around Muir. Before I could realize what was happening, guides and companions suddenly broke into singing the familiar refrains of "Happy Birthday to you!" Liam then handed me a spoon and offered me the first bite, and with tears once again welling up in my eyes, I thanked him and wolfed down the best tasting, rapidly melting ice cream concoction I had ever tasted! The treat was passed around the group and was soon a not so distant memory. What a wonderful birthday surprise! Everyone in the group was now congratulating me. Despite the disappointment of not reaching summit, I had accomplished having my cake and eating it too, well, ice cream at least, on Rainier.

The descent from Muir was much easier than was the previous day's ascent, as we glissaded down the Snowfield and for the most part it went smoothly, although it took the better part of the day. When finally getting back down to solid ground, I tried to stand up and my legs felt like Jello®. Reaching for my trekking pole, I felt a bolt of pain shoot through my left hand and noticed my pinkie finger was the size of a dill pickle! It was quite purple in color and hurt like hell, yet I had no idea what had happened. Most likely I had injured it while clutching my ice axe for all I was worth, glissading full speed down the mountain. Liam looked at my finger and fashioned a splint with a twig he picked up from the ground and some gauze he carried in his first aid kit. It was only when returning home and having it x-rayed that I found out it was fractured.

When finally getting back to my room at Paradise Inn, I collapsed on my bed (a REAL one) and despite overwhelming fatigue, was wide awake. My mind was reeling from all the events of the past two days and reflecting back on the climb, it was so easy to get down on myself for not reaching the summit. I found out later that evening at dinner with my fellow climbers that only 13 out of 23 made summit and three were guides! Mount Rainier is not an easy climb by any means, nor is any other challenging endeavor easy, nor is living with any disability. What I learned from this experience is that I am a far stronger person than I thought, and that one person can indeed make a difference! I accomplished what I had originally set out to do: raise money for ATA and more awareness of the problem of tinnitus.

Barb informed me upon returning from my trip that I had raised $92,000 which far exceeded both my and ATA's expectations! Also, if I inspired at least one person to make their own dreams come true and not let tinnitus or other disabilities interfere with doing the things they love, then I reached my summit after all!

CHAPTER 22
DAISY LADY'S DEMISE (2000-'01)

"Say not in grief that she has gone, but give thanks that she was yours."
— Author unknown

"Hi dear, we're in Colorado!" Gloria's cheery voice echoed on the other end of the phone. It was always great hearing from Gloria whenever she would call.

"Where are you? You sound like you are right next door!" I excitedly exclaimed hoping she would actually come to visit me, as it had been a few years since our last visit when they made a stop in Colorado Springs. Gloria and Skip had an RV and they traveled all over the country in it, yet had never come to visit with us in Broomfield, just outside of Denver, where Gary and I lived.

"Skip and I are on I-25 heading up to Rocky Mountain Park."

"Hey, Glo," as I now called her, "you guys are very close to our house! Why don't you stop by on your way up to the park?"

"Hold on. Let me ask Skip." I could tell by the tone of Glo's voice that it wasn't in the cards this time either. After a few seconds, she got back to me. "Skip is in a hurry and wants to make it up there without stopping. Maybe next time, dear," she apologized.

"Yeah, maybe next time whenever that will be." My heart sank, yet expected her turn down. They were always in a hurry and I didn't quite understand why they never thought to come for a visit. Glo was more laid back and approachable than Skip who was very high strung since first meeting him on the plane to Honolulu for the marathon. Whenever I would ask her about coming out to Colorado, she said she would have to get the OK from Skip and that's where the conversation would end. After the marathon, Glo and I saw each other a lot when Gary and I still lived in Chicago. We did dozens of pantomime gigs together, she in her clown character "Daisy Lady," at hospitals for charity, street festivals and assorted other venues. We were inseparable. She would affectionately call me, "Daughter Who Doesn't Speak."

Skip and I were running buddies. We ran together several times in Caldwell Woods and I enjoyed our runs. Spending more time with Glo, however, I felt closer to her. Glo, who was not a runner, would meet us somewhere in the middle of our run, waiting patiently in her van to offer us coffee and soft drinks when we would stop for a break. She and Skip would volunteer at all the local running races and would be stationed at aid stations along the race course offering refreshments to the runners. Both had time on their hands being retired and put that time to good use traveling and volunteering.

Glo and I kept in contact on the phone. I shared my Rainier climb experience with her and she was extremely proud of my achievements as always, yet the news she would share with me about her situation wasn't as positive. A few months after the climb, she called and informed me she had been in the hospital. The news was a surprise as Glo kept fairly active with swimming and doing all her volunteer work and was always in good health. When questioning her about the hospital stay she replied, "Oh, don't worry dear, it was only a mini stroke and I'm taking blood thinners and the doctor said I'll be fine." Of course, being a nurse, and remembering what happened to Ma, I was concerned.

The phone calls kept coming and with each call she informed me about her declining health. There were more hospital stays and the last call I received from her sometime before September 11, 2001 (9/11), she was diagnosed with a very serious condition known as abdominal aortic aneurysm. Once again, she tried to reassure me that everything would be fine, yet I had my doubts. During that time, I had just started a new nursing job and was preoccupied with that, so I didn't keep in touch with her as often.

A month had passed since last hearing from Glo and I was planning to call her when the phone rang.

"Hi, Donna? This is Skip."

"Hey Skip, how are you and Glo?"

"Well, I'm fine, but I have some bad news about Gloria. She passed away a few days ago." My heart was pounding and I suddenly felt like all my blood was slowly draining from my body.

"Skip... NO!!!! What happened?" I yelled into the receiver.

"I don't know. All I know is we were sitting at the table eating lunch and then her head fell forward and I thought she had fainted. I called 911 but it was too late, she was already dead."

"Skip... no... no... no..." I shouted. Staring at the phone in disbelief with tears welling in my eyes, I knew I would have to make a trip back to Chicago to see her one last time yet didn't really want to see my friend and surrogate mom lying in a casket.

Skip's voice interrupted my thoughts. "Donna, are you still there?"

"Yes…" my voice trailing off. "Skip, when is the wake and funeral?"

"We had the wake two days ago and she was cremated yesterday," Skip replied in a monotone voice.

"Skip!" I was now yelling again. "Why didn't you call sooner?" I asked incredulous that now all hopes of seeing Glo again were dashed to bits.

"Donna, I'm sorry," Skip apologized. "This all happened so suddenly and I couldn't find your phone number until now."

"Did you look in Glo's address book?" I was still in a state of shock.

"Yes, and I couldn't find your name."

"How did you find my phone number?"

"I'm sitting at the table here and found your number written on a piece of paper."

I stood there barely breathing, not knowing what to say. How could this have happened? I couldn't believe that Glo had not written my number in her address book as we were always talking to each other on the phone. Skip was hurting as well over losing his wife and life partner, yet I was angry that I wasn't notified until four days after her passing and was denied the chance to see her again. I remembered he mentioned Glo being cremated and wondered if he still had her ashes.

"Skip, do you have Glo's ashes?"

He paused and replied, "No, I gave them to our neighbor." Cut and dried and totally gone.

"Did she have any special request for the disposition of her ashes?" Staring at the phone, I wondered why he would give her ashes away. His response only increased my bewilderment. "She asked that her ashes be spread in Colorado and our neighbor has a daughter who lives there."

"Skip, you know I live in Colorado, right?" Exasperated, I didn't want to hear any further excuses. "Could you do me one favor? Could you please give me your neighbor's number so I can find out who their daughter is and her whereabouts? This would mean the world to me, Skip!"

He gave me their neighbor's number, I thanked him, expressing my deepest condolences and hung up the phone feeling absolutely bereft. Slumping into the nearest chair, I sat and let the tears fall like a rushing, gushing waterfall. Glo was gone, yet I felt a slim glimmer of hope remaining in a complete stranger I had never met. Perhaps the daughter still had her ashes and, if so, I could at least be closer to her, bid her farewell and bring some semblance of peace and closure to her passing. Clinging to this last ray of sunshine, I dialed the number and left a message. The hour was late and I collapsed on the bed falling into a restless and dreamless slumber.

The next day I received a call from John, Glo's neighbor and he gave me his daughter Alison's number. She lived in Breckenridge, a beautiful ski resort town in the mountains and place where I had spent a considerable amount of time skiing and hiking. I called and talked with Alison explaining I was a good friend of Glo's and asked her if she still had Glo's ashes. She said she had already spread them in the mountains somewhere in Breckenridge, yet didn't recall exactly where. Hanging up the phone, I still felt bitterly disappointed that all was said and done without my knowledge and that I didn't have any choice in the matter, yet took some comfort in knowing that Glo was at least close in spirit somewhere in the mountains of Colorado as per her request. I made several trips to Breckenridge over the next few years and felt her presence knowing Glo was watching from her heavenly new home.

Some months later, I received another call from John notifying me of Skip's passing. John mentioned he underwent knee surgery and never recovered. During many of our past runs together, Skip had mentioned to me that his knee was "bone on bone" from arthritis, yet he was fearful of having the surgery in realizing he might not survive the procedure. I thought this news from John to be ironic and timely. It is a well-known fact that relatively few men survive the passing of their wives, especially true if the relationship was close, and I often wondered how Skip was holding up physically and mentally. The thought of them together again in heaven was comforting.

They say that "time heals all wounds," and I found that to be true. Some years after Glo's passing, I was invited by a friend to attend a women's retreat at a sweat lodge in Aspen. During the sweat lodge ceremony, I sat in the lodge—or rather tent—with several other women from the retreat, sweating profusely and pouring forth our stories to share and cleanse ourselves of all negativity. After sharing Glo's story and feeling tired from pouring sweat and tears, I laid down on the grass inside the small tent listening to my companion's stories. I suddenly felt a sharp bolt of pain shoot down my left elbow and almost cried out loud, but winced in silence not wanting to interrupt my companions from sharing their stories. Quickly sitting up and glancing down at my elbow, I was unable to see anything in the omnipresent darkness inside the tent. I shrugged off the occurrence as nothing more serious than being stabbed by a sharp blade of grass.

A short time later, the tent flaps were opened by our guide, Brandon, and I crawled out of the stifling heat and darkness into the fresh, open air and daylight breathing a sigh of relief to once again be outside. Glancing down, I noticed a quarter size angry red hive on my elbow that hurt like the devil and was sending shooting pains up and down my arm. Reaching for my towel on the ground, my attention was drawn to a curious looking brown spot perched on top of the towel. Upon closer inspection, I noticed the brown spot was a spider with one leg extended up toward me as if in a salute. My first reaction to the spider or any insect in general was to swat at it or squash it and I held my flip-flop in mid-air ready to pounce on the spider. But neither spider nor I moved a muscle. Something was very familiar and comforting about this creature in a strange way and bringing my flip-flop slowly back down towards the towel, I paused to see what it would do. Spider kept its vigil holding its leg in full extension, which I thought very odd.

Usually spiders flee when under attack, yet this one stayed put for whatever reason. The source of my pain was at once obvious and I wondered if this was a brown recluse, whose sting is poisonous. I called out to Brandon, showing him my red arm and asking if brown recluse spiders were indigenous to the Aspen area. He said he didn't think they were and I left it at that.

Somehow, I felt Glo's presence sitting right next to me in the guise of the spider as if to reassure me all was well. Naming my little brown friend "Daisy" gave me comfort and consolation in coming to terms with Glo's passing.

CHAPTER 23
RAINIER REVISITED (2003-'07)

"We know people by their stories: their history, their habits, their secrets, their triumphs and failures. We know them by what they do. We want to know mountains too, but they've got no story. So, we do the next best thing. We throw ourselves onto them and make the stories happen."
— **Bruce Barcott, Public Speaker and leading Author of several books including The Measure of a Mountain: Beauty and Terror on Mount Rainier**

"You have to stand up, Donna!" Jeff yelled down at me from somewhere above in the maddening, swirling maelstrom mixture of snow and sleet whipping around my body lying in the snow. Every pore of my being wanted nothing more than to get up from where I was slumped over in a heap somewhere on the endless snow-field we were traversing, yet the task of reaching my hand towards the top of my ice axe seemed a challenge far beyond what I was capable of doing in that moment. Jeff was now standing over me saying, "We need to head back down." My mind was spinning with thoughts, much like the howling hurricane force winds that blew around our tenuous perch high on the mountain. A vision of Liam turning me around on my first climb came into my mind's eye with amazing clarity. I closed my exhausted eyes as if to shut out the vision, almost succumbing to the intense impulse to lay back and let my body rest, yet another more urgent instinct wouldn't let me surrender just yet. Images of Barb and all the people who supported this climb flooded my mind and I knew in the moment descending was not an option…

Nine months earlier, I called ATA expecting to talk to Barb and was greeted by another unfamiliar voice.

"Hi, ATA, this is Helen speaking. How may I help you?"

"Hey Helen, may I speak with Barb?

"I'm sorry, but she no longer works here. May I help you with something?"

One more time for the road, I thought and introduced myself hoping for some recognition, yet no luck in that department.

"Yes, you may." I was wondering what happened to Barb and now missing her familiar cheery voice. "I did a previous climb on Mount Rainier a few years ago and am planning to do another climb as a fundraiser for ATA next summer. Whom should I talk to in this regard?"

"Did I hear correctly that you climbed Mount Rainier?"

"Well, yes, yet at that time I didn't make summit and that's why I'd like to give it another try this next summer."

"Well, good luck to you," she replied with a slight chuckle in her voice.

"Helen, is there someone I could speak with in regards to this climb or do I talk with you about it?" I persisted.

Pause. "Ummm… let me see if there's staff people I could talk to about your suggestion. Are you sure you want to do this for our organization? I know in the past we have had bike rides and such, yet never climbing endeavors such as you are mentioning."

Sighing and taking a deep breath, I felt the familiar resistance of having to convince a new person that I hadn't gone completely off the deep end.

"Perhaps you can contact Barb and ask about my last climb for ATA and she can fill you in on all the details."

"I sure will, Donna. Thanks for your call. I'll let Barb know you called."

Well, that went over like a lead-filled balloon, I thought. Little did I know, at the time, what an integral role Helen would play in the months leading up to my second climb, Expedition Hopeful Cure 2.

Training for EHC2 began in earnest in 2003, three years after the first climb. Still mourning the loss of Glo, I kept busy pursuing outdoor sports I was passionate about like cross- country skiing. While still working as a nurse for Kaiser Permanente, a leading health organization, I met another nurse who would become a great friend and outdoor adventure partner, named Cindy Davis. We met during Orientation one day when I was new to Kaiser and Cindy was transferring to another department in the clinic. We were given an assignment to introduce ourselves to the group by talking about, ironically enough, the things we were most passionate about in our lives. Cindy stood up and introduced herself as an avid outdoors enthusiast and cross-country skier and I instantly knew I needed to meet her after class and get to know her better. After class, I approached her, introduced myself and we became fast friends. On our ski outings she would tell me of her plans to lead groups of women on back country ski trips to stay overnight at huts that were part of the infamous 10th Mountain Division Huts System, a not-for-profit organization that manages 34 backcountry huts in Colorado connected by some three hundred miles of suggested routes. The name pays tribute to the men of the 10th Mountain Division of the U.S. Army who trained during World War II at Camp Hale in Central Colorado. (24.)

Having never been on a ski outing lasting more than just a few hours, I became engrossed with tales of her visiting and supplying the huts in summer with wood for the wood burning stoves for use during peak winter seasons. She said she was planning a trip that March and asked if I was interested in coming along. I heartily agreed. I will always remember Cindy as our fearless leader and incredible cook! She loaded her pack with tons of food and I wondered how she carried the 50 to 60 pounds on her back up wickedly steep, snowy terrain to the huts we skied miles to reach. She even lugged birthday cakes and balloons as well. What an amazingly strong super woman she was!

The first hut our group visited was called Francie's Cabin, near the town of Breckenridge and I was joined on the trip by several of Cindy's Kaiser co-workers, including nurses, nurse practitioners and physician assistants. During this trip, I met a nurse practitioner, Katy Thach, who eventually became another great friend and partner on climbs and other outdoor adventures.

As we were unpacking our backpacks upon arrival to the hut, and trying to stay warm, I laid down upon one of the bunk beds to try to catch a few winks. That was when I heard Katy mention she was heading back outside for a short ski to explore the area around the hut.

"Does anyone want to join me?" she asked the group.

I heard audible gasps and comments from several of the ladies in our group saying, "Are you for real? We're TIRED!!!"

I felt the same, yet thought it might be a good way to get to know her and explore some of Colorado's pristine wilderness a bit better.

"I'm game!"

The two of us headed out the door and were soon skiing back into a bowl of pure powder surrounded by pretty awesome looking peaks. For a while there was no conversation, just the sound of our heavy breathing as we skied taking in the mountain majesty all around us.

Katy broke the silence. "Have you been skiing for long?"

"Yeah, but have never stayed in any hut until now. How about you?"

"I've been to a few of the huts, though not this one."

During our ski trek, I learned so much about and from Katy that was not apparent when first meeting her. She was more reserved with the group, yet opened up to me as we skied. The first lesson I learned was, when you're with Katy, you go eternally onwards and upwards. I marveled at her ease of climbing hills packed with snow, and even more so at her natural grace of gliding and carving turns on downhill slopes. I lagged behind her going uphill and became quite winded. When finally catching up to her, I gasped, "Wow, you've been doing this forever!"

Taking a well-needed rest break, we chatted and I marveled at her stories. She regaled me with tales of her climbing peaks in Peru, Alaska (Denali, aka: Mount McKinley), and Washington, (Mount Rainier). In her I glimpsed a potential new friend and climbing partner. I shared with her several of my own climbing stories, about our accident on Hallet's and my first attempt to climb Rainier.

After another hour or so of some of the best backcountry skiing Colorado has to offer, Katy and I headed back to the hut and regaled our companions with our shared skiing adventure. When arriving back at the hut, we noticed another group had appeared, and discovered they were doctors. What an irony, I thought, that of all people to share our hut with it had to be a bunch of docs! We passed the evening sharing tons of sinfully delicious food lovingly prepared by Cindy, and gabbed about medical stories, of course. The next morning, we packed up and headed back down the trail in the midst of a snowstorm, eventually finding the way back to our cars. Katy and I exchanged telephone numbers and promised to call each other for more ski adventures and hikes. Thus, began an enduring friendship between Katy, Cindy and me.

Over the next few years, Katy and I were together hiking and skiing as much as our crazy nursing schedules would allow, mostly on weekends. Unfortunately, Cindy and I didn't get together as much except for the yearly hut trips she always organized and led.

On one ski outing with Katy, we were skiing up a steep hill with climbing "skins" (strips of special material applied to the bottoms of skis for better traction) on our skis and I told her about wanting to climb Rainier again for ATA. I had never previously thought of asking her to join me as she was far more advanced in mountaineering skills than myself, yet I decided to ask anyway.

"Hey, Katy?"

"Yeah?"

"Would you consider doing another climb on Rainier? I know you've already climbed the peak."

"When are you planning on doing the climb?"

"Next summer, probably in July."

"I don't think I have anything booked for that time. So, yes, dear, let's plan on it. Let me know the exact dates and let's do it! Have you told anyone at ATA about this climb yet?"

"I talked with a lady named Helen, yet don't think she got what I'm trying to do. Barb, the lady I connected with for the first climb isn't working there anymore, unfortunately, so I have to start all over again to break someone new in as a contact."

"Bummer, man! Good luck with that!" One of Katy's favorite expressions and I was about to hear another one. "We're gonna have to train our butts off for Rainier, you know."

"Katy," I stopped to catch my breath. "What do you think we've been doing with our all-day outings?" Every outing with Katy was an intense training session just trying to keep up with her, being nine years her senior.

"I know, yet Rainier's not an easy climb! I think we should do as many high 13'ers and 14'ers as possible, like every weekend we should ski, hike, or do a peak."

"I'm with you on that one, my friend. I want to make summit this time around."

"I have a feeling you will this time, dear!"

"Thanks for the vote of confidence! Hey, you getting hungry?"

We pulled over to nearby tree and sat taking in the view and munching on trail mix and whatever surprise food combination Katy had in her pack. This time it was apple slices mixed with a jar of peanut butter she was carrying. I chided her about the weird mix of snacks and we laughed heartily. Time spent with Katy was always quality time and went by quickly. Before long we were back down at our cars, hugging each other and driving in different directions to our homes.

During another cross-country hut trip to Jackal Hut, we were out for hours and somehow managed to ski fast and furiously past the hut hidden behind a hill to our right. Cindy, our fearless leader, was searching for the hut in one direction and Katy was heading in another direction. Dee, another friend I met on a hut trip and an avid downhill skier, waited with me standing in the snow looking around for any trace of the missing hut. "There's the parking lot sign," Dee nudged my arm and pointed to the right.

"Yeah, I see it, but where's the hut?" Looking around, I felt the last traces of energy now quickly dwindling. Perhaps we would have to bivy (hunker down in a makeshift camp without tents or cover) if we couldn't find the hut.

Suddenly, we heard Cindy yell to us that she found it! With sighs of relief, Dee and I headed towards the direction of Cindy's voice beneath the hill to our right and sure enough, Jackal Hut came into view with Cindy standing next to it. I looked over my shoulder and saw Katy now skiing in our direction. I waved to her and when she arrived we stood together outside the hut for a few minutes, shedding skis and poles and sharing friendly banter. We slapped each other high five as we did when reaching 13'er and 14'er summits together. I was glad to have Katy as a great friend and teacher, as well as to have befriended some wonderful pals as Cindy and Dee, or hut buddies as we called ourselves.

The next day I called Barb and we talked about the tentative conversation I had with Helen. "She's new to ATA, so give her time to get to know you and I'm sure she'll come around," Barb tried to reassure me.

"Barb, how come you're not working for ATA anymore?"

"After 14 years, it was just time to move on and besides, I'm doing something more fun now like writing articles on all kinds of health and wellness-related topics."

"ATA's not the same without you, Barb!" I heard her appreciative chuckle in the background. "Thanks, but please give Helen a chance."

"Hey, I hope she gives me a chance!"

"She will. I'll talk to her and give some history on you. You have quite a reputation already there, lady!"

"So the word's out already, huh?" We both laughed and I remembered our meeting sometime after the first climb when Gary and I made a trip to Portland to visit her when she still worked for ATA. Her easy-going and free-spirited nature instantly attracted me and we became fast friends thereafter.

"This time I'm going to make summit, Barb, and I would love to see your smiling face at journey's end after the climb. Do you think that will happen?"

"The summer's a long way away, but I think the possibilities are good. Regardless of whether I'm there or not, I have no doubt you will go all the way this time. You're a strong lady, a lot stronger than you think!" Barb was my biggest fan and despite only knowing her a short time, I felt like we had known each other for a whole lifetime.

About a week later, I called ATA with some apprehension about talking with Helen, yet I needed to find out if she and Barb had connected. After talking with Helen for several minutes, I discovered our conversation was going a lot smoother than previously.

"So, I heard from Barb. You have a bit of history with ATA!" her tone of voice more friendly and less formal.

"Helen, I seriously want to try to find a cure for this problem and this time I'm going to make summit!"

"Well, you certainly have a lot of determination and courage! Barb tells me you are planning to do the climb this July. Do you have dates yet?"

I had just solidified my travel plans and trip dates with International Mountain Guides (IMG) upon Katy's recommendation. She referred me to Jeff Ward, her guide when she climbed Mount McKinley a few years prior and recommended I send him an email and do the climb arrangements directly through him, which I did. We were scheduled to do a three-day climb this time, leaving on July 12 and returning to Denver on the 17th. After sharing this information with Helen, she told me that ATA was planning another fundraising event that spring that would bring attention and essential funding to increasing numbers of veterans returning from war with tinnitus. Feeling a bit dejected about another event taking priority, I thought this would divert attention from the climb, but realized that any funding for tinnitus research was a step in the right direction. Any doubts I had about Helen were quickly dispelled during weekly phone conversations with her.

Over the next few months, Helen proved herself to be an invaluable contact person and ally; as with Barb, we developed an incredible rapport. She kept me informed as to how many donations they were receiving for EHC2 and even fashioned a page on ATA's website dedicated specifically to the climb. The page included a short article on my personal history with ATA and a creative graphic of a mountain depicting heights on ascent akin to monetary amounts of donations generated by the climb.

As my time was occupied with daily weight training sessions, cross-country ski trips, peak climbs, hikes, and teaching weekly yoga classes, I had little time for fundraising. Gary stepped up to the plate and began contacting audiology and hearing organizations, music magazines, local and out-of-state ENT doctors, as well as other affiliate organizations online to publicize EHC2. He worked tirelessly and got the attention of a local radio show host, had a number of articles written by audiologists, and even managed to get the support of the British Tinnitus Association in the UK! I made a few contacts with TV reporters, and got a few articles published in the *Rocky Mountain News* and *Denver Post*, yet Gary did the lion's share of work related to fundraising and publicity. I couldn't have done the climb without his support. I had hoped he would be able to accompany me to Seattle, yet was disappointed when he told me he had to work and couldn't get the time off. Helen, as Marketing Director of ATA, did her part to publicize the climb to all ATA members and kept the ATA website updated as funds came pouring in. She informed me that an "anonymous donor" had made an incredible donation of $100,000 and said he would match any donation of $100 or more. When hearing the news, I was ecstatic and stunned that someone I hardly knew would make such a generous donation.

A few months before the climb, I made another attempt to connect with a TV reporter, Kathy Walsh, from Channel 4 news (KCNC) in Denver and shared my story with her. She said she was busy and didn't think she would have time to cover the story, yet said she would keep in touch. I didn't hear from her and with total immersion in training soon forgot about hopeful thoughts of media coverage.

Three days before leaving for Seattle, I was preparing for an early morning appointment when the phone rang and there was Kathy asking if it was possible for us to meet that same morning within the hour. After recovering from the shock of hearing from her, and noticing that it was 9 a.m., I told her that I could meet her at Apex Recreation Center where I did my weight and elliptical machine training, between 10 and 10:30 a.m. Springing to action, I ran around the house like a maniac gathering backpack loaded with gear, trekking poles and boots, dashed outside to my truck and managed to make it to Apex still intact by 10:15 a.m. Kathy and photographer arrived soon thereafter and after exchanging greetings we headed downstairs to the weight room. Kathy asked if she could film me training on the elliptical machine and I was soon huffing and puffing away and trying to make the exercise appear effortless. After the elliptical episode, she interviewed me in a nearby conference room, told me the interview would be aired that evening, wished me good luck, and hurried out the door with photographer and huge camera in tow.

The story was aired as promised, and I marveled at the fact that my story received a full four-minute segment. At the start of the segment, Kathy surprised me with her humorous comment. She introduced the story with, "There's no spandex in this lady's future…" and I could hardly keep a straight face! Indeed, I was not ready for retirement just yet despite my advancing age of 55! Katy also caught the clip and we had a good laugh on the phone afterwards.

The day of our departure, July 12, 2007, finally arrived and Gary drove Katy and me to the airport amidst the flutter and flurry of craziness that always accompanies travel plus Katy's vet appointment that same morning. I noticed Gary whispering something to Katy as he dropped us off at the check-in, yet quickly forgot about it as we hurried to catch our flight.

We soon were whisked off to Seattle and our two-hour flight went without a hitch. It took us another three hours to drive from Seattle to Ashford and our destination for the evening, Alexander's Bed and Breakfast. It was a neat little place complete with beautiful wildflowers galore in the back garden and a quaint water wheel overlooking a pond behind the inn.

Katy and I stashed our gear in our room, headed downstairs for a quick bite, then back upstairs for a fun-filled night of packing and repacking our gear for the climb the next day. Katy crashed early and I crashed late as per usual. Katy slept like a log as she makes it her habit and I was awakened from a sound sleep by a familiar eye agony, (aka: corneal abrasion) that I've come to know all too well and often. Having dry eyes, I have developed a nightly routine of using eye drops and gel and this night was no different. Our room was hot with only a fan blowing on us and that was most likely the culprit. Recognizing the searing pain, I flooded my eyes with drops and gel, and fell back into a restless sleep hoping that the eye pain would resolve. It wasn't. The pain the next morning was relentless. *This is gonna be one long day, I sighed.*

DAY ONE (July 13, 2007)– The Journey Begins

I lay on the bed with a warm wet rag over my eye wondering how in hell I was going to do the climb with one good eye and the other on FIRE!!! Katy was looking at me with concern and trying her best to get me moving. She drove us and gear to IMG headquarters and we were a few minutes late, yet there nonetheless. I went on remote control from that point on with more packing and unpacking, loading and unloading gear, and meeting our guides and fellow climbers. After introductions, we got instructions from our guides as we stood in a garage amidst a torrential downpour outside. Just when I thought we would start our climb in the rain, it stopped. We piled all our gear in a huge van and away we drove to Mount Rainier National Park to begin this incredible adventure. While riding in the van, I tried to rest my eye and catch a few winks with my head resting on Katy's shoulder, yet due to nervous anticipation, failed miserably.

When we arrived at Paradise, I looked around for familiar landmarks, yet nothing seemed familiar due to everything being under construction. Even Paradise Inn was being remodeled. *What a difference seven years makes, I thought.*

By the time we hit the trail it was 11 a.m. Stumbling along with my flaming eyeball, it was difficult trying to keep up with Jeff and Katy. Trekking up Muir Snowfield that looked nothing like what I remembered, was a long and arduous plod especially carrying our heavy 40 pound packs. Finally reaching Camp Muir at 6 p.m., I was so tired I could barely stand much less try pulling my sleeping bag out of my pack. After carving out a place to crash in the hut, it was time for dinner in the form of a spicy hot Jambalaya. Not fond of spicy foods, yet feeling rather ravenous from the day's climb, I tried a few bites and my mouth felt like a raging inferno! I reached for my water bottle and practically drank the whole bottle! *So much for dinner, I thought,* until Jeff came through with another less flamboyant pasta dish he created and I ate ravenously.

After dinner, as we prepared to crawl into our bags, one of our guides, Mike Haugen, regaled us with stories of his Everest climb a few months earlier. We all sat transfixed at the chilling tale of his daring rescue of a Nepalese female climber who collapsed at around 27,000 feet and was left for dead by her teammates. Apparently, she was found lying unconscious in the snow and was thought to be dead, yet was suffering from either High Altitude Cerebral Edema, (HACE), or Pulmonary Edema (HAPE). In either condition, fluid accumulates in the brain and /or lungs and are both fatal without immediate treatment. After enlisting the help of his teammates, they managed to get her safely back down to a lower altitude where she could be transported by helicopter to a medical facility in Katmandu. Our mood was somber as we settled in for the night with thoughts of our own summit bid weighing heavily on our minds.

DAY TWO (July 14, 2007)– Ascent To High Camp

Mike woke us at 6 a.m. and after eating a quick breakfast of powdery cereal packets mixed with hot water, we headed outside to review self-arrest and crampon techniques with our guides. This is where the real climbing begins! I was so nervous I stood shivering in the early morning hours as Jeff, Katy and I donned harnesses, crampons and packs, roping ourselves together with Jeff in the lead, myself as middle man, and Katy bringing up the rear. Jeff informed us before leaving for high camp that this would be an easy day, estimating our climb to be around two hours. Jeff was right about the short part, yet the climb was far from easy. Jeff lead out around 9 a.m. and setting a steady pace we headed up Ingraham Glacier, a moderate slope. It was fairly windy at that point, yet the wind paled in comparison to what we would encounter the following day ascending to the summit.

Climbing steadily uphill into the wind for at least 45 minutes, we approached "Cathedral Gap," a huge prominence of rock and loose gravel that we needed to scale. Gazing up at this massif, I was filled with a sense of foreboding wondering how we would traverse up this very rugged terrain with crampons. I soon discovered that wearing crampons was far better than none and they proved themselves to be absolutely vital tools for providing traction and good foothold on extremely slick and treacherous terrain. The higher we climbed the more valuable they became.

We slowly and tediously made our way up The Gap, stopping for a few minutes rest break to catch a quick snack and check out some awesome views in every direction. As we sat eating our snacks, I tried to imagine where I stopped and was turned around on the first climb. Nothing about our current location was familiar. I certainly was tired, yet seeing the surrounding majesty from that dizzying height made me realize I had reached the highest point I had ever been on Rainier. This along with other thoughts of carrying the banner and all the people supporting me on this climb re-energized and spurred me onwards. By the time we reached the top of The Gap, I felt the effects of altitude and a wave of nausea and dizziness overcame me. Katy kept reminding me to eat and drink, yet I could just barely nibble on pieces of cheese I carried in my pack. We took another hour to cross the snowfield just past The Gap and finally reached High Camp at 11,500 feet by 11 a.m.

Seeing the tents already set up was a welcome sight, as the wind was blowing harder and making the temperature grow colder. I couldn't imagine having to set up tents with relentless and merciless winds thwarting our attempts. Katy and I picked a tent, stashed our packs inside and hunkered down. Katy took a nap and I wrote feverishly in my journal, documenting the day's events. So much had happened in the course of a few days it was difficult to describe it in words much less wrap my head around it. The only sounds I could hear were the flaps of our tent ferociously flapping in the wind and Katy's snoring. I envied Katy's uncanny ability to sleep through a hurricane! A short time later, I heard voices outside our tent and realized the other guides and climbers had arrived.

We passed the time resting and preparing for the arduous challenge of ascending to summit that lay ahead of us, only crawling out of our tent for latrine stops and a quick pasta dinner prepared by Jeff and guides in the mess tent. Our tent with gear strewn everywhere would have given the mess tent some stiff competition! Jeff told us during dinner that we should try to get as much sleep as possible as he would be giving us a wake-up call at 11 p.m.

Sometime after dinner, Katy and I hurried back to our tent and began packing for our summit bid. By the time we were done, it was getting too dark to write, and Katy was already snuggled into her bag. I tried to catch a snooze, yet found it impossible to sleep with the wind's relentless commotion outside. I tossed and turned and when facing towards Katy, would catch her peeking at me to see if I was asleep. I don't think either one of us got much sleep, yet Katy told me that I was snoring! Laughing aloud, I told her, "You should hear yourself some time!"

"Uh huh… she groggily agreed then drifted back into her snoring routine.

DAY THREE (7-15-'07)—Summit or Bust!

Spending endless hours lying awake, staring into the penetrating darkness and listening to the monotonous chatter of the wildly flapping tent, many thoughts were racing through my head. I imagined what reaching summit would look and feel like. I asked myself, *What would it take to go beyond what one expects the body to be capable of and break through self-imposed barriers?* And did I have that critical component lying dormant somewhere deep within? What if I didn't? I recalled the bitter disappointment of turning around and feeling so defeated and did not want to have to live with that same dejection this time around. My thoughts were interrupted by a male voice outside the tent, "Hey guys, it's time." *Too late to turn around now!*

Jeff came to wake us up at 11 p.m. as promised. I nudged Katy and after a few a moans and groans uttered from her side of the tent, I heard her say, "Oh hell, already?"

"Yep, its show time! Feeling nice and rested?"

"Shit… how about you, Donna dear?"

"Feeling feisty!"

"OK, dear, gotta go!" Suddenly, Katy sprang up from her bag and ran around the tent donning warm outer layers of clothing, headlamp, helmet and gathering her gear. Feeling dazed, confused and dog-tired, I marveled at her energy at that ungodly hour of nighttime. I made a feeble attempt to sit up in my bag and started looking around for my headlamp in the dim intermittent flashes of light shining from Katy's headlamp as she bounced around the tent. Donning her pack, she dashed outside the tent and disappeared into the night, then poking her head back through the front tent flaps, yelled at me, "You coming?"

Stirred out of my lethargy by the urgency in Katy's voice, I hesitantly emerged from my cocoon and instantly started shivering in the dark, bitter cold infiltrating what little warmth was generated in my bag. I quickly donned numerous layers of fleece, down jacket and climbing boots, grabbed headlamp, pack, helmet, and crampons and crawled out of the tent, bracing myself against the fierce, biting wind that greeted me.

Katy blew over to me and said, "Hey Dear, you need to get something to eat!" Turning into the wind, she headed for the mess tent and I followed. Jeff and Mike were inside slurping on hot drinks and preparing breakfast. I wasn't really hungry, yet gladly accepted the origami cup Katy handed me containing hot powdered cider. I remembered she bought the cup at the store the day before the climb and that seemed like eons ago. We had tons of gear, yet no real cups or eating utensils. Unable to stop shivering from the cold, I could barely hold onto the cup and spilled the cider all over myself. Jeff glanced over at me from his breakfast duties with a slight smile on his face.

"Ready, Donna? Drink up! You'll need the fluids to hydrate and keep warm!"

Why isn't he shivering? I wondered. Nodding at him and shaking was the best I could do at the moment.

After a few bites of whatever breakfast was prepared, it was back out into the fiercely frigid, relentless wind. Jeff and Mike sprang into action and started emptying our packs of everything other than bare essentials, such as food, water and an extra layer of warm clothes. Before long my pack felt light as a feather as compared to the load I carried up to that point. Sitting down on the cold, frozen snowy ground, I managed to get one crampon on, then started fidgeting around with the other one and felt my hands getting numb. Mike was suddenly by my side and, within a few seconds, the crampon was strapped onto my boot.

At around midnight, we were finally roped together and heading out of High Camp with Jeff in the lead and Katy behind me just as we had arrived hours before. We steadily climbed through the darkness with only thin beams of light shining from our headlamps. I wondered how Jeff could find the route in the darkness, yet he never wavered.

Dead ahead of us was a very challenging section of the mountain known as Disappointment Cleaver, and thus, the route we were on was called the D.C. route. Prior to the climb, I had read about this section and seeing pictures in books had filled me with fear in anticipation of navigating this route. Comprised of mixtures of snow, loose gravel and plenty of large rocks, the main danger is falling rocks. Being up close and personal, I had to face my fear head on, yet was glad to be climbing in the dark to not have to see where I was climbing.

My crampons, scratching and scraping against the gravelly and rocky sections, gave me confidence and good purchase on the treacherous terrain. Jeff scrambled up this section with amazing grace and the agility of a gazelle and would often stand above me gazing down as I struggled up the steep rocks and boulders yelling words of encouragement, like, "Way to go, Donna!" *Yes, we still have a way to go, yet I am remembering all the people with tinnitus who are with me in spirit and spurring me onwards and upwards...*

We finally took a rest stop atop The Cleaver and I sank down on my pack in exhaustion. Jeff reminded us to put on our down jackets and Gore-Tex® pants, as the 30-to-40 MPH winds would certainly do their best to give us hypothermia (dangerously low body temperature) in a heartbeat. He also told us some disappointing news that he might have to turn us around due to the blustery winds that were bombarding us from every direction. Katy and I exchanged nervous glances. After a short ten-minute break, we hit the icy trail once again.

After perhaps another hour or so of steady climbing, we reached the Icefall, an area of huge ice blocks (seracs) and wide crevasses (deep open cracks in glaciers), both plentiful enough to fulfill your wildest dreams and nerve-wracking nightmares! This section of the climb felt surreal as we plodded along a narrow, slippery ledge with only the light from our headlamps to guide us through the darkness. The sound of our crampons biting into the snow and ice beneath us put me into a trancelike state and made me feel remote and desolate. The only thing keeping me awake was the cold, biting wind pummeling us from above and below.

A female voice suddenly yelled something unintelligible from somewhere behind, awakening me from my reverie. The figure of another climber rushed by me still yelling to someone ahead. All I could see was a headlamp light fading into the frozen, barren distance ahead. Jeff was too far ahead of me to ask about the situation. Glancing behind me, I saw Katy keeping the pace and her presence was reassuring. To this day I don't know what had transpired.

Peering up ahead of me, I noticed Jeff was standing still and signaling for me to keep coming towards him. Drawing nearer, I noticed Jeff standing on the other side of a sizable expanse of crevasse. He called for me to stand at the edge of the crevasse and to "just jump over it!" With heart pounding and sweat pouring from every pore, I stood at the edge feeling an icy draft wafting up from the depths beneath my feet and dared not look down! Who is he kidding? "Donna, just DO IT!!!" he admonished. Scenes of the baby bird flying solo were bombarding my mind. *You can either stand here and freeze to death or feel the fear and do it anyway, I reprimanded myself.* Choosing the latter and throwing all caution to the wind, I did it! Backing up and running toward the edge, I leapt into the air over the crevasse, landing safe and sound on the other side next to Jeff. He grabbed my shaking hand, pulling me away from the edge and gave me a high five. With great relief, I watched Katy jump over the crevasse and soon thereafter with more high fivers all around, we proceeded onwards. There were more crevasses to cross up ahead, and we all made it across without incident, but another hair-raising section was soon to follow.

A short distance ahead was a huge serac towering over us, obstructing our path. There were only two ways to get around it: either ascending or descending. Jeff's plan was the latter and he pulled the rope with me in tow towards him with instructions to anchor down into the slope with my axe. Digging my axe into the snow above me, I leaned against the slope bracing my feet underneath for purchase and clung to my axe for dear life. Jeff told Katy to go first and I watched her slowly descend down the dark, narrow ledge hugging the serac and disappear from sight. Jeff stood next to me slowly paying out the rope as Katy progressed and called out to her periodically asking if she had found her way around the mammoth ice block. "No, not yet!" Katy's voice sounded far away. Waiting for what seemed like an eternity, we heard Katy yell back to Jeff that she made it! Knowing I was next in line, I felt relieved to finally release the death grip on my axe yet nervously anticipated trying to navigate around the serac. Slowly descending along the precarious ledge, I was hit with waves of intense anxiety. *Just keep moving and don't look down! I scolded myself.* Placing one foot at a time in front of me, searching for a solid foothold, I clung to the smooth, glassy ice with heart beating out of my chest. Finding solid purchase with one foot and praying that my crampons would hold me upright, I finally slid around to the other side. The anxiety now replaced with sheer relief at seeing Katy in front of me and we slapped each other more fivers.

"Hey, Katy?

"Huh?" she turned towards me.

"Slap me upside my head if I ever decide to do this insanity again, OK?"

"Remind me to remind you… she started and before she could finish her sentence, Jeff was standing next to her prodding us ever onwards.

A short while later, Katy suddenly pulled on the rope and yelled to Jeff to stop. Her headlamp went out and Jeff turned around to help her. I reminded her the night before the climb to change the batteries and wondered if she ever did? I welcomed the rest stop nonetheless. They were somehow able to get the light to work and we were finally once again on our way. It was slow going and as the terrain became steeper the higher we climbed, the wind felt like a battering ram crashing against us, making it difficult to stand. Leaning into the wind, I tried forcing my body to stand, yet was repeatedly being knocked down to the ground. While lying on the ground once again digging my ice axe into the snow with every last ounce of energy I had left, I looked up and saw the headlamps of my fellow climbers in a long procession winding their way up towards the summit, bringing back memories of the first climb. Recalling how I watched them so enviously from below sitting on my pack unable to stand, I realized that I was now part of that procession and was cheered at the thought! With renewed energy, I pulled myself back up and continued ascending. This pattern would repeat itself over and over again, being blown over after a few steps, struggling to get back up to a semi-standing position, only to be knocked down once again.

The relentless wind was now blowing snow and spindrift in my face and I discovered in amazement that it was daylight already. Glancing at my watch, I noticed it was after 6 a.m. and wondered how much farther we still had to climb. At another rest stop, we saw the familiar faces of the other team of climbers who left high camp after us and were now moving ahead. Exchanging words of encouragement, we watched them ascend toward the sky.

After our short rest stop, we continued ascending and once again I found myself lying on the ground, energy totally depleted and unable to get up.

"Donna, you have to stand up!" Jeff yelled down to me from above. Now he stood next to where I lay speaking words I had dreaded hearing from him and Liam years before, about turning around.

With every ounce of will power and energy I could muster, I somehow managed to grab my axe and pull myself upright to face Jeff. My heart sank as I fought back hot tears that seared my eyes despite the chilling snow and wind biting into my face.

"No, Jeff, please!" I knew we were somewhere close to the summit and thought about how difficult the climb had been just to get to this point, all the training Katy and I had done and about all the people I would be letting down if we turned around.

"How much farther to summit?"

"Another half hour at least."

"Jeff, I can do this! Give me another 15 or 20 minutes, OK?"

"OK." He stared at me, tiny flecks of ice clinging to his eyelashes. I'll check in with you in ten minutes."

Glancing quickly at his watch, we were once again ascending for another eternity and I followed close behind him somehow managing to stay upright. Thoughts of Gary, Barb and Helen came into my mind, giving me strength and renewed resolve.

The terrain was now beginning to level out and Jeff never did turn around. I noticed we were descending toward what appeared to be a huge crater where other climbers were congregating. Jeff suddenly turned around to face me and smiled.

"Guess where we are?" I stood there staring at him in disbelief at the realization of the moment. Tears of joy fell from my eyes and all I could utter over and over again was, "OH MY GOD!!!" "Donna, you did it!!! Jeff shouted at me amidst the swirling vortex of snow and raging wind.

Glancing at my watch, I noticed it was 7 a.m. and realized we had been climbing for eight hours almost non-stop with only a few short rest breaks. Throwing my arms around Jeff, I sobbed uncontrollably in pure ecstasy! I couldn't stop thanking him, yet he reminded me that our success was a team effort. Hearing his words reminded me that there were so many people working as a team to make EHC2 successful, and Gary's face suddenly popped into my head. He worked just as hard promoting the climb and I wished he were there with me sharing the experience! Katy passed us at that moment, and we slapped each other fivers; as we did on countless other peaks we scaled together. We hardly spoke, yet words didn't seem to matter at the time. The expression on her face spoke volumes as she sauntered onwards a short distance to check out another area of the crater.

Weary, yet elated, I sat down on my pack and looked around to try to catch a few glimpses of views from atop of Mount Rainier, yet the conditions were absolute white out, rendering checking out views next to impossible. Nothing else seemed to matter at that moment in time as I took in the whole experience. Jeff asked for my camera and handing it to him I remembered the ATA banner in my pack. Trying to get it out of my pack was an effort and trying to hold onto it so it wouldn't blow right out of my hand was a supreme challenge. Jeff shot a few pictures of me shaking like a leaf from exhaustion and exhilaration with the banner flapping wildly in the wind. I tried to smile, yet the tears kept on flowing, freezing and contorting my face. The realization of accomplishing a long sought-after goal was overwhelming!

After the short photo session, Jeff sat down next to me with a look of concern in his eyes. Handing me back my camera he said, "You need to eat and drink!" Wearily stashing camera and banner back in my pack, I stiffly turned to face him.

"You sound like Katy." Eating and drinking were the last things I thought of in that moment, yet realized he was right. All traces of appetite were worn away from effects of altitude and exertion. On the ascent, all I could eat were a few bites of cheese and bits of bread from Katy's sandwich creation given to me pre-climb, seemingly a million years ago. Jeff sprang into action pouring packets of Cliff Shots, a syrupy sweet energy supplement, down my throat. The raspberry flavor actually tasted pretty good and revived my dwindling energy reserves. "Thanks, Jeff!" I tried to smile between slurps. "I'm good!"

"C'mon, let's finish this off and then we need to start heading back down."

Jeff called out to Katy standing in the distance talking with a few climbers and before long we were roped together and descending with me leading out, Katy behind and Jeff bringing up the rear.

Starting descent, I was suddenly confronted with some of the most awesome panoramic vistas imaginable and stopped for a brief moment to take it all in. The winds were relenting and the clouds were starting to scatter, allowing the sun to peak through highlighting the surrounding mountain majesty with hues of lavender, peach, and blue. "Stunning!" I gasped glancing back at Katy who nodded and we shared the moment. Wishing my camera was within reach, I recalled it was stashed somewhere in my pack and inaccessible. Hearing Jeff's voice from behind reminded me to keep moving. The terrain we descended was every bit as steep as the ascent, only now I could see it very clearly in the daylight and focused my gaze and concentration on where my feet were stepping.

Descending at a fairly steady pace, we reached the Icefall within an hour or so and encountered the bottleneck. Before this climb, I had read about climbers backed-up and unable to move due to sheer numbers of other climbers, for example, at the Hilary Step, the last obstacle to climb before reaching summit on Everest. Now we were confronted with a similar situation. Jeff walked in front of me saying he would go first. Peering over his shoulder, I saw a huge serac perched precariously over heavily crevassed terrain and realized that same serac we encountered in the wee morning hours on ascent was the cause of the bottleneck.

Nervously watching climber after climber pulling themselves up the fixed rope with one hand and axe in the other, I was glad that Jeff offered to lead! *Thank God, I couldn't see this hideous beast in the dark on ascent or I surely would have turned around!* After perhaps a half hour wait, we finally reached the serac and Jeff started climbing up with the ease of a monkey frolicking in the trees of a jungle. It was soon my turn and Jeff yelled words of encouragement from above. I clipped my biner (locking device with safety closure) into the fixed rope, said some silent prayers and climbed up the serac. Making it to the top, I breathed a sigh of relief, said a few Hail Mary's, and watched Katy do a decent ascent. Slapping more fivers all around and we were once again descending.

After an hour of steady descent, we arrived back at High Camp. Heading for our tent, Katy and I started gathering all the gear we left behind in the wee morning hours that seemed more like days ago rather than hours. Realizing we had been on the move for 12 straight hours, we yearned to crawl into our sleeping bags to catch a nap, yet the guides kept reminding us to keep moving. We were pretty comical trying to pack in our exhausted state and after being on a roll, would suddenly stop and stare into space. It took us another hour to pack and grabbing a few handfuls of trail mix and cheese bits, we were once again on descent with heavy packs in tow.

In another few hours, we were approaching Camp Muir and I once again flashed back to my first climb recalling watching my fellow climbers returning from the summit and how envious I felt. Realizing that now, seven years later, I was returning from a successful summit bid brought tears of joy to my sleep-deprived eyes!

Back down at Muir, we shed crampons, ropes and harnesses, pausing for another brief rest. It was good to be able to move freely again and the realization of the hardest part of the climb now behind me brought feelings of indescribable relief. Watching teams of other climbers donning their climbing gear, I felt glad to be going in the opposite direction! Overcome with longing to be back down on solid ground once again and to finally stop moving, I knew we still had a few more hours to go descending the Muir Snowfield. Struggling to my feet, I tried hoisting my pack on my back for the last leg of the climb, yet the pack felt like I was carrying huge boulders on top of all the gear. I carried two water bottles and my pack had only one pouch for a water bottle, so the other was left dangling from my hip strap. Too exhausted to reattach the last bottle to the strap, I left it behind lying on some rocks outside the hut for another climber to put to good use.

Our guides and fellow climbers were anxious to glissade down the Snowfield and Katy was already sitting on the snow raring to go. As my legs felt like jelly and could barely hold me up, I decided to follow suit. We left Muir sailing down the Snowfield on our butts and making quite the commotion in the process. What fun to be cruising down the slope full speed ahead using our feet and axes to navigate, wind in our faces and whoops of jubilation filling the air! Cruising along I was reminded of sledding as a kid, yet soon the others were far ahead and I paused to catch my breath. Mike suddenly appeared standing over me offering a ride. Before I could even respond, he grabbed my trekking poles shouting over his shoulder to "hold on" and took off running like a cheetah down the Snowfield!

Gasping in amazement at how little effort he expended loping down the slope with me in tow, I wondered if he was going to pull me all the way down the mountain! As if reading my mind, he stopped long enough to ask how I was doing and we were off again in a heartbeat. Hanging on and enjoying the ride of a lifetime, I suddenly lost my grip on one of the poles and slowed to a grinding halt in the snow. Mike paused looking back in my direction and I waved him onward. Holding his hand to his chin and pondering the situation, he disappeared over the lip of the Snowfield. Trying to stand was fruitless, so I just sat there taking in the awesome scenario and a well-deserved rest break.

Before long, I was going it solo and enjoying a saner glissade. Cruising along, I saw someone was glissading at warp speed past me yelling, "Yeeehaaaaaaaa!" and recognized the voice as Katy's. I followed in close pursuit and caught up with her after a few minutes, then soon fell behind once again. I noticed the wind was beginning to die down, yet clouds were steadily rolling in and creating a grey, overcast sky. In the foggy distance, I saw one of our guides, Jenny, trekking at a good clip with the faster climbers down the Snowfield and Katy got up stepping into pace with the group. They were heading down to an area where other climbers were resting. Glissading over a few remaining hills, with more gusto, I soon caught up to the group and paused for a well-needed rest. Once back amongst the group, I gulped some water, stuffed more handfuls of trail mix into my hungry, parched mouth, and snapped a few pictures. Soon we were back on our descent.

Once back on solid ground, it felt good to be upright and walking on a paved trail again, yet the hike back down was not an easy one. My feet were hurting big time from hitting against heavy boots and my toes felt like shredded meat! While each step brought more agony and pain, it also brought us closer to Paradise and REST! Katy was far ahead of me descending at a good clip and when I would catch up with her at brief rest stops, there was not much conversation between us. We both just wanted to stop moving!!! During that endless descent, I often wondered where Jeff was and assumed he was somewhere ahead with Katy or even as far down as Paradise. Then suddenly, I'd hear footsteps behind me, turn and see Jeff following me. A few times he would pass me with a "Hey," and then I would lose track of him, only to catch him following me again. The hours passed in a blur of feet pain and utter exhaustion.

Glancing up from dazedly staring at the ground, I noticed numerous hikers passing me along the trail. Recognizing familiar landmarks from our days-ago ascent, I knew we were finally close to Paradise. As the temperature got warmer, I shed my too-warm outer layers, yet still wore the blue liner gloves my friend Roz had given me months before. I knew Helen and other ATA staff members were waiting somewhere at Paradise, planning a celebration party back at Alexander's and longed to be back there with them. I also thought about Gary, missing him tremendously and wishing he could be waiting at trail's end, yet sadly remembered him saying he had to work. A few times I imagined seeing him standing up ahead near the trailhead, yet was disappointed seeing it was someone else. Approaching the trailhead, my pace quickened as I noticed Katy and Jeff now standing directly up ahead. Wearily dragging my body those last few steps after seventeen hours of continual motion, I finally reached trail's end and was suddenly filled with an overwhelming sense of relief that this journey was finally complete!

After slapping Katy and Jeff fivers, I asked Jeff to put my gloves in my pack, as any further movement was a supreme effort. Intending to shed my heavy pack, I glanced around the area for a place to sit, and saw out of my peripheral vision a lady seated on a nearby bench with camera in hand snapping pictures in my direction. Thinking she was photographing someone else I stepped back, yet she followed me with her camera. She then lowered the camera revealing her smiling face and called to me, "Hi, Donna!" Her voice was instantly recognizable as that of Helen Connor, the ATA staff person I had been in contact with for months prior to the climb. With sewing machine legs and whole body shaking, I staggered down the steps leading down from the trail and was soon wrapping my arms around Helen in a huge bear hug embrace. All trace of exhaustion quickly dissolved into the warmth of her embrace and jubilance of the moment! Sobbing with joy into her blouse, I apologized for giving her a good and proper soaking. I can't recall what words were exchanged during our embrace other than her sincere congratulations, and her saying, "Donna, there's someone else waiting to see you!" Just when I thought, *it doesn't get any better than this,* it did!

Helen pointed to some shady-looking guy standing a few feet away wearing a big sun hat that partially hid his face, who was pointing a video camera at me. It didn't take very long to recognize who this shady character was! "OMG!" I screamed at the realization that it was Gary behind the camera filming the whole scene. His description of the moment would probably go something like this: "All of a sudden, this lunatic lady wearing a huge pack on her back came charging at me smelling like an overheated pit bull with arms wildly flailing and legs all akimbo, and only when she tackled me to the ground did I discover it was my wife!" His description would have to suffice as words at that moment for me were non-existent. Watching what little video footage was retrievable, gave us a bird's eye view of that magical moment in time and a bit of comic relief seeing a body catapulting through space at Gary and watching the video camera bouncing wildly around on the ground.

After more photos and conversations with Helen, Katy, and Jeff, we said so

long to Helen, who was heading to Alexander's for the post climb dinner celebration. Katy and I hobbled after Gary who lead the way back to where he parked
his rental car claiming it was right around the corner, which was actually at least
another mile hike down the road. We made it back to Alexander's in about ten
minutes flat and after dropping me off, Gary drove Katy back to IMG headquarters to chat with Jeff and Jenny.

Walking gingerly towards the lobby of Alexander's, I noticed a tall brown-
haired lady approaching me wearing a huge grin. She warmly greeted me and
introduced herself as Jennifer DuPriest, an ATA staff member I hadn't ever
met. We had spoken a few times on the phone and suddenly we were wrapped
in a warm embrace. I recalled that Helen informed me two weeks before the
climb that she was dismissed from ATA and that Jennifer was replacing her.
I felt disappointed as I did when Barb left ATA since I had developed a rapport with Helen over the months we were in contact prior to the climb. But
I got to know Jennifer quite well over dinner that night and established a connection with her as well. Helen then approached me. I saw that another lady
was standing behind Helen, yet I couldn't tell who she was, since I was involved in more bear hugs and conversation with Helen and Jennifer.

Glancing over Helen's shoulder as we embraced, I suddenly recognized the
lady's voice. It belonged to none other than Barb, my long lost friend and initial
ATA contact person. I gasped in surprise to see her again with memories of meeting her at the ATA office after the first climb flashing through my mind as though
it happened just yesterday.

"Barb!" I stammered and before she could reply we were like magnets drawn
to the other madly embracing and as previously with Helen, I flooded Barb's shirt
with tears of joy.

"Congratulations, you mountain woman, you!" Barb's familiar cheery voice
chimed in my ears. Finally breaking free from Barb's warm embrace, I tried to
find the words to describe the jubilance I felt at that moment, realizing that Barb,
Helen and Jennifer had driven three or four hours from Portland, Oregon to join
in the celebration of achieving my seven-year dream!

"Barb, Helen, and Jennifer, thank you so much from the bottom of my heart
for being here!"

"No, Donna. Thank YOU for all you have done for ATA and for millions of
people across the country with tinnitus!" Barb declared, her face beaming. Engrossed in the moment, I had totally forgotten about the climb and all the fatigue,
aches, and pains involved. Here these ladies were congratulating and gushing over
me and I felt they were the ones to be honored for their role in helping pull off
this harebrained stunt!

Katy and Gary arrived shortly thereafter and after introductions all around we took more photographs in the beautiful flower garden behind Alexander's. Then it was off to dinner. The hours flew by interspersed with good food and conversations with our new friends. During our conversation, Jennifer told me that my climb had already generated $220,000 in donations. My jaw dropped to the ground. She continued by saying that thus far my climb had generated the largest sum of money raised for ATA by any previous fundraising campaign, and I stared at her in disbelief. She then invited Gary and me to be guests of honor at their next board meeting in October in Dallas, Texas. Stunned at her offer, I could hardly respond. I had seldom before been honored for anything, yet felt thrilled at her invitation and accepted her offer. I was later to find out at the meeting that people were still donating well after the climb and the amount soared to an incredible $350,000! A few acclaimed musicians, Al Di Meola, lead guitarist of Return to Forever with Chick Corea, and Sonny Landreth, slide guitarist extraordinaire added their own donations, much to my amazement.

During dinner Helen asked me, "So, what's next for you, Donna?" and I paused with uncertainty not knowing how to answer her question. My body, running on adrenaline for months on end, was now wanting nothing more than to sleep. I felt a tremendous sense of accomplishment of a goal and satisfaction that the money generated by the climb was going to a good cause.

"I think I'm ready to do absolutely nothing for a while and catch up on some sleep!" Everyone present appreciatively nodded.

The evening finally ended as ATA staff had to get back to Portland. Waving goodbye to them, I felt a sense of sadness for the departure of newfound friends. To this day, the fond memories of this incredible adventure of a lifetime still linger. The ending of an era always precedes the dawning of yet another.

CHAPTER 24

SECOND CHANCES
(2011-2013)

"You can do the impossible, because you have been through the unthinkable."
— Christina Rasmussen

Life is full of opportunities and risks. We can either take advantage of them or choose to postpone them, yet whatever our decision may be, we can be certain they will find us when least expected. Either way, it's a choice. And if we come to realize over time that it was an unwise choice, do we live the rest of our lives regretting it? Or if miraculously we get another chance to do it over again and choose differently, do we take that second chance? In 2012, Gary and I found ourselves unexpectedly faced with that choice. It started with a phone call that changed our lives and turned our world upside down.

Wednesday, Feb. 1, 2012

"May I speak to Donna Brown?" a strange male voice eagerly asked on the phone.

"Who is this?"

"My name is Rob Sevier from Numero Group and I am calling from Chicago. Are you Donna?" Puzzled by the mysterious voice and purpose of the call, my first thought was that this was a prank.

"Yes, this is she. Why are you calling and what is Numero Group?

"I understand you used to play in a band back in the '70s called Medusa and I heard your music and am a big fan," Rob replied. Stifling a laugh, I thought, *This has to be a telemarketing prank!*

"How did you get hold of our music and how did you find us?" I was incredulous and ready to hang up.

"A friend gave me a 45 of yours. I have also been in contact with your old singer, Peter, and he said you and Gary were living in Colorado."

"We played that music back in the early '70s. Where did this friend of yours find the 45?" I wondered whatever became of those 45s that each band member received, but was drawing a blank. I suddenly recalled seeing a 45 lying somewhere around the house collecting dust.

"He found it at a record convention and gave it to me." Rob's voice interrupted my thoughts.

"OK, so I still don't get why you would be so interested in music of the '70s? What's your connection to this music?"

"Seventies music is hot right now and vinyl is making a resurgence as well."

"NO WAY!!!" *That music went out with the dinosaurs, for God's sake!*

"Do you still have the original recordings of your music?"

Once again, I wracked my brains trying to recall if Gary had kept any of the old tape recordings from when we rehearsed way back when in his garage.

"Perhaps Gary has a few old cassettes that Pete recorded, yet little else. Besides, what would you do with them anyway?"

"I would like to try to get a hold of the original recordings and release an album." Dead silence. I found myself barely breathing. *Is this guy for REAL???*

"Don't tell me you're a music producer?" It was actually more sarcasm than a question.

Rob chuckled. "Well, I guess you could call me that, but I'd say more of a musical archivist."

"So, let's do a recap here. If I understand you correctly, you're telling me you'd like to make an album of our music?"

"Yes, most definitely." My heart was pounding away. I wanted to believe him, yet my inner critic was not a believer at that moment. *Things like this just don't happen to everyday ordinary folks like you, the critic reminded me.*

"Do you know if Lee has the original recordings?"

"We haven't heard from him in years. He lives in Nederland. You could try calling him and, oh, by the way, tell him to give us a call sometime."

"OK, I plan on contacting him next. I'd also like to talk to Gary sometime. Gotta get going here. Nice talking with you, Donna." And that's how it all started.

After our conversation, I sat for a few minutes in a daze, feeling like I had just been hit by a hurricane. Memories of Lee, Kim, and Pete wearing his brown fringe vest and shaking his tambourine flooded my mind like a tidal wave. *Wouldn't it be something to reunite with them again and play the great music we used to play back in the day?* Picturing Kim brought feelings of deep sadness, as he had passed away around the same time as my last Rainier climb and I missed him tremendously. I was right back in Gary's garage immersed in the moment and music we created. Picturing Gary in the garage playing guitar reminded me that I needed to let him know what had just transpired with Rob. I called him at work.

"Hey, what's up? Gary asked.

"Are you sitting down?"

"Yeah, why? I'm always sitting in front of a computer."

"Well, I just got a very strange phone call from a guy named Rob Sevier from Numero Group in Chicago and he wants to make an album from our Medusa music."

"Really? Who is this guy anyway and how did he get hold of our music?" Gary excitedly queried. As I recounted the whole story to him, I heard dead silence on the other end.

"Are you still there?" *Gotta love these cell phones, I sighed thinking we were disconnected.*

"Yeah, I'm still here. Wow... ain't that some shit?" Gary was just as floored listening to the story as I had been hearing it from Rob.

We bantered back and forth for another 15 minutes not knowing what to make of the situation. We were both in a state of shock that anyone would be even remotely interested in our music. Chicago's music scene at the time focused on horns rather than what was called, "Prog Rock," (aka: Progressive Rock), or music that was more experimental and psychedelic, not the typical pop songs you heard on the radio. Rob's phone call was the catalyst for reigniting our passion for playing music and reuniting the band after almost 40 years.

A few days after the call, we were all writing emails to each other on a daily basis and talking periodically on the phone. It was strange, yet wonderful to be in communication with the guys after so many years and hearing about life on their side of the world. Pete was married to his lovely wife Dawnn, had a 29-year-old son, lived in the Chicago suburb of Bloomingdale, and worked in a bolt factory. He regaled us with his sob stories of getting hit with tons of snow. Remembering all the snow and blizzards that I ran through when living back in the Windy City generated a few appreciative chuckles and little sympathy. I wrote him an email reminding him to bring his skis if he ever came out to visit in Colorado. He had joined another band and we would send mp3s back and forth of our music with lengthy reviews on a daily basis.

We found out that Lee still had the original four- and two-track reel-to-reel tapes we recorded in his basement. They had been sitting in his closet collecting dust. Luckily for us, he dusted the tapes off, drove down to a place in Greenwood Village called DVD Memories and had them all transferred to a CD to listen to. He stopped by our house to visit on the return trip to drop off the CD. We had since been up to visit him and his wife, Kathy, at their cabin in Nederland and it was good seeing them again and renewing old times. Lee, unfortunately, told us he had hung up his drumsticks which made us sad, as we knew he played some mean drums once upon a time. Although Lee didn't want to play anymore, he played a key role in the process of turning the old worn out, rusty tapes into an album.

After listening to the music on the tapes converted to CD to make sure the music was still there after so many years, he prepared the actual tapes and mailed them off to Rob as per his request. A year later our album, First Step Beyond, was released by Numero Group and our lives would never be the same.

At the time of Rob's phone call, I was anticipating surgery on my right wrist to repair torn cartilage resulting from a zip-lining excursion. The previous summer Gary and I drove down to Buena Vista to celebrate my birthday. We were enjoying zipping with wild abandon through mid-air above the trees, but we were in for a rude awakening at the end of the ride. The guides sent a wooden block along the line to stop us that slammed against the cam, a mechanized wheel, that hit our hands. Neither Gary nor I recall the guides informing us to take our breaking hand off the zip-line when finishing the ride. Consequently, both our right hands were sore and swollen. Gary's hand was far more swollen, yet he escaped from the experience relatively intact. I suffered a broken wrist and torn cartilage, unknown at the time. Early the next morning, I donned a hefty backpack and climbed Mount Antero, a 14'er, broken wrist and all. After several months of outdoor activities and unrelenting wrist pain, I saw a hand specialist who took x-rays and informed me of my injuries and the need for surgery.

It was an emotional roller coaster after Rob's call, yet it provided welcome distraction from the nervous anticipation of undergoing surgery. There were other distractions to deal with at the time like having to put down our beloved canine companion, Jack, and getting bitten by my neighbor's dog on the other arm a few days afterward, then spending Valentine's Day in the ER. Those were some of the worst "Dog Days" I can remember. On a more positive note, a certain incident that occurred the previous summer inspired a songwriting flurry creating, in my opinion, some of my best and most heartfelt songs.

On a scorching hot summer day sometime in June 2011, Gary and I were hiking through the Grand Canyon. After a while he was lagging behind along the dry, parched trail that led down into the canyon. Both of us carried plenty of water, food, and gear and thought we were prepared for any mishap we might encounter. Not by a long shot. Soon Gary came to a halt next to a bunch of boulders, and wearily sat down on a boulder informing me he was "done!"

After making sure he was alright, I left him drinking water and eating a snack, telling him I would hike on ahead for another mile or so to check out more of the trail and scenery.

About a half hour later, I noticed a lady limping on the trail just ahead of me and grew concerned. Catching up to this lady, I asked if she was OK and she seemed pretty tired, yet told me she was doing alright. Striking up a conversation, she told me her name was Ava, and that she had knee surgery just a few months prior. Staring at her, I couldn't believe that she was undertaking such an arduous activity like hiking the Grand Canyon so soon after surgery! She was barely able to walk, much less hike. She was also low on her water supply. Seeing her in a dehydrated and incapacitated state, I somehow convinced her to turn around and we walked back down the trail to where Gary was resting. During our rest stop, I gave Ava some water from my supply and wrapped her knee with an ace bandage in my pack.

The heat was unrelenting, Ava and Gary were both exhausted and we still had a good three or four miles of steep, rocky terrain to hike to get back up to the trailhead. Realizing the urgency of the situation, I started heading back up the trail toward the trailhead with Ava and Gary following behind, stopping every few minutes to give them brief rest stops. With each stop, Ava and I conversed, and I got to know her better and felt an instant connection. She informed me she was an opera singer and was planning on traveling to Vienna to continue her operatic studies. Each step was a struggle for her and ongoing concern for me, yet she continued onwards fueled by mere adrenaline.

Passing a few horses and riders heading down into the Canyon, I yelled to the leader asking if he could take some tired hikers back up to the Rim. He shook his head, telling me he was heading down, not up! After spending hours plodding along with Ava and Gary on the dusty trail, we managed to safely reach the Rim trailhead where Ava's mother, Donna, was anxiously awaiting Ava's return. We exchanged contact information and then went our separate ways. I often thought of her in the following months, sent her a few emails and wondered whether she ever made it to Vienna, yet heard no reply.

After the release of our album, in February 2013, things started to swing in an uphill direction. Our album was a worldwide hit! First Step Beyond received rave reviews in several magazines, (i.e. *Mojo, Uncut, Record Collector,* and *Terrorizer*) and was receiving airplay on a number of radio stations in New York and New Jersey. We were even interviewed on a few local radio stations including KVCU radio 1190 in Boulder and KUHS Radio in Denver. Our music was all over the Internet. After someone downloaded our whole album on YouTube, our music was listened to by thousands, our albums selling like hot cakes in record stores, and fans writing to us everywhere from Sweden to Australia! It was hard to imagine that dinosaurs in their 60s were suddenly rock stars. Rob wasn't joking when he told me that "music of the '70s is hot!" Good thing I didn't hang up on him!

Around the end of March 2013, I received some shocking news online. Noticing I was receiving a number of odd emails from total strangers expressing their sentiments about missing Ava, I tried sending her another email, yet again got no reply. Desperate to hear some news about Ava, I sent an email to Donna asking if she was OK. Donna's response was immediate and devastating! She informed me that Ava had taken her life just days prior to my email at the tender age of 33. I sat gazing at the computer screen in shock and disbelief feeling a flood of tears pouring down my face. "No! No! It can't be," I sobbed envisioning Ava so full of life just months before hiking with her through the Canyon. In the weeks following Ava's desperate deed, I felt her presence several times. On one occasion, I heard an actual choir being sung amidst the sound of water falling all around me while I showered.

Feeling utterly desolate and inconsolable one day, I tried to make sense of Ava's senseless act and wrote a tribute song to her called, "Ava Bella." The song recounts the story of our chance encounter in the Canyon and, although never published, it helped me grieve and eventually come to terms with her loss. It also inspired me to keep writing songs and hammered home the fact that we need to keep doing the things we are passionate about as LIFE IS SHORT!

Anxious to reunite with Pete, and meet Rob, we traveled back to Chicago in May 2013 and had quite the reunion. It was good spending time with Pete and Dawnn in their tiny apartment with two cats, walking down once familiar streets now more crowded with traffic than I ever recalled, and having a surprise breakfast get-together with Art Shan, the once frizzy Hendrix-haired guitarist who took my place in the band when I left for nursing school.

We talked for hours about old times in the band and he caught us up with his life post-Medusa. His hair was more civilized yet still fairly curly, and it seemed like married life, and playing daddy to two small children, agreed with him.

After spending time with Art, we took a trip to the south side of Chicago to visit with Rob Sevier and tour the Numero Group office. From the outside, the building looked more like a refurbished brick brownstone house rather than a record label headquarters.

It was great finally getting to meet Rob and other staff members in the office and get lavished with praise for our music. We heartily thanked him for giving our music worldwide recognition, reuniting band members and pulling us away from the abyss of eternal obscurity. Rob thanked us in return. "The honor is ours. We listen to your music every day and really dig it! Smiling, he shook our hands enthusiastically as did all office staff. He took us on a tour of Numero Group and regaled us with history of the company, how it got started in 2003 with just himself and another business partner, Ken Shipley, and how they built their name and reputation to achieve world-wide acclaim and even a Grammy nomination. (25.)

The next day we visited some record stores and received the same enthusiastic response from the owners who raved about our music and likewise told us they were big fans. We were amazed and bewildered by all the fanfare we received, yet enjoyed the attention and adulation nonetheless. Even more confusing was trying to relearn all the songs on *First Step Beyond* after so many years. Playing guitar in those days without a proper tuning device, I just tuned my guitar by ear and the guys tuned to me, so there was never any definite key we played in. Also, trying to replicate the intricate time changes and spacey guitar jams was a bit of a challenge and kept our brains from dissolving into sawdust.

A few days later, Pete arranged for us to do a jam session that was another moment in time! He introduced us to his friend, Mark, a drummer, and told us he had a surprise guest who would be sitting in on the session. We met at Mark's house and started setting up our equipment. Mark's house was rather small and the only room big enough to accommodate all of our equipment was up in his sweltering hot attic. Carting equipment up the narrow stairs was task enough, and when we got up to the attic the temperature felt like at least 100 degrees in the shade! I had to settle for playing an old broken down mini-keyboard that belonged to Mark, as I didn't feel like lugging both my Hammond SK-1 or Korg X3 on the airplane.

As the guys were setting up, I sauntered outside to cool off and catch some fresh air. Not outside for more than a few minutes, I noticed another car pull up and a tall, lanky, sandy-haired guy got out and approached me. Watching him draw nearer, I thought there was something familiar about him yet I couldn't figure out what it was.

"Hey, Donna! Good to see you!" he exclaimed. Suddenly recognizing who this surprise guest guy was, I ran into his arms and we clung to each other for some time. Breaking free of his hold, I stood for a few moments looking into the eyes and face of Fred Porzelt, our old roadie! The last time we saw him, he was just a 16-or 17-year-old kid, stringy of hair and spindly of frame, putting extra flash powder in our light pods, almost setting the place and whole band on fire! He looked older of course, yet still had a youthful appearance and exuberance about him.

"Fred! I exclaimed. "Man, what a surprise! Will you be joining us for the jam?"

"Yep! I'm gonna jam with you guys." He was holding a guitar case in hand

and I didn't recall him playing any instrument back in the "Gary's garage" days.

"Are you playing guitar?"

"Nope, bass." I vaguely remembered a phone conversation last year with Pete mentioning something about Fred learning to play bass and made the connection.

"Wow! COOL!!! Can't wait to hear you play. Let's head upstairs and by the way, hope you brought your swimsuit for the sauna." Fred just laughed. We had a great jam with Pete once again at the mic, Mark on drums, Fred getting down on his bass, Gary wailing away on his guitar and myself banging away like Schroeder of Charlie Brown fame on a broken-down excuse for keyboards. Time flew by, yet it seemed like no time had elapsed.

While there in Chicago, we visited with another person I hadn't seen in forever—my cousin, Susie. She and I had more in common than I thought. We were both into the same music scene in the '60s and most likely even attended the same concerts back then, even though we were each doing our own thing at the time. It was good catching up with her, and of course, stuffing our faces at our favorite pizza place, Barnaby's. When the going gets tough in Chicago, the tough eat pizza!

Returning back to Colorado, we were inspired to somehow keep our jam session going despite thousands of miles between us. We kept in contact with Pete and Fred and recorded separate musical tracks of songs to send via mp3's back and forth via email. Fred, Pete, and Mark tried their best to dub in their separate tracks, yet it was difficult to keep the project going over the distance and we soon gave up on it. Gary and I decided we would reform the band locally, and somehow it finally all came together over the next few months and into 2014.

CHAPTER 25

ANOTHER MOUNTAIN TO CLIMB (2013)

"The mountains are calling and I must go."
— John Muir

In between trying to audition new band members, I decided to do another fundraising climb for ATA in the summer of 2013, and added the challenge of training for the climb to the mix. With the experience of climbing Mount Rainier six years prior still fresh in my mind, I still craved more outdoor adventure and wanted to relive the whole experience this time on Mt. Hood (11,250 feet) in Oregon.

Gary and I flew to Portland, Oregon, on July 10. Leaving the plane and walking through the terminal, I heard my name being called. Glancing around, I saw Cara James, my contact person, and several other ATA staff members waving and holding signs that said, "Way to Go, Donna!" I was thrilled to see them and once again put faces to their names. At the time of our meeting, Cara was the Executive Director of ATA. I first spoke to her a few months prior to the climb when she first started working at ATA. Jennifer was now married, pregnant with her first baby, and living in Arizona. In pre-climb conversations with Jennifer, she told me about staff changes at ATA and introduced me to Cara who then was Jennifer's assistant. Like Helen, during our initial phone conversation, Cara was a bit skeptical when I informed her of my plans to do a climb on Hood, but after several chats she became more enthusiastic. I had also been in contact with Barb and informed her of the climb and she mentioned she might be available to meet with us afterwards.

About a month before our departure to Portland, my cousin Susie sent an interesting email notifying me that Becky, another cousin I hardly knew, had climbed Hood the previous month and put me in touch with her. The only time I recall meeting her was when she was just a kid of 13 at my Aunt Dolly's house. Every time we went to Dolly's house it was an event. Dolly was a fabulous cook and made tons more food than a house full of people could possibly eat. I knew as little of Ma's and Dolly's sister, my Aunt Butchie, as I did of Becky, Butchie's adopted daughter. Ruth Popel, (aka: "Butchie") traveled around the globe and brought us small souvenirs from the exotic places she visited. She stayed around long enough to hand us dolls, pens, and assorted trinkets as souvenirs, then out the door she went to fly off to another foreign paradise.

Eventually, she married and settled down in Pottstown, Pennsylvania. Becky and I didn't have much interaction that day many years earlier when we met at Dolly's. But the stage was set for our future encounter.

When hearing the news from Susie about Becky's Hood climb, I immediately called her wanting to reconnect. She was glad to hear from me and we talked at length about her Hood experience and shared a few laughs about the irony of our situation. I learned that Becky, much like her mom, also had wanderlust and traveled around the country with her husband Tom in their RV. Luckily, they were still in Oregon vacationing at the time. She said she would like to connect with me post-climb and I could hardly wait to meet her after so many years. Whatever compelled me to do the Hood climb a month after a long-lost cousin would climb the same mountain is either a good story for sitting around the campfire or perhaps a twist of fate. The universe does indeed work in strange ways!

Cara had arranged for complimentary rooms at Best Western Mt. Hood Inn for Gary, me, and Katy to stay that night and for Gary the next night. Katy planned to fly in on her own and was to meet us sometime later that afternoon. Gary and I passed the time doing some sightseeing around the small town of Government Camp where we stayed. As it drew close to 5 p.m., Katy had still not arrived and I started to get worried. As Gary and I hiked around the area looking for a place to eat dinner, I received a call from Katy explaining she had missed her plane and wouldn't be arriving in Portland until later that evening.

"Hey, make sure you don't miss this next flight, OK? Otherwise, Jeff and I will just have to start without you!" I chided. "We're supposed to meet Jeff bright and early tomorrow at 8:30 a.m."

"Don't worry, dear, I'll be there eventually." Katy tried to be reassuring, but was obviously pissed that she missed the flight. I recalled her telling me that she had to work the day we were leaving for Oregon and wondered why she didn't take the day off. But I knew she was far more work-oriented than her climbing partner.

Later that evening, still waiting for Katy, Gary and I had a lengthy get-to-know-each-other conversation with Cara in her room. We talked about many topics, mostly about ATA and her goals for the organization to become a better source of information and support for people with tinnitus. I shared my story with her and we found her to be very sympathetic and open to us sharing our ideas and comments. She even told us she planned to see Katy and me off on our journey the next morning.

As Gary and I were grabbing a quick breakfast in the dining area of the Inn the next morning, I looked up to see Katy stumbling down the stairs to join us and was relieved to see she had made it. She joined us for some coffee and snacks and told us she had arrived fairly late the night before and was still pretty wiped out. I wondered how she would do on the climb, yet quickly got involved in the commotion of final preparations for our journey.

After breakfast, we met with Jeff in our room and did a gear check with him, then rushed off to meet with Cara in the parking lot. Cara took pictures of Katy, Jeff and me holding the ATA banner for the climb before we headed up the trail leading to the ski lift that would take us up to the ski area where we would start our ascent.

As we hiked along the trail, Gary was doing his best paparazzi imitation of jogging along beside us snapping pictures to document the three of us embarking on our adventure. I wondered how he got all his energy, as Gary was not really a runner. The only time I saw him run was to get to his car in a hurry. Hiking along, I felt slow and very tired with the weight of my pack weighing heavily on my back and I wondered how Katy was doing. Glancing over at her walking beside me, she looked strong and steady as did Jeff.

I was not fond of ski lifts and would normally have preferred hiking up to the ski area, yet Jeff suggested we take the lift to help conserve our energy for the climb.

We took two lifts up to the ski area with Gary snapping pictures of us from below. As we rode, the panoramic vistas of Hood from the lift took my breath away and presented glimpses of the challenge that lay ahead. The day was bright and sunny and Hood appeared directly in front of us like a huge mass of volcanic rock and glaciers protruding from out of nowhere.

The ski area (elevation 8,600 feet) was packed with skiers rushing around us and we were anxious to begin the climb in earnest. Jeff lead the way up the snow-field and soon we were climbing high above the skiers and glad to be away from the maddening crowd. We climbed for a few hours at a steady pace. At our first rest stop, we ate a few snacks for energy and took in some awesome views of surrounding peaks such as Mt. Adams, St. Helens, Jefferson to the north, and my old friend, Rainier, to the south.

After about three-to-four hours of steady climbing, we reached High Camp at

9,500 feet around 3 p.m. and made our camp for the night. There was little wind to speak of, unlike on Rainier, which made our tent set-up a breeze. Jeff set up his tent a short distance below where our tent was situated and settled in for the evening leaving Katy and me to do our own settling. Katy busied herself with cooking dinner and I busily started taking pictures from our rocky perch. High Camp looked like one big lopsided rock quarry and our tent was precariously perched on a downward facing slope that made me feel dizzy gazing down at it from above.

We didn't need to worry about it sliding down the slope as it was tightly cinched down with ropes tied around rocks.

Katy and I passed the evening gazing at the stunning view and talking about the next day's summit climb. With packs ready to go and spirits soaring high, we retreated to the tent for some shut eye around 6 p.m., as we had a 3 a.m. wake up the next morning. I was so full of adrenaline, sleep was the last thing on my mind and spent the next few hours walking around the tent area taking more photos. Katy was sound asleep and didn't hear me get up and leave.

Jeff was nowhere in sight and I assumed he was also tucked in for the night. As another hour passed, I sat on some rocks staring out into the twilight distance at the city lights down below and decided to give Gary a call. He was glad to hear from me and said he had just awakened from a nap and wondered why I wasn't doing the same. We talked for five minutes or so and he wished me good luck on tomorrow's climb. The wind was picking up a bit and feeling the chill of cold mountain air biting at my exposed face, I headed into the tent for the night. Curling up inside my bag, I fell into an intermittent, restless sleep.

Three a.m. came fast, and suddenly we heard Jeff's voice outside the tent giving us a wake-up call. This time both Katy and I lingered for a few minutes inside our bags not wanting to move. Katy needed her coffee and I longed for more sleep. I sat outside the tent watching Katy busily preparing her cup of java and when she offered me some, despite not being a coffee drinker, I eagerly gulped down the hot fluid along with a few bites of warm, mushy oatmeal.

After a 4 a.m. gear check with Jeff, we started up the snowfield towards the summit, our headlamps dimly lighting up the surrounding surreal rock and snow-strewn landscape. Feeling a bit more awake after the coffee, I fell into stride behind Jeff and noticed another group of climbers were now behind me. They asked Jeff if they could tag along with us as they had been climbing for some time and said they lost the route. Jeff greeted them with a smile and nod of his head and we were back on ascent. After an hour of steady climbing, I noticed the first glimpses of daylight breaking around me and to my left caught a peek at a fumarole (opening in a volcano through which hot sulfurous gases emerge) that we were passing. This was quite the sight as I had never before seen one and it gave the first indication that we were climbing an active volcano. A nauseating scent of sulfur filled the air and I recognized it immediately. Becky had told me that we would know when passing through Devil's Kitchen by the smell and she was right!

We stopped for a brief rest stop at the base of a snow covered, narrow spiny ridge known as The Hogsback that lead up to the summit headwall. I sat on my pack with Katy next to me taking in the incredible views from 10,600 ft. My gaze focused on the climb up ahead and I felt a bit sick to my stomach at that point. I tried not to think about the challenging terrain we would soon be ascending and suddenly broke out in a cold sweat that made me feel very chilly in the cold mountain air. Part of me wanted to stay right there in that moment, immersed in the breathtaking vistas of the slowly breaking dawn, yet another more urgent and colder part reminded me that I needed to get moving. As if reading my mind, I heard Jeff announce, "OK guys, let's move on."

We made our way along the narrow ridge of The Hogsback and I was aware of little more than air on both sides of the ridge. Nervously, I measured each footstep cautiously up the ridge. Ice axe and crampons were once again welcome and necessary companions, providing steadiness and traction on this and the even steeper terrain that lie ahead.

Within an hour of steady climbing we reached the summit headwall, a 600-foot tall wall of 40-60 degree steep snow and ice leading up to the summit ridge. We steadily ascended the wall with Jeff ambling up with the grace and finesse of a spider dancing on its web, and I following behind more akin to a plodding, lumbering bear. Pausing only long enough to catch our breaths, we continued our eternal journey upwards heading to the ridge, the minutes seeming like hours. Feeling whole body exhausted and sore, I wanted to turn around, yet dared not look back or down and kept climbing wearily upwards toward the crystal blue sky and ridge now in sight.

Reaching the ridge was a definite highlight! Hefting myself up onto the rocky ridge top took every ounce of energy I had left. The welcoming rays of sunlight warmed my face and rejuvenated my depleted body. With gasping breaths, I took a short pause to rest and contemplate the panoramic spectacle that met my eyes. From 11,000 feet high, I could see far below the outline of Oregon and surrounding peaks in the distance. Gazing upwards to the now visible summit, my stomach once again did several flip-flops at the thought of traversing across the narrow knife-edge ridge. The summit, hidden behind several forbidding rock pillars and beams of piercingly bright sunlight, seemed miles away. Katy climbed up next to me on the ridge pausing to take in the view and "wow" was the only word uttered between the pair of us.

Jeff snapped a quick shot of Katy and me on the ridge. Unbeknownst to us, he was sending text messages and photos back to Cara reporting our progress on the climb. I imagined Cara, Gary, and ATA staff cheering us on as we wearily scraped and clawed our way to the top, and I felt their energy spurring us on. Glancing at my watch, I saw it was 6:30 a.m. and calculated we would reach the summit in perhaps another hour. Jeff was scrambling over rocks and patches of slick snow and ice some distance ahead of me and Katy and I were moving at a snail's pace. Jeff would turn around at intervals watching our progress and yelling words of encouragement at us. Everything seemed to be moving in slow motion, and I kept my focus straight ahead on the next rock pillar I needed to ascend at that moment. My foot suddenly caught on a rock, throwing me off balance. With heart pounding out of my chest, I steadied myself with my ice axe, catching a glance over to one side at a sickeningly steep drop off to my right.

"Hey guys, looking good! Keep on coming!" Jeff's voice got me back on track and we continued our hectic ridge traverse towards the top.

"How can he yell like that? I gasped.

"Keep going, girlfriend. We are getting close!" Katy panted.

Noticing Jeff now standing on some distant shore, taking off his pack and throwing it on the ground, I felt tears streaming from my eyes while recalling Jeff's smiling face on Rainier yelling at me, "You did it, Donna!" With more energy and urgency in our step, we picked up the pace and covered the last mound of snow in record time before joining Jeff on a flat and barren expanse of rock, gravel and snow with nowhere else to go! Nor did I want to be anywhere else in the world than atop Mt. Hood!

We reached summit somewhere around 7 a.m. Katy and I exchanged high fivers, and yelled whoops of joy and jubilance. I meandered over to Jeff and we hugged and exchanged fivers and posed for photos in attempt to try to capture the moment. Looking back at the photos always seems strange and somehow anticlimactic, yet photos are reminders and documentation of highlights of the seasons we pass through in our lives.

Entranced in contemplation of breathtaking panoramic vistas all around me, I stood on the summit of Mt. Hood still wearing my heavy pack, oblivious of its weight. The wind had picked up and I felt its biting chill penetrating through layers of down and fleece. Suddenly, remembering the ATA banner in my pack, I let it slide off my shoulders landing with a thud on the ground. Fumbling around in the pack, my hand pulled out a sopping wet banner. I discovered my camelback sprung a leak and of course, its target was the banner. Jeff shot a few photos of Katy and me standing in a freezing wind holding a wet white banner with ATA insignia flapping in the breeze. A Kodak moment!

After spending about a half hour on the summit, Jeff reminded us it was time to descend. Not really wanting to leave the moment, I gathered my pack and took one last glance back at the summit as we started down the mountain. Making our way back across the ridge, my legs felt like silly putty. Arriving back at the junction of where the ridge met the headwall was a wake-up call. On ascent, the headwall was in front of me and I didn't dare look behind and for good reason. Now confronted with the vast white expanse of air and wicked steep terrain we still had to descend, I realized that one false step could be my last. Jeff warned us to proceed with caution and my stomach was tied in as many knots as the rope attached to our harnesses connecting us together. Katy led out with Jeff behind me, and with slow deliberate steps we side-stepped our way down the icy slick headwall. The often-quoted expression of making summit only being "half-way there" took on a whole new meaning and brought an intense awareness to mind of the inherent hazards of climbing mountains. Therein lies the challenge and your reward, living through the experience to tell the incredible tale!

When we finally reached The Hogsback, the terrain leveled out somewhat, yet we still had to climb down its spine before I could breathe a sigh of relief. We took another rest stop at the bottom, took more pictures of awe-inspiring scenery, refueled on handfuls of trail mix and drank as much water as we could pour down our parched throats. Scanning the horizon below, I searched for some signs of the ski area, yet realized that it would still be hours before we got there and perhaps another hour before finally reaching the trailhead where the climb began the previous day. Once again, the familiar sulfurous stench filled the air and, glancing behind me, I noticed the same fumarole area that we passed hours ago on our way to the summit. The fumarole looked very distinctive in the bright sunlight of day as compared to the early haze of dawn, and I could make out all its features with great clarity. The sunlight warmed my chilled body despite the cool ambient mountain air.

The next few hours were a blur as I tried to keep up with Jeff. He was on a mission of sorts to beat us to the bottom and fulfilling that goal. After shedding our harnesses and ropes, Jeff took off his crampons, packed them in his pack and in a flash, was off glissading down the snowfield towards the ski area. Katy and I watched him with some dismay knowing we could never keep up in our exhausted state.

"Where's the fire?" I asked Katy.

"I think he needs to be somewhere like maybe a friend's wedding or something."

"Well, I think he'll be early wherever he's going!"

We saw him wave to us from a distance away, signaling for us to follow suit. Katy and I sat down on the snow and took off our crampons. After packing them away, Katy looked at me and declared, "I'm going for it!" and suddenly took off glissading down the snowfield with pack bouncing chaotically behind her. Watching her for a while and seeing her reach where Jeff was standing near the ski area, I prepared for my glissade. Katy's was more of a skyrocket and mine comparable to a stalled cargo plane, yet I eventually slid and skidded down to join Jeff and Katy.

Once again on descent, Jeff took a detour to our left to avoid the jam-packed ski area atop the snowfield. In the distance, I could make out the parking lot and saw Jeff ahead of us talking on his cell. I wondered if he was talking with Cara and letting her know our whereabouts. Looking at my watch, it was 1p.m. and I figured we were perhaps an hour away from the trailhead. Excited about seeing Gary and Cara again, I picked up the pace and fell in behind Jeff who was moving like a racehorse sensing the finish line. Katy was lagging some distance behind us and I wondered if she was OK. Pausing for a few moments, she caught up to me and I could tell she was pretty well spent. She said she wasn't feeling well yet told me to go on ahead.

Catching up to Jeff who was now making tracks towards the trailhead, and occasionally glancing back at Katy, I noticed she was still trailing behind, making slow progress towards the lot.

Finally reaching the trailhead, I squinted in the bright, warm sunlight searching for signs of the vehicle we arrived in just yesterday, yet couldn't even remember what the car looked like. Thinking that Gary and Cara might be waiting there for us, I scanned the faces of people rushing past me, yet felt disappointed that none were familiar. I asked Jeff if he was in contact with Cara and he said she would be meeting us at the trailhead. I suddenly remembered our detour and realized they were waiting for us on the other side of the lot. Jeff found his car and started piling his gear in the trunk. Feeling a bit dazed and confused by our re-entry back into society, I stood watching him pack in his gear and offered to help, yet he declined my offer. Katy slowly made her way towards us and I walked over to meet her. After slapping each other fivers, she let out a long sigh of relief. "We did it, girlfriend. Man, I'm wiped."

"Yeah, me too! I was worried about you, my friend!"

A figure with camera bag swinging from his shoulder rushed at me sweeping me into his waiting arms. Letting go a squeal of delight, I embraced Gary with every last bit of energy left in my body. "Congratulations, mountain mama!" Gary exclaimed in between bear hugs. "Where were you guys? We were waiting at the trailhead yet didn't see any trace of you!"

"We did a detour to avoid the ski area and came down a different route," I explained. Suddenly aware of other folks milling around us snapping photos of the two of us caressing, I recognized the smiling face running towards me was Cara. I felt a river of hot tears flowing down my face as we embraced. She wished me congratulations and we talked for a few minutes about the climb.

"I just need to tell you that you guys raised another $52,000 with your climb!" she gushed.

After recovering from the shock of realizing the total amount generated from the three climbs was just shy of $500,000, I was soon to discover yet another surprise. Engaged in conversation with Cara, I noticed someone approaching and was now standing beside us waiting patiently for us to end our conversation. I just happened to glance over at her and recognizing her immediately, let out an excited gasp, "Barb! You made it!!!

There was my old friend, Barb Sanders, who came to visit me for the third time after my climbs. It was so good to see her smiling face again after six years of only brief communication through emails sent back and forth. Just when I thought that I had no more need of Kleenex®, the dam broke once again and I kept wiping my face with my sweat and salt-soaked fleece shirt. Seeing my predicament, she offered me a Kleenex® that I gladly accepted.

After another round of bear hugs and infinite photo shoots, we headed to Ice Axe Grill, a small café near Timberline Lodge for an early dinner where we would meet up with my cousin Becky. I looked forward to meeting her after so many years and wondered what she looked like, since I had only vague memories of her as a teen.

Entering the restaurant, I noticed in the waiting area a short, muscular, strawberry-blond lady and a guy with short-cropped hair. I instantly knew it was Becky and her husband, Tom. It was so great reuniting with Becky and getting to know her and Tom. After more hugs and introductions, we proceeded to our table where Gary, Katy, Cara, Barb, and Barb's husband, Bob were waiting. Jeff had to leave early to attend a friend's wedding. The hours passed by too quickly with us all immersed in good food, great company, conversation, and post-climb celebration. All too soon the festivities ended and everyone went their separate ways, Becky and Tom dealing with vehicle repairs, Cara heading back to Portland, and Barb and Bob heading back to their home. The next morning would be an early one for Gary and me as we planned to do some camping and hiking through The Cascades region of central Oregon and Washington.

Katy was planning on doing some exploring of the area on her own before heading back to the airport the next day.

Gary and I left on our vacation the next day taking with us some fond memories of mountains, lasting friendships and promises to reunite with Becky and Tom in the fall when they planned to travel back to Colorado in their RV.

CHAPTER 26
ALL TOGETHER NOW (2013-2014)

"Great things are done by a series of small things brought together."
— Vincent Van Gogh

With the Hood climb now behind us, Gary and I immersed ourselves in trying to put together a "New Medusa." Every bit as challenging as gathering members was relearning the music we played back in the '70s! Having no tuning devices back then like we have today, the band was forced to go with whatever key my guitar was tuned to, which was tuned by ear and fell more into either sharp or flat keys. I thought I had a pretty good ear for tuning in those carefree, pre-tinnitus days. But with our new band, we found we had to change keys into either minor or major chording so the songs would be easier to relearn. Back in the day, band members would ask what key a song was in and our reply was, "Whatever key Donna's guitar was tuned to!" We still to this day have a good laugh about it.

For our new band, our first singer, Arlo, was thrown right into our laps so to speak. Arlo, a radio DJ for station 1190 in Boulder, hosts a program called "Hypnotic Turtle" every Thursday evening, and plays an eclectic mix of music. Arlo heard our music and invited us to do a live performance and interview on his show shortly after we returned from our Oregon trip in July. We lost contact with him until August, when we bumped into him and his wife, Kim, at a Cheap Trick concert in Winter Park. Kim regaled me with stories of how Arlo was such a great singer and front man, and invited us over to their house for dinner the next week. During dinner, he informed us he was in an alternative punk rock band, Dead Bubbles. We liked his quirky, witty personality and eclectic taste in music and decided to get together for a jam session.

Hearing his alternative style voice for the first time sounded a bit abrasive, yet we heard tones somewhat similar to Pete's and decided to give him a chance to learn and get a feel for the songs. Gary and I worked with Arlo on the songs, although he found little, if any, time to practice, being overextended with his weekly radio program, attending concerts, and family obligations. Even though he stayed with the band for six months, we realized his vocals were more suited for singing alternative style than old psych metal. Pete's strong and melodic vocals were an integral part of Medusa's sound and, with our goal to play live shows once again, we wanted the best representation of this genre of music. We just didn't feel Arlo was a good fit.

While still in the band, Arlo introduced us to Kam, another guitarist, although we were hoping to find a bass player rather than another guitarist. Arlo told us that Kam knew a bass player, but he never materialized. When he auditioned for our band, Kam was barely twenty years old. He was an old soul in a young man's body, had a good knowledge of musical history and was a great guitarist. He was soft spoken and said very little during rehearsals, yet his guitar playing spoke volumes. Kam had a friend named Grady who was a year older and they were inseparable. Grady accompanied Kam to many of our rehearsals and on every gig we would eventually play. He had a lot of opinions on every topic and was not shy about voicing them. Perhaps Grady was the mystery bass player?

A few months after Kam joined the band we auditioned a drummer, named Duff, who stayed for about a month. It was obvious to us he was not working out, as his focus was more on timing rather than finding the right beat for our music. One day he came over, picked up his drums and said he needed to find more gainful employment. That was the last time we saw him.

Sometime around Christmas, Arlo found Dean McCall, our next drummer, and this time it was a good fit. Dean had played in some twenty or more bands before hooking up with us, the most recent being a Rush tribute band. His drumming style was very similar to that of Neil Peart, the drummer of Rush. Dean was a great drummer, well versed in playing everything from classic rock to orchestral music and every genre in between, yet his plate was every bit as full as Arlo's having to divide his time between job, family, and other cover band commitments.

The new Medusa rehearsed once or twice a week and the more we rehearsed the tighter we sounded, yet Arlo's vocals were not progressing. We discussed this matter with Dean and Kam to get their feedback and Kam was the only one who was impressed with Arlo.

Gary and I decided to talk to Arlo and honestly let him know what we thought. Trying to be as diplomatic as possible, we told him we didn't think his vocals were a good match for the band. He defensively said, "Well, that's my voice, take it or leave it," and walked out never to be heard from again.

Over the next few months, I tried taking over the vocals, but I had a hard time trying to project my soft voice over loud guitars and drums. We clearly needed a singer with more powerful vocal abilities. Kam decided to put an ad up on Craigslist for a singer and got an immediate response from a guy named Randy Bobzien, who played guitar as well as sang. Gary talked with him on the phone. Then after listening to a few mp3's Randy sent of his songs from previous bands he played in, we decided to invite Randy over to audition.

A few days before Gary's 60th birthday, we met with Randy. Clad in camouflage pants with black knee-high combat boots and short cut spiked hair, he wasn't exactly our idea of what a front man for our '70s band would look like. But there was something in his loud and raucous voice that clicked. Despite being a guitarist, he agreed to play bass as well. He wasn't always spot on with his vocals, yet he was eager to learn our songs and seemed to jive with the other band members, at least at that point in time.

Gary was unaware I was planning a birthday bash party for him on April 4th, the Saturday before his actual birthday, and that I had decided to have the band entertain for the party. What better way to celebrate this milestone birthday than to do something we loved, playing music? I secretly informed Randy, Dean, and Kam about the party and thought this would give Randy the perfect opportunity to showcase his musicianship in front of friends. At first, he seemed a bit hesitant, yet he agreed to perform with us nonetheless.

Trying to keep the party a secret from Gary was a supreme challenge, yet I had sent Gary out to run a few errands to get him out of the house an hour or so before the guests were to arrive. Kam and Grady were the first to arrive as I was busily running around the house trying to prepare for the party. I hid Gary's cake out in the garage with candles and matches and hoped the guests would show up before Gary did! Shortly after Kam and Grady, Dean and his wife, Leonore and several other friends arrived. They sat and chatted while I continued my food preparations. Randy was the next to arrive along with my hut buddies, Katy and Dee, plus Cyndi and Tami, my yoga students and their husbands, and soon the party was in full swing. Randy disappeared down in the basement to set up his equipment.

Gary walked in the door sometime after all guests had arrived wearing a big smile on his face when he heard everyone yell "Happy Birthday!" Looking in my direction he said, "I knew something was up when I saw a shit load of cars outside!" After a delicious potluck dinner, I brought in the carrot cake, Gary's favorite, with candles quickly melting on the butter cream icing. After everyone had their fill of birthday songs and dessert, we headed downstairs and started playing our first song, "Strangulation." Soon, the whole basement was full of guests watching us play. Randy remembered most of the words to songs he had just learned a few days before and his voice sounded strong! Receiving rave reviews from our guests, Randy passed the audition with flying colors. Gary and I thought he was the right match for our band, yet not all band members would agree.

During one rehearsal shortly after Gary's party, Dean informed us about a popular local music festival over the 4th of July weekend, and I made a phone call to the festival promoter to try to gather more information about the festival. He was rude and condescending, telling me I would have to sell tickets to gain entrance to this event and I almost hung up on him! He told me to talk with Jake, the person in charge of the festival, and I gave his information to Gary so he could follow up with him. Things were radically different when Gary talked with Jake. He told Gary he was definitely interested in Medusa playing at the festival and even came over to our house to meet us with his girlfriend. We seemed to hit it off and talked with them at length about our music. They especially dug our music and we felt an instant connection with them. Gary signed a contract to play at the Fest and handed it back to Jake. There was even talk between Jake and Gary that we would be playing on the main stage and that he would pass our information along to the folks in charge of another popular event. We were excited about finally getting an opportunity to play out and looked forward to playing at this Fest and other venues to get our music heard.

Shortly after our meeting with Jake, we learned of some underhanded money laundering by his partner that led to a name and management change of the Fest. Things became rather complicated thereafter. A lady named Sara sent Gary a few emails asking for stage plots, promo material, and a W-9 form. Our hearts sank when she informed us that we shouldn't get our hopes up to play on the main stage and that our playing time slot and date was up for grabs. Gary was also informed that our contract was lost. Sara told Gary to contact a lady named Heather with any further questions about the Fest and good luck trying to get in touch with her! Gary sent several emails to her without response.

In the meantime, Gary kept checking the website to see if we were even listed, and found we were listed under another band's logo. That was the straw that broke the camel's back. After several tries, Gary finally was able to reach Jake by phone and complained about our situation. Shortly thereafter, we heard from Heather. She sent an email apologizing about the advertising error, and fixed the website so that our logo and correct contact information was listed. Trying to play at this Fest was a comedy of errors from the start, and it didn't stop there.

A few months before the Fest, we still didn't have a contract or the correct information about our band on their website. Gary spoke with Dean a number of times on the phone and he offered to take over communication with Jake, yet as Gary had developed a rapport with Jake, thought he could work things out. Gary kept all band members updated at rehearsals about the latest turn of events, yet he felt as the band's leader that he would soon need to make a decision on whether or not it was worth it to play at the Fest.

Frustrated at Jake and his assistant's lack of organization, not answering his calls, and uncertain if we would even be getting paid, Gary decided not to play this Fest. He called Jake and left a message that Medusa would not be playing and sent emails to all band members to notify them of his decision, receiving backlash from Jake and Randy. Later that same day, Jake left Gary an angry text message. Randy at least called, yet angrily lashed out at him about making the decision supposedly without first discussing the situation with the band. Later that evening, Randy came over and we had a discussion, worked things out and learned a few things in the process. First and foremost, it's best to talk things over with band members in person before making any decisions. Second, always get a copy of the contract you sign. And third, when in doubt, as in Murphy's Law, always refer back to #1! Little did we know at the time, that this was the first in a series of events that would eventually lead the band on a wild roller coaster ride.

During one rehearsal, Randy informed us that he got us our first live gig at Toad's Tavern in Denver and this lifted our spirits tremendously! Gary and I were excited to play out live for the first time in almost 40 years. We decided to take band photos for publicity for this show and Gary chose a cemetery, no less, for the photo shoot. I thought his choice of locations was a bit weird, yet he refreshed my memory by showing me pictures of Medusa's original photo shoot in the '70s taken in a cemetery. I was not in the photo as the shoot occurred after I left the band.

A week before the Toad's gig, the phone rang. It was Chris Vanderveen, from Channel 9 News in Denver telling me he was interested in doing a story on the reformed Medusa. I had written a blurb on the "News Tips" website about our reforming the band and didn't expect any reply. The previous year, when leaving several messages for Chris to notify him about our story and album release, I got no return call. At that time, Gary and I were still trying to relearn all the old songs from *First Step Beyond*, (no easy task), and hadn't yet reformed the band. Funny, how things can change from year to year.

Chris said he wouldn't be in town for our gig, but he would have his photojournalist, Rico, call us in the next few days to schedule a time to shoot us rehearsing and playing the actual gig! He also mentioned he would interview us sometime after the gig as well when he got back in town. Excitement and morale ran high for all band members at the time and bolstered our sagging spirits still reeling from the cancelled Festival fiasco.

Wednesday, June 4, 2014

A knock on the door and enter Rico, photojournalist from Channel 9 News with his huge camera in hand. Our band was there waiting. We talked with him before rehearsal about our music, how the band was formed and reformed, and our musical influences. He seemed genuinely interested in our story and had a big smile on his face as he filmed us rehearsing for our gig the next day. While filming he asked Gary and me about our thoughts and feelings preparing for our first gig in almost forty years, and we told him it was hard to describe, and a bit surreal, yet exciting as hell! We described in great detail our appreciation for Kam, Randy, and Dean and how integral a role they each played in the band as well as helping to recreate the '70s sound we once had. He asked Kam, Dean and Randy how they felt about playing in the band, and it was great hearing their heartfelt sentiments. Kam spoke about Gary being a great role model for him, and about listening to Black Sabbath and other bands of the '70s and how they influenced his becoming a musician. Randy talked about how after hearing our music and story he wanted to become part of the band. Dean spoke about the great chemistry we have and being excited to finally get a chance to play our music live.

Thursday, June 5, 2014—Toad's Tavern

The day of our gig was the longest day ever! We weren't due to start playing until 10 p.m. since there were two other bands playing before us. I tried keeping busy with nursing paperwork, yet I couldn't concentrate.

After Gary got home from work, we started packing amps, guitars, and keyboards into my truck and we were so nervous the truck was packed in no time flat. Later that evening, we headed down to Toad's Tavern and were the first to arrive. We started the eternal process of unloading equipment and carting it into the club. The first band, Tin Star Charmer, was already set up onstage so we put the equipment on the floor next to the stage forming a hefty pile of amps, guitars, keyboards, and stands in a very short period of time.

Soon thereafter, Randy arrived with Alyssa, a lady I met the week before when Gary and I went to see him perform with his Kiss tribute band, Rockissity. I thought she was a friend of Randy's, yet would soon find out otherwise. After finishing with unloading, we worked up king-size appetites and decided to head out for a bite to eat. Randy and Alyssa met us outside holding hands, and I saw they were an item. They were also heading out to eat and invited us to a place called Texas Roadhouse to celebrate Randy's birthday. We accepted their invite, as Dean,

Kam, and Grady were doing their own thing for dinner. The staff at Texas Road-house put on a great show in honor of Randy's birthday, and although it wasn't nearly up to the standards of the show Medusa did later that evening, it was fun watching Randy sitting on a mock saddle eating ice cream, his face beaming.

We headed back to Toad's in time to catch some of El Problemo's show and to interface with Rico from Channel 9 again. He asked us many more times that evening how we were feeling and if we were nervous, and I felt like an actual rock star standing in front of his huge camera trying not to look at the camera as instructed. This made me more nervous than being asked numerous times if I was nervous.

Time passed and soon it was show time! El Problemo was tearing down their equipment and all I could do was stare up on stage at all the commotion in a state of disbelief that Medusa would soon be up there playing. Then I was part of the commotion, carting equipment up and down the stairs leading to the stage, hearing Grady's voice shouting, "Donna! Where does this go?" pointing at my keyboard stand. I felt like the scene was reminiscent of some weird dream, yet I realized it wasn't a dream at all! Yelling back to Grady, "Over there," I signaled towards stage right next to Dean's already set up drum set. Everything was a blur of activity, Gary standing below the stage trying in vain to untangle the mess of cables belonging to my keyboards, the sound guy asking me if I would like a mic placed by my amp, interspersed with Rico passing in front of me shoving his camera in my face asking if I was nervous. When Randy and Kam tried to lift the Medusa sign Randy had fashioned, one of its legs fell off, and I chuckled. *So much for having an official sign… OMG, is this really happening?* "Slowly The Madness Creeps In," a song Pete and I collaborated on, flashing through my mind as I set up my keyboards in preparation for our show. So many emotions passing through me like scenes from a staccato slide projector flashing on a screen…

"Sound check now for keys," the sound guy's voice interrupting my train of thoughts, bringing me back to the stage. I plunked a few keys and heard the sound guy say, "OK, sounds good to me. We're ready for the guitar, now. OK, maybe not…" Gary was kneeling on one knee down on the stage floor fiddling around with his guitar and mess of 10,000 foot pedals only he could figure out. Then he was up in an instant playing a few ripping leads and the sound guy's voice again, "OK, sounds good!"

"OK, I think we're ready!" and then it was show time. "We are Medusa playing for you after some forty odd years!" Randy introduced us to the audience and smiled at Gary and me as the audience yelled their raucous and rowdy approval.

As we started playing and rocking the house, all nervous energy was dissipated and redirected into the music that poured from within our collective souls. Playing onstage again felt surreal! All things seemed to be moving in slow motion, yet before long we were well into our set. We played for over an hour to the yells and cheers of an appreciative audience of friends, fans, and club owners.

Playing my keyboards, I would gaze up, from time to time, at my fellow band members, to see Randy smiling back at me, and Kam, the most animated and youngest of the group, with his hair flailing back and forth in time with the hard and heavy solid beat of our music engaging and assaulting the audience. I gazed over my shoulder at Dean behind his drums, looking cool, calm and collected amidst the organized chaos of musical madness, free flowing and all-encompassing as though driven by some unforeseen force beyond our control. Gary would even look over his shoulder at me from time to time with an expression of enormous enjoyment, as if to say, "Yeah, this is fucking great!" Meeting his gaze, we shared the moment. Closing my eyes for a few minutes, I listened to the music flowing from the stage and was enveloped by the sheer energy and magnitude of our sound. It felt as though the music was playing us and we were mere conduits aiming musical currents at the audience with overwhelming ferocity!

After the show, we started tearing down our set and carting equipment off the stage. Then I stood below the stage talking with friends and fans, and hearing their compliments and rave reviews brought tears to my eyes. We stood and delivered! Caught up in the moment, I didn't want it to end. As I conversed with folks who came to see us play, I noticed a guy standing a few feet away from me looking in my direction and turned to meet him. He approached me with a huge smile and introduced himself as Garrett, one of the owners of Toad's Tavern. I held my breath for a moment waiting to hear his feedback. "Wow! That was awesome and your story is pretty incredible as well!" *Guess he liked us! COOL!* "I hope you guys come back to play here soon on a Friday or Saturday night next time!" *Even COOLER!!!* We chatted for a while about music in general and he finished the conversation by handing me a business card of the other owner of Toad's, Mark, telling us to contact him regarding setting up another date to play there.

It had rained pretty hard outside when we were playing and we didn't even know it, until we started carting equipment out to our vehicles. Just before midnight, Randy and Alyssa left Toad's followed by Dean, and we waved them off standing outside as a light drizzle fell upon our heads. Gary and I looked at each other, exhausted from the day's events yet grinning from ear to ear. "We did good!" Gary sighed and I nodded affirmatively. We loaded the rest of our equipment into my truck, and went back inside to check for anything else we might have left behind. As we were heading for the door to leave, the bartender, a guy with hair as grey as mine, approached us praising our music. We stayed for a while and reminisced with him about the great music of the '60s and '70s long gone by. We left Toad's after midnight with musical refrains in our ears and fond memories in our hearts.

Tuesday, June 24, 2014

"We'll be over by 3 p.m. if that's OK with you," Chris Vanderveen announced on the phone. Looking at the clock, I noticed it was noon. "Sure!" I reply trying not to sound too excited. The phone call from Chris once again surprised and spurred a quick phone call to Gary shouting something like, "Be home soon!!!" followed by a flurry of house cleaning activity. The hours flew by in a furious cleaning-throw-things-everywhere-but-where-they-should-be frenzy, until Gary came home. At promptly 3 p.m., I heard a knock on the door and there they are, Rico Meyer, the photographer, and Chris, the Channel 9 reporter up close and personal. Handshakes all around and then Rico pulls out a few chairs from the table for Gary and me to sit in, sets up an umbrella-like light shade and then its lights, camera, action! Chris pulls up the hassock to sit down and starts firing numerous questions at us.

"Is she good?" Chris asks Gary.

"Yes, she's a great nurse!"

"What about as a musician?"

"Oh, I thought you meant as a nurse," Gary laughs. Yeah, she's one helluva keyboards player as well!"

"Is he good?"

Yeah, when he remembers the question! "Yes, he's a fantastic guitarist and I've told him since day one that he needs to get off his duff, (*can you say that?*), and let his music be heard!"

"Can you describe the music you play?" Chris directs the question to Gary.

"Hard rock and old school metal music of the '70s fashioned after a few of our idols, such as Black Sabbath, Hawkwind, and progressive rock favorites like Epitaph, Amon Duul ll, and Can."

"How would you describe the music of the '70s?"

"Long-winded guitar solos that seem to go on forever with a spacey psychedelic feel," Gary replied after a few thoughtful moments.

"Add to that a lot of wah-wah guitar sound effects with a Hendrix feel… and echo-plex effects that continue for all eternity!" Glancing over at Gary, I nudged his arm affectionately, as this perfectly described Gary's guitar-playing style.

The interview lasted for perhaps an hour and then we chatted with Chris while

Rico was packing up his lights and camera. Chris was very down to earth and told us he would be in touch with us after reviewing all the footage taken of us during rehearsal, the Toad's Tavern show and the interview, to let us know when the story would be televised. When Rico was all packed, we shook hands and they were gone, leaving behind their words of encouragement and support, taking with them our musical legacy for the world to see.

Our interview was aired about a month later on a Sunday night episode called "Storytellers" and we excitedly watched it in the company of all band members. Grady, especially enjoyed our new roles as dinosaur rock stars. We were surprised and disappointed that the praise we shared for each band member was left out of the interview.

Over the next weekend, we recorded demos of our newest songs, "Turn To Stone," "Headin' for Armageddon," and "Into the Night," in a garage-turned-studio owned by Randy's friend, Ace. I was in a furious writing frenzy at the time. Kam had suggested during rehearsal one day that I write a song about the story of Medusa and I based it on the popular mythological interpretation of Medusa. This story depicts the tragic and unfortunate fate that befell an unlucky maiden named Medusa, a one-time high priestess of the Goddess Athena. Medusa was raped by Neptune, God of the Underworld, and worse yet, bearing the wrath of Athena, had a spell cast upon her that turned this once-beautiful woman into a hideous creature with serpentine mane in place of what used to be her hair. According to the story, every man who even glanced in her direction is immediately turned to stone. "Headin" for Armageddon" is my rendition of the consequences of choosing to follow a very violent and destructive path that has befallen the modern-day world we live in. Pete and I wrote "Into the Night" during our frequent flurry of emails shortly after Rob's call served as a catalyst to reunite four original band members after years of obscurity.

After recording some decent sounding demos, we sent them to several record labels including Shrapnel Records, Ripple Music and Numero Group, the same label that released *First Step Beyond*. Mike Varney from Shrapnel and Rob Sevier from Numero said they liked the music, but we heard nothing more from either one. We didn't get a reply right away from Ripple, yet we had a few more gigs to prepare for which kept our spirits up.

Friday, August 8, 2014—Hi Dive, Denver, Colorado

This was truly one of our best shows! We played with three other bands, Gingaso, Cloud Catcher and Space In Time, the headliners. Gingaso opened the show with their loud, raucous metal music, followed by Cloud Catcher, another local band. Gary met Rory, the singer and lead guitarist of Cloud Catcher, at a Penta-gram concert a few months previously. Pentagram was a band from back in the '70s, who played music similar to our style and, like Medusa, never really got the recognition they deserved at that time. Finally landing a record deal forty years later, they achieved considerable worldwide notoriety and popularity. Gary and I saw a documentary about Pentagram and when learning they were playing the Summit Music Hall, Gary decided to go to their concert. Rory and Gary met when Christina, Rory's girlfriend, approached Gary and made comment about the Medusa t-shirt Gary was wearing.

"Those guys are pretty awesome!"

"I'm the lead guitarist!"

"No way!" Christina called Rory over to introduce him to Gary. Rory and Christina told Gary the story of how they met over our album at Black and Read, a local record store in Arvada. Rory and Gary became friends, and Rory invited us to play the Hi-Dive gig with them.

By the time we hit the stage, the house was packed with people, even more so than at our first gig at Toad's. I was a bit nervous about playing in front of so many people, yet the nervousness quickly dissipated when hearing the enthusiastic yells and cheers from the crowd as we started our set. During breaks between songs, I looked down toward my feet and noticed fans were peering up at me through an opening in the wall to my right. They were giving me thumbs up sig-nals and wanting to slap my hand with fivers, and the feeling was surreal that after so many years people were really digging our music! After playing for 45 minutes, the crowd kept applauding and yelling for more. We did an encore and were then immersed in the chaos of tearing down equipment and clearing the stage for the next band, Space In Time. The steps leading up to the stage were steep and it was difficult carrying heavy amps and instruments down the stairs without losing my balance. With stage lights glaring in my eyes, I could barely see where the steps were and almost took a tumble. Finally making it down the steps with all body parts intact, I headed through the sea of smiling faces in the crowd for the back of the room carrying my two keyboard cases, being inundated with enthusiastic comments and kudos.

Suddenly a guy stood in front of me blocking my pathway and leaned towards me. As I stared directly into his eyes, I recognized him as Vaughn, the keyboard player from Space In Time. He grabbed my shoulder and yelled into my ear. "You were fucking amazing! You're a fucking legend! I should be taking lessons from you!" He was gone in a flash heading toward the stage to set up his keyboards, and I stood there at a loss for words. Having never before been called a "legend," and thinking that legendary status was reserved for the likes of The Beatles, Hendrix, Santana, and numerous other super groups of the '60s, Vaughn's comment was unexpected to say the least. I hardly considered playing music you love playing as "legendary," yet I felt honored to be held in such esteem by fans and fellow musicians alike.

Continuing towards the back of the room to drop off my instruments where Gary, Randy, Dean and Kam were doing the same, I pulled Gary aside and shared Vaughn's comment. He also relayed similar comments to me that he received from our fans.

We stayed well after midnight to hear Space in Time's set and really dug hearing their music. They are all seasoned musicians and despite being half our age had made a name for themselves in the Denver music scene, establishing quite the cult following. We chatted with the band members for hours after the show and once again heard from Vaughn that we also have a considerable cult following of fans all over the country and world. This was one of many heart-to-heart talks we would have with band members well past our bedtime, establishing lifelong bonds and friendships.

CHAPTER 27

GAINING MOMENTUM (2014)

"It's not enough to be a musician. You must also be an entertainer."
— Donna Brown

Monday, September 22, 2014

Out of the clear blue sky came the reply from Todd Severin from Ripple Music, that he really dug our demo, describing it as, "…very warm and organic, heavy. Great stuff." His positive comments amazed us all that a record label was finally pursuing us, and opened lines of almost daily email communication. He asked if we had any other material to send him and, as a matter of fact, we had just written and learned a few new songs, yet hadn't had a chance to record them. Knowing he was interested in our music gave us reason to ask him what it was in particular that he liked about the demo so we could record more of the same on our next demo. He responded, "I loved the recording, it had very organic '70s feeling, as did the instrumentation and tone of the guitars. The playing was excellent and the songs themselves were quite strong. I like the heaviness and the big organ. It all sounded so genuine. Very of the day, which I loved." Excited and encouraged by his reply, we busied ourselves with the task of trying to record three new songs to send as a follow-up demo to Todd, as well as playing numerous gigs in between recording sessions.

Monday, September 29, 2014

Mutiny Information Café—Lecherous Gaze, Cloud Catcher and Medusa

This gig was held in a small bookstore. Lecherous Gaze, a band from Oakland, California contacted us a few months prior about this gig and invited us to play with them. And what a rowdy and raucous night it was! Cloud Catcher got the party started and rocked hard and mighty.

Then it was our turn and we responded with more hard and heavy music and the audience loved it! Lecherous Gaze came on last and literally closed the show. They were so blazing LOUD the police came and shut their show down! Highlights of the evening were: meeting Zaryan, the lead singer of Lecherous Gaze. He had such an interesting persona. Dark, mysterious and of Mediterranean decent, he spoke about Medusa as elders in the music business setting the bar with high standards for those young future torch bearers to follow. Our conversation made me realize we were considered role models for the kids of today's Generation X and Millennials who grew up in a very different world than ours. Kids of today are adept at operating every kind of computer imaginable in our technology-driven society, but they never experienced the barrage of great rock music we Boomers were very fortunate to be exposed to throughout the '60s and '70s.

After the show, I went outside to chat with a few fans standing outside the Café and met Alex and Olivia who complimented me on our music. Their comments such as, "it's an honor to be in your presence," or "I'm just gushing right now!" made me feel unworthy of such an honor. They were too similar to comments I would make to my rock heroes. I'm just doing what I love to do at a rather-late-yet-better-late-than-never stage of the game," I told them as they smiled and continued to gush.

As Alex and Olivia expressed their adulation, I realized the awesome power of music to move people regardless of age, denomination, or gender, and walked back into the bookstore feeling fortunate for being so honored.

Friday, October 3, 2014—3 Kings Tavern, Denver, Colorado

This gig was a total surprise, well almost. Medusa was invited to play with Cloud Catcher, Titan Arum, and Space in Time at 3 Kings, a popular local venue. We looked forward to playing there as many locally and nationally known bands have graced the stage of Denver's Premiere Rock Establishment, as it's often referred to. A few days prior, Gary received a phone call from a member of one of the bands informing him the gig was cancelled as a more well- known band, Uncle Acid and the Deadbeats, were playing a concert that same evening at a different venue. Gary looked at the website billboard of bands scheduled to play at 3 Kings and, noticing that Medusa was still listed, called Jim, the owner, and found out that we were indeed still playing the gig. When he told me, I was shocked. "What? I thought that gig was cancelled! Are the other bands still playing?"

He called them and found out that one band wasn't even notified that they were supposed to play the gig and the other had made other arrangements to play elsewhere when they found out the gig was supposedly cancelled.

Luckily for us, most of our band members were available to play on such short notice, except for Kam, who decided to attend the Uncle Acid concert. Randy informed us he knew of another band, Dredneck, who was willing to play and be our back up for the evening. Breathing sighs of relief that we wouldn't have to play solo that night, Gary and I crammed our equipment into my Ford Ranger and headed down to 3 Kings. Figuring out parking logistics in downtown Denver is another story in itself and my least favorite aspect of playing out live. We, of course, couldn't find a place to park to unload, and had to circle around the block several times before Gary remembered a place nearby—a credit union's parking lot across the street from 3 Kings. We had to make several trips with our instruments in tow, stockpiled on top of the dolly Gary had grabbed from our garage before leaving our house. When we got to our venue feeling tattered and torn, we saw Dean looking cool, calm and collected as usual, carrying a few pieces of his drum kit into the tavern. He saw us hustling our gear, and told us he was parked in the alley behind the tavern and suggested we do the same. "Now you tell us," I joked.

"Hey, it's a lot easier and closer than where you parked," he chuckled.

We met the guys from Dredneck backstage as we unloaded equipment and chatted with them for a while, thanking them for helping us out with the gig. I sat with Tami, one of my yoga students, and her husband Roy, at a small table listening to them play. The band was pretty loud and raucous and I ran to the bathroom and shoved toilet paper in my ears having forgotten my earplugs. Tami asked me for some TP I had in my pocket when I returned to the table, so I didn't feel so bad. They played for about an hour and, after they finished their set, I headed backstage and we started carting equipment onstage for our set. We did a sound check with the sound guy and starting playing around 11 p.m. The rest of the night was filled with our music, and we played, as usual, with wild and gleeful abandon and had a small, yet appreciative, audience. We sounded great even without Kam and played some new songs (i.e., Turn To Stone, Rage On, and House of Usher) for the first time in front of a live audience, and they loved it!!! I was a bit nervous about how House of Usher would sound, as we had barely learned it during the last few rehearsals, yet we managed to pull it off with only a few minor glitches. We ended our set after 1 a.m. and were pretty tired, yet jubilant that we received such a great reception from the crowd despite missing a band member. Gary and I chatted with Jim, the owner, after the show and he dug our music big time and told us we could play there anytime. We didn't get home until late and after loading and unloading our equipment, didn't get to sleep until even later; so much for the glamorous life style of the not so rich and famous.

Over the next few months, we headed back to Ace's studio to finish recording our three newest songs to send to Todd for demos. We also played more local gigs and did an interview with Tom Murphy from *Westword Magazine*. Somewhere around Thanksgiving, we sent the finished demos to Todd with high hopes of landing a record deal with Ripple Music by year's end.

A few weeks before Christmas, Todd gave us the go ahead to record our second album in an actual recording studio. We contacted and visited several local studios and after much deliberation decided to go with Colorado Sound Studios in West-minster. Having recorded big name bands such as Yes, James Taylor, Stevie Ray Vaughan, and The Doors, we felt we would be in good hands in producing a quality recording. We still had several more gigs to play throughout December and into the New Year, including an invitation to tour in early February with JOY, a San Diego band who contacted us. So we set our first recording session for late February. Gary had recorded in a studio with his previous band Backstreet, so it was rather anticlimactic for him. But never having set foot in an actual studio, I was nervous as hell!

Touring the studios, and seeing all the recording equipment, seemed intimi-dating at first, yet made it all worthwhile knowing we were taking another step towards securing our rightful place in musical history.

December 13, 2014—Squire Lounge, Denver, Colorado

We were contacted by a popular local skateboard company, 303 Boards, who wanted us to play for an event they were holding at Squire. We played with Cloud Catcher and Arctic, from California, who are also professional skateboarders. Medusa closed the show. It was a wild and crazy night! Cloud Catcher was smok-ing hot and so loud you couldn't hear Rory's vocals. Arctic traveled from Califor-nia just to play with us and played an all instrumental set similar in sound to Earthless, another band from California. The stage was so small it barely fit Cloud Catcher and Arctic, both three-piece bands.

When it was time for our five-piece band to take the stage, Dean spread out his drum kit as usual taking up most of the cramped space, relegating the remaining members to set up on the floor amidst the maddening throngs of 200-250 undulating people in attendance that night. I was playing my key-boards in a puddle of beer, people in the audience in their mad outpouring of adulation, pulled wires out of Gary's foot pedals as he tried to play. Tossing his guitar down on top of his guitar case, he jumped on the stage and not so politely yelled back at the crowd, "Are you fucking done?" One guy replied, "Hey, sorry man!" I was wondering what he was doing standing on stage wildly waving his arms at the audience rather than playing our opening song, "Transient Amplitudes," yet we persisted without our lead guitarist and pulled the song off in his absence.

Most of the time I look down at my keyboards trying to focus on what I'm playing rather than looking around me at the audience, yet this time, I noticed the faces and expressions of the people watching our show. I was AWESTRUCK by the demonstrations of adoration surrounding and overwhelming me! There were guys playing air keyboards with their hands flailing in my face as I tried to concentrate on playing keys. Numerous fans were yelling things at me, and I could barely hear what was being said over the deafening decibels pouring from the band and fanfare from the audience. One young man shouted, "Wish you were my grandma!" and I realized at that moment I was indeed old enough to be his grandma! *GO GRANNY GO!!!*

Christina, Rory's girlfriend, sat next to where I played, and I felt her staring up at me for most of the show. Flashing back to gazing up at Grace Slick, it was evocative of my idolization of her. Glancing at Christina from time to time and smiling, she'd return my smile with thumbs up and high fives. She was my guardian angel, bodyguard and most avid fan all rolled up into one small, mighty package! The mic stand was being pushed into my keyboards and almost knocked over numerous times, yet she managed to retrieve it from the clutches of doom time after time.

We saw fans that follow us from place to place such as Nick Lasar, who we met at 3 Kings Tavern, Mike, an ex-singer of Space in Time, Shaun Goodwin from the Munsens, with whom we were going to play a show at High Dive in January 2015, and Brian Castillo, a DJ who hosted the last gig we played at 3 Kings. It was good to see that MEDUSA 1975 had made quite a name for ourselves!

Randy's vocals couldn't be heard for most of the night. The PA system at the club wasn't the greatest. It was mostly Kam that we heard blasting everyone's faces off with his brand-new Fender Bassman amp! We finished up at 1:45 a.m., got home at 3 a.m. and didn't get to bed until almost dawn. The toughest part of doing this insanity at our age is playing the brutal late-night gigs and having to lug heavy equipment around, yet seeing the response we get from our fans makes it all worthwhile.

SQUIRE LOUNGE—December 31, 2014-New Year's Eve Party

Back again to play at Squire. Despite it being a very cold night, around one hundred or so people showed up to party. Usually, Gary and I never go out on New Year's Eve, but this year was different. We were the entertainment!

I didn't want to leave the house and hit the road with all the other "crazies," yet we had a gig to play and play we did.

Speed Wobble opened the show trying to combine speed metal growling with mediocre skateboarding at best. I don't know what was more painful—hearing their music or watching the singer fall off his skateboard repeatedly.

Medusa finally took the stage around 11:30 p.m. and we played one song, then took a break to countdown to the New Year. Gary broke into an impromptu Hendrix-style rendition of "Auld Lang Syne" that would have given even Hendrix himself some stiff competition. But it got a rather subdued response from the audience filled with fans young enough to be our grandchildren. I'm not sure they even recognized the song to be honest! The audience gave us a less enthusiastic reception than when we last played there a few weeks ago. But looking out at their bobbing heads from on stage behind my rack of keyboards, it appeared as though they were getting into the show in spite of themselves. Perhaps they were preoccupied with the New Year festivities and less into being inundated with the inane, insane wall of music from the '70s being thrown down by folks old enough to know better, yet still young enough to pretend not to care.

CHAPTER 28
ON THE ROAD AGAIN (2015)

"The road to success is always under construction."
— Steve Maraboli, Keynote Speaker, Life Coach and
best-selling Author of several books including Life,
The Truth, and Being Free

The new year brought a roller coaster of new adventures to share and a flutter and flurry of activity. In a band, it's share and share alike, and share we did! Randy was sick with a flu bug during our last gig that he shared with me after the gig when we hugged. The gigs we played throughout January at the Hi Dive, were for me a blur of coughing fits and extreme fatigue.

The first gig we played was on January 9, 2015, with Sugar Skulls and Marigolds, Cloud Catcher and Bronze. I felt like crap and could barely stand up to play my keyboards for the show, yet managed to push through the set. We were second in the band line-up and despite Nick, the sound guy barking orders and telling us we were only playing for twenty-five minutes, was actually a blessing in disguise. Usually our sets were an hour or more in length. We made it home some-time after midnight rather than our usual wee early morning hours routine, and I breathed a sigh of relief to finally be in my recliner where I belonged rather than shredding in our heavy metal band.

Tired of being sick and tired for weeks, I went to the doctor and discovered the flu had turned into pneumonia. After a round of antibiotics, I started feeling a bit perkier, yet the constant gigging was taking its toll. Usually when you're young, your body is quicker to recover. But when you reach dinosaur status, re-covery seems to take forever! I tried to rest as much as possible between gigs, yet our hectic schedules dictated otherwise.

Saturday, January 24, 2015
Back again at Hi Dive, this time with The Munsens', Shaun and Mike Good-

win, we had another great show with an enthusiastic audience. A local band, Still Valley and a band from North Carolina called Toke joined us on the same bill. We played songs from our newest album that we had barely learned for playing live, yet the response from fans was encouraging. Before the show, we went out for pizza with Shaun and Mike and during lengthy conversations established lasting friendship bonds with them. They informed us that some favorite bands of ours The Shrine and Electric Citizen were playing at the Hi Dive the following week and after talking with the guy who books shows for Hi Dive, we were confirmed for that show as well.

Thursday, January 29, 2015—Hi Dive—The Shrine, Electric Citizen and Medusa 1975

It was a bit sobering being the opening band for this show, as we were usually the headliners, but it gave us the experience nonetheless. As we pulled up to the gig, we saw a guy step out of a white van parked in front of us. Gary jumped out of our vehicle to talk with him. The guy turned out to be the manager of The Shrine and Gary had an interesting conversation with him. So interesting, that Gary forgot to ask him for payment. In fact, he thought Mike, the guy who booked the gig for us last minute, would be paying us, which was not the case. As local musicians just getting our start in the music biz, we certainly weren't getting paid top dollar and we didn't expect to. But we did expect to get paid! It turns out we didn't get paid for this gig and it wouldn't be the last time. We found out a few days later that the company who sponsored the show never intended to pay us from the start. They had most likely spent their stash on The Shrine and Electric Citizen. Another opportunity for growth and learning!

We got a chance to meet Josh, Court and Jeff from The Shrine, a well-known Psych rock band hailing from Venice, California and shared great comments of mutual admiration. Also, Gary and I talked a bit with vocalist, Laura and husband/guitarist Dolan Ross from Electric Citizen before they took the stage. It was especially great to talk with Laura and get a female perspective of rock music, as most of the time I'm surrounded by males in a predominately male- dominated musical arena. Electric Citizen hails from Cincinnati, Ohio and plays hard-driving metal music reminiscent of Black Sabbath with more melodic vocal refrains. Still recovering from pneumonia and feeling weak and fatigued, I was both anticipating and dreading the Midwest tour we would be starting the next week with JOY. As this was our first tour ever with another band, I hoped my health would hold out and wondered what life would be like on the road with all male companions. I was excited about heading back to Chicago for our last show, playing in front of our hometown crowd and reuniting with Pete.

Wednesday, February 4, 2015—LOST LAKE, Denver, Colorado

Our tour started with a gig at Lost Lake, a small music club in downtown Denver that offers a stage for local and indie bands. Some bands choose to be independent from major record labels and record and produce their own music and Medusa 1975 fits into this category. In the '70s, cover bands were preferred over bands, like ours, that played original material, and we were relegated to playing drunken Frat and Sorority parties in that era. So we welcomed the opportunity to play at new venues for audiences that would appreciate our music.

We arrived at the club around 7 p.m. and met with JOY, the band from San Diego, who invited us to tour with them over the next four days through Kansas and Missouri, ending with a show in Chicago. JOY consists of three playing members, Zach, Justin and Thomas, and two roadies, Tyler and Magic. All are in their early-to mid-twenties with long hair, either straight or Hendrix style and dress in the garb of the '60s with jeans, jean jackets, psychedelic t-shirts and head bands. Zach, the lead guitarist, is a born leader, has a quick sense of humor, and charismatic presence. When he plays guitar onstage, his style of playing and presence are reminiscent of Hendrix. Justin, the bassist, is a bit shy until you get to know him and he then will hug the shit out of you. Thomas, the drummer reminds me a bit of Frank Zappa with his dark brown hair in long, curly ringlets. Magic has electric frizzed-out hair and an outgoing personality. Tyler, the chauffeur, is a lone ranger sort and sleeps outside in the band's van. An incredible bond between our bands was formed from time spent together on the road.

Cloud Catcher was up first and played their loud and raucous set. In previous shows, their music was so loud that Rory's powerful voice was lost amidst the endless feedback of mics and amps. But this time, I could actually hear his voice. We were up next and played old and new songs plus new ones from our second album. JOY came on last and really jammed hard and heavy, their music an intermingling of the straight ahead and unrelenting, ball-busting heaviness of Blue Cheer with a bit of bluesy Hendrix flavor added to the mix. The audience yelled their enthusiastic cheers and waved fists in the air in appreciation of all the bands.

After JOY's set, we began the long and arduous process of hauling and loading equipment back in our vehicles. I saw Zach standing outside JOY's van and asked him where the band was sleeping that night. "Not sure, man, yet no worries, we'll find a hotel or something," he casually replied. I offered our house as a place to crash and he gratefully accepted. Dean already had his place to sleep upstairs in my yoga room, and I chuckled at the thought of our house becoming a crash pad. After we finished loading equipment, I gave Thomas some hurried directions to the house and wondered if he understood any of them at the ungodly hour of 2 a.m. We got home somewhere around 2:30 a.m., followed by

Dean and the guys from JOY. Gary and I bid the guys goodnight and left them to carve out sleeping spots on our living room floor.

Thursday, February 5, 2015—The long and winding road to Kansas City, Missouri

The next day Gary and I were up at 8 a.m. expecting Randy's arrival to help us load his truck with equipment, as he told us the previous night. Gary sneaked downstairs and took a photo of the JOY boys scattered across our living room floor huddled in sleeping bags, or in various stages of awakening. I wasn't aware that he took the photo until after the tour when he showed it to me. Randy, Kam and Grady met us at the house, and when everyone was finally awake, we all headed outside and took some great photos of the two bands together. We headed over to IHOP to grab a bite to eat, and the JOY boys said they would meet us somewhere along the road. Ironically, we didn't catch a single glance of them along the way until our final destination in Kansas City. Gary drove with Randy and I drove in Dean's car with Kam and Grady. We hit the road around 10 a.m. and arrived in Kansas City, Missouri around 9:30 p.m., almost a 12-hour slog. We were originally booked to play that night at the Jackpot Saloon in Kansas City, Kansas, yet found out a few days before the tour that the gig got cancelled and was changed to a place called The Union in Kansas City, Missouri. When trying to confirm our show, Gary and I were unable to find a phone number for The Union, so were unsure if we even had a gig for the night. Gary had made a previous hotel reservation in Kansas and we had to change to a different hotel in Missouri, which we luckily found at the last minute.

By the time we finally reached our destination, it was freezing cold outside and there was no place to park, as the neighborhood around The Union was right in the middle of the city. Gary got out of Randy's truck to check on logistics for the gig only to discover the place was not yet open. After circling around a number of times, Dean parked in a public parking area a few blocks away. Dean talked with Gary on the phone and after finding out about the place being presently closed, called Randy who was still circling the area. Randy soon parked next to us in the lot, and a very frozen Gary hurried towards us and hopped in Randy's truck to warm up.

After grabbing some dinner, we drove to another parking lot behind The Union, then unloaded and carried our equipment down some very icy and treacherously steep stairs into the club. We found out that another band, Gnarly Davidson, was opening for us and watched them set up after our gear was all settled in. The sound guy greeted us and seemed excited about us playing there. He said he had friends who also wanted to hear us play and sent out many text messages letting them know we would be playing that night. Gnarly played for about a half hour, then we played a 45-minute set. The audience was small, yet enthusiastic and gave us a warm reception. After our set, I headed back to the merchandise table only to find it unattended once again. I looked around for Kam or Grady and saw them watching JOY setting up. During the tour, they spent some time manning the merchandise tables, yet more often than not, they would approach Gary or me and ask if we could watch the table so they could watch the bands. JOY started playing sometime after midnight and I was enjoying their music standing back at the merch table when suddenly their music stopped. I wondered why they only played two songs. Apparently, the club had a 12:30 a.m. curfew and the DJ promptly shut them down. We chatted with them after their short set and they seemed to take the situation in stride. After chatting with fans and band members, JOY helped us load our equipment into our vehicles. By the time we reached our hotel, we were all pretty wiped out. Once again, another late to bed and early to rise morning awaited us.

Friday, February 6, 2015—A Hot Time at The Melt Tonight and Adventures En Route to St. Louis, Missouri

After a decent breakfast at Denny's, we hit the road for St. Louis around noon. We drove for seven hours and feeling the need to take a break, we stopped at a rest stop. I did some yoga stretches and Grady just laughed at me.

When arriving at The Melt, Dean pulled his car around to the alley in back, and we started the relentless process of loading and unloading equipment in through the back door. Getting out of the car, I was not paying attention to where my left hand was and slammed the door on my thumb! Wham! "OWWWWWWWW… !!!$**t, F**k!" I cursed. Luckily, I had gloves on my hands and they absorbed some of the initial blow. I ran inside and pulled the glove off my hand, not wanting to see the damage, yet curious nonetheless. Staring down at my bloody thumb in disbelief, I wondered how I would be able to play this gig and the next evening's show in Chicago. One of the cook's in the kitchen came over and seeing my situation offered me the first aid kit he held in his hand. I eagerly opened it hoping to find antiseptic and Band-Aids®, yet found only a few butterfly strips and an old alcohol pad. I asked the cook for a Band-Aid but he just shrugged his shoulders and walked back into the kitchen saying, "Nah, if there's none in there then I guess we're out."

After gingerly dabbing at my bloodied thumb with the lone alcohol wipe, and wrapping it around the sore appendage, I wandered out into the main room where the rest of the band had congregated. They were all seated at a table waiting for their dinner of waffles and lord knows whatever other sinfully delicious garbage food they ordered. Watching me approaching the table holding my sore thumb, they all stared at me like an alien had just arrived from Mars.

Gary got up from the table, his face full of concern. "What happened?"

"Slammed it in the car door." I headed over to the bar to ask the bartender for a Band-Aid®. The bartender, Luc, engaged me in conversation about the band. Luc was a friendly and outgoing sort of guy and avid Medusa fan. We chatted for some time about music and I enjoyed our banter. As fate would have it, he produced a Band-Aid® from behind the counter and I gladly took it and applied it to my battered thumb and thanked him.

"Hey, are you still gonna to be able to play? We have a lot of folks here that are really into you guys!"

"Yeah, she's a survivor!" I heard a familiar voice and turned around to see Gary standing right behind me. We laughed yet I winced in pain with every thought of banging my thumb around on the keyboard.

The first band was starting to set up on stage. We were playing second in the four-band line-up that evening. Gary tapped me on the shoulder and reminded me we needed to eat before our show. He had heard from the band members that the waffles weren't that great, so we decided to head out and grab some pizza, the main staple of any touring band. We found a small pizza place and chatted while waiting for our dinner.

Gary's ever-ringing cell rang and it was Zach wondering where we were.

"We're grabbing some pizza down the street… yeah, she's doing OK. It's hurting, yet she's a trooper…" *What's he talking about?* Between coughing my lungs out from a lingering cold and a smashed thumb, I felt like absolute crap! They talked for a few minutes more and then Gary informed me that Zach was making a special trip out to find me some Advil.

"No way! He doesn't have to do that!" I was grateful for and touched by his generosity and thoughtfulness. I knew we had some Advil somewhere in the mess of bags and equipment that used to be Dean's car, yet didn't want to even attempt to find it amidst the chaos.

After dinner, we headed back to The Melt with full bellies and nervous energy enough to rock people's socks off! When we arrived back at The Melt, everything was a blur of motion: gulping down a handful of Advil® tablets with water, setting up our equipment on stage in between the chaos of bodies from the first band tearing down their set, and JOY helping with ours. I looked out from the stage and saw a small crowd of people standing around waiting for us to start playing and felt a bit disappointed that there wasn't a larger crowd. Peaking back at my fellow band members, I asked, "Are we ready?" Gary nodded and we were off!

From the opening chords of our first song, "Strangulation," I noticed the place suddenly come alive. The crowd had grown to at least one hundred people and the air was charged with electricity that felt like a bolt of lightning hitting me square in the chest. The room was filled with heads bobbing and fists pumping in the air in time to the intense rhythmic beat of our music! Yells and cheers filled the air before, during and after each song we played. I would have pinched myself to make sure I was awake, yet dared not take my hands off the keyboard, reveling in the moment.

Gazing out at the crowd, I saw Zach staring back at me as if mesmerized by our music, with similar expressions on the faces of our audience. We were playing the universal language of music immediately understood, appreciated, and applauded with raucous hoots and hollers emitted from beaming, euphoric faces! Taking in the whole scene, I was a bit overwhelmed by their rowdy reactions, yet savored every moment. My thumb was precariously perched atop the edge of my Hammond SK1 and my fingers were doing a decent job of substituting, yet it would have to be used in the next song, "Turn to Stone." I managed to make it through our whole 45-minute set with only occasional thumb soreness when hitting my keys. All too soon, we finished playing and stood onstage taking in the wild and thunderous ovation from the crowd, followed by loading and unloading of equipment off the stage and into our vehicles waiting outside to take us on the last leg of our tour to Chicago.

We hung around to watch JOY play and to chat with the many fans who besieged us from all sides with enthusiastic and heartfelt displays of praise and admiration. Making my way over to the merchandise table, I saw that Kam and Grady were manning the table and thanked them for doing so. Grady proudly showed me the inventory sheet he fashioned to keep track of merch that we sold that evening. Noticing we sold a bunch of t-shirts and had only a few albums left, I wondered whether we would have enough to sell in Chicago. Luc came by and gave me a huge bear hug, interspersed with numerous "wows," and "hell, yeahs!" and extended an invitation for us to return in the fall to play at a festival sponsored by The Melt called Tu Fest. It was well after midnight by the time we left The Melt, exhausted to the bone and exhilarated to the max.

Saturday, February 7, 2015—From Mud Hut to Cobra Lounge—Chicago, Illinois

We had a sinfully huge and delicious breakfast with JOY at a neat little café in St. Louis called The Mud Hut and then hit the road for Chicago. Gary and I were chomping at the bit to get back to our hometown and to see familiar faces once again. I was looking forward to seeing Mo and cousin Susie again.

After a short six hour drive as compared to the past three days' marathon driving sessions, we arrived at Cobra Lounge around 7 p.m. and parked in an actual lot instead of our usual alleyway sprint unloading our gear on crowded street corners with hazards flashing. As I got out of Dean's car, I felt the familiar cold and damp atmosphere of Chicago amidst piles of snow, and thought *welcome home!* Visions of running through heavily snow and traffic-laden streets years ago with horns honking when still living here flashed through my mind. Chicago had just experienced a blizzard the week before, and I breathed a sigh of relief that we had missed it and made it safely to our last destination.

After unloading equipment, we met up with Dead Feathers, a local band whom we would be playing with that night, and chatted at some length with the lead singer, Marissa, and Tony, her husband and lead guitarist. I especially enjoyed talking with Marissa about music, of course, and our experiences as the only females in all male bands. Gary and I had listened to their music before we left on tour and marveled at their ability to create and play with a psychedelic quality so reminiscent of the '60s.

Pete suddenly appeared out of nowhere with his lovely wife, Dawnn, and we hugged and exchanged pleasantries for a few brief moments. Then Dawnn disappeared into another part of the lounge while Pete and the band headed to the stage for a sound check. We played a few songs with Pete yelling into the mic, and the scenario was so amazing, yet the full impact of being together again playing onstage after almost forty years hadn't quite hit me yet.

Being the headliners for the evening, we had a few hours to kill before playing. I meandered around the lounge, and saw my cousin, Susie, and her boyfriend Nick sitting there. When I walked over to talk with them, Susie beamed as we hugged and introduced me to Nick and informed me they were engaged. I extended heartfelt congratulations, as she was previously focused on her career rather than relationships, and I felt happy that she finally found her soul mate. We chatted for a while and then, feeling quite hungry, I excused myself and headed into the bar to find some food.

Walking into the bar, I noticed Gary had found us a table and was sitting waiting for me. Mo and my nephew, AJ, joined us and we engaged in conversation as we ate. After dinner, Gary and I headed back to the music area to catch the latter part of JOY's set and prepare for our show.

Once JOY finished their set, Gary nudged me towards the stage. It was hard to believe that the moment we had anticipated had finally arrived! I took a deep breath and felt my heart skip a few beats. Making my way to the stage, I saw that Gary and the guys were already onstage setting up equipment for our show. With heart pounding, I was almost to the stairs leading up to the stage, when suddenly a big burly guy with a goatee and huge grin stepped in front of me.

"Hi, I'm Dan," he extended his hand towards mine. "Donna, right? Are you excited about playing?" Dan vigorously pumped my hand. I searched his face for some familiarity, but I did not recognize him.

"How do you know me?"

"I'm the guy who found your 45," he exclaimed, his grin widening.

At that moment, my mind filled with memories of sitting at my desk, answering the phone and hearing Rob Sevier's voice at the other end, echoing words that would forever change our lives. I recalled talking with Gary then going downstairs to our computer and finding that Pete had already emailed telling us that Dan Schlosser, a friend of his, is the guy that gave Rob our 45. In an instant, the connection was made.

"Dan Schlosser! No way!" I gasped at this gentle giant standing in front of me realizing the monumental role he played in bringing Medusa back from the brink of oblivion and obscurity. I flung my arms around him and we embraced. We had just met, yet I felt like I had known him all my life!

"Man, I'm so psyched to see you guys play!"

"We are too! We've been waiting for this moment to play with Pete again for 40 years!" I could barely hold back the tears that were now freely streaming from my eyes. "Speaking of which, I should be heading to the stage right about now!" Breaking free of our bear hug, I took one last glance at his beaming face and wiping the tears from mine, ran up the stairs and onto the stage with heart pounding and adrenaline surging through my veins.

The guys were already setting up their gear as I dashed towards my keyboard stand and looked around for my keyboard cases. Gary was already setting up my keys and I pushed him over towards his set up area reminding him to set up his own stuff. In the chaotic moments of plugging in power cords to my keys and hoping I got the right cord in the right outlet, I also hoped to remember what chords I would be playing for the songs. Time seemingly stood still, although the moments raced by, and I glanced up from my keyboards to see Gary heading over to the mic to greet the crowd and recite a beautiful tribute to our old and prematurely deceased bass player, Kim. The tears returned when hearing the audience respond with a profound and reverent silence, sharing the moment with us. Gary then nodded in my direction and I found myself nervously playing the opening chords to "Into the Night." The atmosphere was electrified and filled with yells, cheers and fists pummeling the air, and I soon noticed Dan standing right in front of the stage smiling and adding fists, yells and cheers of his own to the pulsating melee.

After two songs, Randy announced, "We have a special guest we would like to have come on stage at this time," and introduced Pete to a welcoming and appreciative roar from the audience. My heart jumped right along with him onto the stage. He was wearing his brown fringe vest with Medusa logo on the back, waving and greeting the rowdy crowd. With much shorter hair than I remembered and tambourine in hand, he broke into the opening "ah haaaaa's" of Strangulation, and it seemed like no time had ever elapsed. The crowd roared their approval and one fan's voice was heard above the commotion, "HEY, YOU GUYS ARE OK!" We played five original songs that night —"Strangulation," "Frustration's Fool," "Temptress," "Black Wizard," and "Unknown Fear," — basking in the glow of shimmering lights and music that came full circle back to its place of origin.

After playing the old songs from the glory days with Pete, he left the stage to thunderous and deafening applause. We played the rest of the set including new songs, with high-octane energy as ever present in all the shows we played well into our Golden Years. An hour and a half seemed more like five minutes and then our show was over. We all clasped hands, and savoring forever the moment, took our bows and left the stage surrounded by throngs of gushing fans and blinding flashes of cameras capturing the moment. Following our show, there were blurs of faces, brief encounters, and exchanges with cousin Susie, Mo, and AJ. After a few thousand group shots with Pete, JOY and Dead Feathers, we left the Cobra somewhere after 1 a.m., exhausted yet exuberant.

CHAPTER 29

BEGINNINGS AND ENDINGS (2015)

"We can't even remotely fathom that whatever is ending for us is always more than an ending."
— **Craig D. Lounsbrough, M. Div., LPC, and Author**

Still flying high from our triumphant tour of the Midwest, we drove back to Colorado settled back into our separate work and life routines, and eagerly anticipated going into the studio to record our second album. Gary and I looked forward to our next Thursday evening rehearsal in which we would practice all the new songs once more despite having played them countless times during our past gigs. Although there were warning signs along the way, we didn't anticipate the fast approaching storm that would shake us to our very core.

Thursday, February 12, 2015

Ending the phone conversation with sullen expression, Gary walked back to the couch and slumped into it.

"Who was that?"

"Kam. He says he's coming over and wants to talk to us."

"Wonder what he's going to talk about?" I mused, as though trying to ignore all the conflict between Kam and Randy that, despite Kam's best efforts, was glaringly apparent. Ever since Randy joined the band, Kam had complained about everything from his combat fatigue boots to the camouflage pants he wore on stage. Kam and Grady, in their youthful minds, had their own ideas of what image our band should portray, and apparently Randy didn't fit the bill. Randy, on the other hand, was very amiable towards them, even taking time out of his busy work and school schedules to be a companion to Kam in recording sessions he had missed. Kam did, however, play a significant role in helping us reform the band and in his social circle having access to numerous contacts for getting us gigs, such as connecting with Dusty Brooks, a key organizer for South By South-west Fest in Austin, Texas.

An hour or so later there was a knock on the door, and in strolled Kam with a gloomy demeanor.

"Hey Kam," Gary and I greeted him.

"Hey." He sat down on a chair Gary pulled out from the dining room table, and got right to the point.

"It's either Randy or me," he calmly declared.

Gary and I exchanged glances not really knowing what to say and we all sat in silence pondering the weight of his words. In the past year and a half, we got to know him and appreciate his musical contributions to the band. But we were weary of the conflict between him and Randy. Although his words hit us like a ton of bricks, we knew it was only a matter of time before the shit was going to hit the fan.

"Well... Gary's voice suddenly broke the silence. I guess you have to do what you have to do."

"What do you have against Randy?" I asked.

"I don't think he fits the band."

"Who do you think would be a better fit?"

"I don't really understand why you made Arlo leave," Kam firmly stated his case. "I thought he was a good singer."

"Kam, that's your own opinion. We didn't make him leave. He chose to leave on his own." Kam had his mind made up and nothing we said moved him. He got up from the chair and walked towards the door.

"See ya."

"Yeah..." Gary dejectedly stared down at the floor.

"Nice knowing you, Kam," I told him in earnest. We briefly exchanged glances as he headed out the door.

Gary and I sat in silence for a few moments. We thought highly of Kam and his proficient level guitar playing he added to the band despite his young age.

"Well, it's done," Gary sighed with a mixture of relief and regret.

"His timing is spot on. Here we are two weeks away from going into the record-ing studio. What do we do now?"

"I was thinking either myself or Randy could do his parts in the studio. It will be interesting recording with just the four of us, yet we've done a few gigs already without him, so we'll survive."

Gary called Randy and Dean to let them know what had gone down with Kam. Randy told Gary that he knew a bass player named Phoenix Johnson, whom he had played with when they were in their Kiss tribute band, Rockissity. He asked Gary if he could bring Phoenix to rehearsal the following week and let him audition for the band. Gary asked Randy who would cover Kam's guitar parts, and Randy, originally a guitarist, offered to switch to playing guitar instead of bass. We decided to give it a try, and this decision turned out to be fortuitous.

The following week, Phoenix showed up for rehearsal and as he furiously flew around the room setting up his amp and bass, there was something familiar about him. Gary and I had attended a Rockissity show at Toad's Tavern a week or so before our first gig there. He looked a bit different bouncing around on stage donned with tons of the typical whiteface make-up and glitter-glam attire of Kiss band's tongue-wagging bassist, Gene Simmons. It was hard to believe that this was the same guy with his petite stature, frizzed-out jet-black hair and orange Bronco sweatshirt, looking rather unassuming, yet his bass playing spoke volumes. It took him all of three days to learn our songs and it astounded us that he was able to accompany us into our studio recording sessions playing Randy's old bass lines without missing a beat. It was obvious we had stumbled on a true professional who blew us away with his thunderous, lightning fast bass riffs and steadfast, melodious vocal ability that added another dimension to our music. We were now psyched and ready to record our second album.

Colorado Sound Recording was a studio recommended to me by Danielle, a musician and yoga student of mine, who had previously recorded in the studio. Gary had gone in to check out the studio on the first visit and spoke to Kevin, the owner, at length about our project and was impressed with Kevin's knowledge of the recording process and industry. He was under the impression that Kevin would be our recording engineer, yet we were in for a surprise. I had accompanied Gary to several other studios, yet he liked this studio the best and we decided to go with it. When we went in the end of February for our first session, we merely dropped off our equipment so we could be ready to roll early the next day. Kevin was there to help us get set up and after many sound and drum mic checks, it was already late and time to head for our weary beds. We shook hands with Kevin and bid him a good night.

The next morning, we were met by Brandon, who introduced himself as Kevin's assistant and told us he would be our engineer, as Kevin was busy recording at another location. Brandon was young enough to be Kevin's son and we were a bit skeptical about his recording capabilities. I recall questioning Gary about the situation, and he was just as puzzled as I was. He had even told Kevin that he was glad to have someone his age with all his experience and knowledge of the '70s sound working with us. Nonetheless, Brandon became our engineer and eventually won us over with his laidback manner, competent work ethics and proficiency in operating Pro Tools, the recording software program.

The guys in the band had already been in recording studios previously. But for me, stepping into a recording studio for the first time was a bit nerve-wracking. Entering the studio for the first time, I was inundated with all the high-tech recording equipment scattered around the studio and the experience seemed unreal. I imagined the musicians I had idolized as a youngster, such as Paul McCartney and Jimi Hendrix, walking into the studio for the first time. I wondered if they felt nervous as well and marveled that I was now sharing their musical legacy, albeit less legendary. Perhaps even more worrisome was having to come up with a marketable product and wondering if it would be considered good enough by industry standards.

In the early days of Medusa, I had struggled to come up with lyrics and music for the rudimentary songs I wrote and didn't really give much thought to themes, much less marketability. My current song-writing process is far more theme-oriented and most songs are created in the shower! Melodies come into my head much like a full orchestra playing at a live concert, and I hear every note as though the orchestra were playing right there in my bathroom. This led to numerous midnight forays down into the basement to bang out unmerciful melodies on my keys when I should have been doing the more sensible thing, sleeping! Since the senseless passing of Ava, my Grand Canyon friend, I have written songs covering every topic from parents to road rage and everything in between. Little did I know at the time how a tribute song could ever evolve into the depth of songs we were now about to record, some based on Edgar Allen Poe stories and Dante's Inferno.

So, there we were in the studio laying down basic instrumental tracks of the new songs over two ten-hour long days at the end of February. They actually sounded pretty decent despite Kam's absence. Vocals and additional instrumentation were added on dates dictated by Colorado Sound, extending from March through August. I didn't have a clue about how much work went into recording an album, financially, physically and emotionally until actually going through the experience. I discovered the biggest obstacles in recording were getting the songs to sound the way we wanted them to sound and trying to get the recording engineers on the same page.

After finishing the actual recording of the songs, we were all given mp3's to listen to and make sure we were happy with the sound and finished product. Of course, there were a few blunders and mistakes both in instrumentation and vocals, and we made several more trips back to the studio for Brandon to work on them, especially getting the drum parts down to Dean's satisfaction. Then there was the final mastering of the mixes and it wasn't until September that we finally had a mastered product we were pleased with. We soon discovered there were more surprises in store for us in the near future. In the meantime, while still in the recording process, we eagerly looked forward to playing at the prestigious music Festival, South By Southwest Fest in Austin, Texas, to break up the recording routine.

CHAPTER 30
HEADING SOUTH BY SOUTHWEST (2015)

"The road to success is a very lonely road. You're not going to see too many friends. It's only you with your shadow. Once you get there, many people will love you, also many people will hate you. Because your success is a huge spotlight, shining on their failures."
— **Greg Plitt, Actor, Entrepreneur and Motivational Speaker**

"We're excited to meet y'all! We've heard all about y'all and dig the shit out of y'all's music!" Dusty exclaimed to Gary on the phone a few months prior to the festival we would be playing in March. Of course, we were just as excited and stoked about playing this event as was Dusty upon our acceptance of his invite! Dusty also worked as a bartender at The Lost Well, a popular bar and musical venue in Austin. Gary and Dusty had a number of prior phone conversations to discuss details of playing at The Lost Well.

South By Southwest, abbreviated SXSW, is described as, "the world's leading music industry event that provides attendees with the ability to explore the future of music during the day with its trade show, music gear expo, panels, and discussions while at night experience the absolute best mix of regional, national, and international performers." (26.) Known for hosting acts in every genre of music from new artists to music legends such as: Stevie Nicks, Prince, Bruce Springsteen, and Lou Reed, SXSW attracts bands and crowds worldwide.

Getting a chance to play at this festival was for us, the chance of a lifetime to achieve even more recognition in the music arena than we had already attained. During twice weekly rehearsals in preparation for the Fest, we excitedly talked about travel arrangements with Dean, Randy and Phoenix. Dean said he was going to fly to Austin with Leonore to visit with his family, leaving us to figure out how we would get all our equipment, including his drums, into Gary's cramped 2008 Ford Focus or my old 1998 Ford Ranger.

Gary's Focus was a more logical choice than driving my dilapidated Ranger which could possibly break down on the road. But the car was too small to accommodate amps, guitars, two keyboards, and Dean's drums. After giving up on the idea of using Gary's vehicle, we decided to rent a bigger and newer car and drive in style. Randy had offered to help carry some of the equipment and the four remaining band members in his truck, but Gary and I knew it would be a tight fit just for equipment, never mind the humans! So, it was finally decided that Phoenix would ride with Randy, and Gary and I rented our luxury ride. Despite our best efforts, we were still packed to the max! Somehow, we managed to make it all fit and finally hit the road heading for Amarillo.

After a grueling nine-hour drive, we finally made it to Amarillo, checked into our hotel, grabbed some dinner and prepared for bed as we were exhausted from the day's long drive.

Wednesday, March 18, 2015—Awesome Austin

After another long day of driving, we hit the big city of Austin, Texas, around 7:30 p.m. and were super stoked and LOST! Amarillo paled in comparison to the endless winding highways, byways and hustle and bustle of Austin. Approaching the city, we took a few wrong turns and ended up on I-45 instead of I-35. After driving in circles, we managed to navigate ourselves to La Quinta, our hotel for the next few days and actually found Carino's, a decent place to eat this time. Afterwards we headed downtown to check out the Gypsy Lounge and see the JOY boys. We parked a few blocks away from Gypsy Lounge, then walked over and met up with the JOY boys, Arctic, and another local band, Crypt Trip. Justin greeted me with his usual smile and bear hug, and after our embrace I asked him when they were playing. He informed me that they were the headliners and wouldn't go on stage until 1 a.m.

"Man, that's a bummer!"

"Yeah, no shit," Justin grinned at me. I wondered why his bandmates nicknamed him "Nasty," as he always seemed good natured and mellow whenever we would meet. I never did find out.

We chatted for a while with members of the three bands. Sam Bryant, the bass player from Crypt Trip, engaged us in a lengthy conversation. Gary and Sam had corresponded a number of times on Facebook, and it was evident Sam was especially enamored with Gary, looking up to him both as musician and role model.

A band I was not familiar with, Ruby The Hatchet, hailing from Philadelphia, was now onstage. Watching them play, I was especially taken by the delicate presence and powerful voice of the lead singer, Jillian. Their music is reminiscent of the psychedelic sound of early Jefferson Airplane, complete with echoplex and fuzz guitar sounds intertwined with vocal strains similar to that of Grace Slick.

After they finished playing their set, I met up with Jillian who was sitting at a table selling their CDs, and I discovered she was as huge a fan of our music as was I of hers. We instantly bonded. Gary and I wearily headed back to our hotel around 1a.m., deciding we were too tired to stick around to see JOY play.

Thurs. 3-19-15—Lost and Found at The Lost Well

Donnaaaaaa! Donnaaaaaa! Donnaaaaaaaaaaaa… The crowd's deafening cheers persisted, echoing through my sleep deprived brain. Glancing at the sea of faces blurred by the intense stage lighting, I could barely make out where the stage ended and the crowd began. Energized by the thunderous roar of the crowd, I played with an intensity and fervor summoned up from a deep reserve within. Sweat was now pouring from every pore like the music I was playing.

Gary and I started the day with breakfast then headed to The Lost Well and sat outside at one of many tables set up in the back yard around the bar. As our show didn't start until 1a.m., we had plenty of time to kill and chatted with Dusty and some fans. Dusty introduced us to an artist named, Phillip Reader, who said he said he was a big fan of our music. We got into a lengthy conversation with him and viewed some of his artwork. Gary and I really liked what we saw and thought the Medusa logo he created would look good on the cover on our newest album whenever it was ready for release. We exchanged phone numbers and told Philip we would keep in touch with him.

Randy and Phoenix arrived sometime in the early afternoon looking road worn and torn, an entertained us with their stories from the road. They told us they had driven for two days straight through from Colorado to Austin, stopping only for brief naps and pit stops and pit washes. It was good to see them again and hear their humorous stories. Dean arrived sometime afterwards looking composed as usual.

As the hours dragged on, in anticipation of finally hitting the stage, we peeked inside to check out other bands as they took the stage and played their sets. We watched several bands, heard loud, though barely discernable vocals, then retreated back outside to wait our turn. We knew that a local heavy metal band, Mothership, was playing at midnight right before us, and looked forward to hearing them play live. Gary and I had listened to their music online and we'd even sent a few emails back and forth. Mothership was originally listed as the headliners, yet Kelley, their lead guitarist, was kind enough to give us the top spot as headliners for the evening. Though grateful for this offer, we were a bit apprehensive about the reception we would receive from the audience. Looking around at the crowd hanging in the back yard, I wondered if we'd even have an audience when we took the stage after Mothership.

While still back in Colorado, we had received an email from Whitney, the bass player from Voidstrider, another band from Austin. Whitney said she was a fan of our music and looked forward to playing with us at The Lost Well. We shared mutual admiration and ironically that we were both married to musicians and in bands together. I looked forward to meeting Whitney and hearing her band play at the Fest.

Needing a break from The Well, Gary and I took a walk to grab a bite to eat before our show. When we returned, Voidstrider was getting ready to do their set and I met with Whitney and enjoyed talking with her and meeting RJ, her husband and drummer, and Clint, the guitarist. Fervent fans of our music, they expressed their eagerness to hear us play live and I felt buoyed by their encouraging words. I enjoyed their heavy, yet melodic music reminiscent of late '70s with a taste of Rainbow and Deep Purple minus keyboards.

It was fast approaching midnight and Gary and I were engaged in a conversation with Kelley, Mothership's lead guitarist and bantered on and on about music. Kelley then excused himself from the conversation, shook our hands saying, "Can't wait to hear y'all!" and disappeared into The Well to prepare for their show. Randy, Dean, Gary, Phoenix, and I were hanging just outside the side doors leading into The Well and soon heard thunderous, raucous guitar riffs pouring from Kelley's guitar and just as thunderous yells and cheers radiating from the crowd as they started their set. After listening to Mothership for five minutes, I decided to sneak inside to catch their show, and was a bit surprised to see the place only half filled with people. Now I was really nervous, wondering if we'd have any audience by the time we took the stage after 1a.m. and what kind of reception we'd get. Glancing at my watch, I saw it was 12:30 a.m. and knew I had to get ready for our show. I walked back outside, grabbed my clothes bag from our car and hurried inside The Well heading for the ladies room.

Slipping into the slinky blue paisley dress Gary bought me, especially for wearing onstage, I felt a bit overdressed yet thought if I was going to be a rock legend, I might as well look the part. Wondering if older ladies should wear short dresses, I nervously pulled down on the dress hem, and walked outside where the guys were hanging out. Gary was the first to notice me approaching and smiled his approval as he slipped his arm around me.

"That dress really looks good on you!"

"Thanks for getting it for me," I smiled, squeezing his hand.

Turning around to face the guys, they briefly glanced in my direction then refocused their attention on finally taking the stage.

Suddenly, cheers erupted from inside The Well, signaling the end of Mothership's set, and we were once again in motion hauling our equipment into the smoky and dimly lit room. Involved in the chaos of setting up equipment and getting ready to play, I hardly took notice of the crowd of people now filing into the room. The stage was fairly good sized and I set my keyboards up on the far right somewhat behind where Gary would be playing. Chuckling to myself, I recalled watching the video of our first show at Toad's Tavern and noticed that I wasn't in any part of it. Coming back to the present moment, I pulled my keys out farther to the right in attempt to be more visible onstage.

It was 1:10 a.m., and I suddenly felt exhausted. Gazing out towards the audience, I saw a miraculous sight before me. The place was packed with people crowding the stage and filling the dimly lit room to capacity. Before I could even react to the sight, it was show time and Randy grabbed the mic and greeted the crowd with, "Hey, how y'all doing tonight?" The crowd roared back their enthusiastic response, intensifying the already super-charged ambience. I stood onstage taking in the moment, the crowd's deafening cacophony, the bright lights from the stage shining a seductive, sultry blue, gazing out to hundreds of bobbing heads barely visible in the dim, hazy bar hall atmosphere. Pastel pink lettering of The Lost Well behind the stage mixed with the blue, immersed us in splashes of iridescent purple. I thought this so unreal yet I reveled in each passing second.

With renewed fervor, we broke into our first song, "Strangulation," adrenaline coursing through our musical veins. We played with an intensity spilling from the very depths of our souls. Each song built on the intensity of the previous song, igniting the flames of kindred musical spirits setting the night on fire. "Looks like we're headin' for Armageddon!" Randy's voice ominous and threatening and the crowd roared back their approval, as if to say, "Yeah, we're going there too!"

There were so many highlights of that night, it's hard to put into words. Feeling the magic of playing "Black Wizard" in front of a live crowd, beyond description. Another highlight, jamming with uninhibited anarchy on "Transient Amplitudes," taking the audience on one hell of a roller coaster ride and breaking into a keys solo, hearing my name being yelled out by the crowd! What a moment!

After the show, someone jumped up onstage and began vigorously pumping my hand, yelling, "Great show! You guys killed it, man!" I stared at him trying to figure out where I'd seen him before and suddenly it dawned on me that he was Vaughn, the keyboards player, from Space in Time. Embracing with my face buried in his shirt, I mumbled an apology, "Vaughn, sorry I didn't recognize you! What are you doing here?" He explained his band was playing down the street and he decided to stop by and check out our show. After we chatted for a short time, I thanked him for stopping by and headed through the crowd towards the front of the club with keyboards in tow. Glancing behind me, I caught sight of Vaughn and Gary engaging in conversation.

Searching for some space to store equipment, I made my way through the throngs of throbbing humanity to the entrance of the club and was intercepted by my good JOY buddies and several fans I recognized from before our show. Pausing for a few minutes to chat and hear their praise and admiration for our music, I was approached by a long, tall lanky guy wearing a snappy looking Stetson who engaged me in conversation, shook my hand and introduced himself as Aryn Jonathan Black, vocalist of Austin-based heavy psych rock band, Scorpion Child. After a long discussion about the ins and outs of the music business, I finally reached the front entranceway and wearily set the keyboards down on the ground. Breathing heavily with a mixture of exhaustion and exhilaration, I noticed Tasha, owner of The Lost Well, approaching me. She was also complimentary about our music, remarking that our show was "the best she had seen at The Well to date..." Instantly liking her down-to-earth and good-natured manner, we connected. Smiling and grabbing my hand, she followed up with, "Medusa is welcome here anytime and hope y'all come back soon!"

After packing all equipment in our vehicles, Dean bid us farewell and said he was heading over to his daughter's house to stay the night. Randy, Phoenix, Gary, and I drove to the house of Deb Dangerfield, a good friend of Dusty's to try to catch some welcome sleep. It was around 3 a.m. and we were feeling pretty wiped from all the events of a very long day. Two ladies were sitting on the front porch, waiting for our arrival. A blonde, outgoing lady waved and called out to us in her best southern drawl, "Hey there, I'm Deb and this is my friend, Jennifer.

Y'all must be the Medusa band!" Deb was kind to open up her house to a scruffy bunch of road warriors and total strangers. She practically bolted down the stairs to shake our hands and welcome us to her humble abode. I wondered how she could be so perky at this ungodly morning hour when I was barely able to stand up.

Taking Gary and me on a tour of their house, Deb and Jen showed us our room. We then spent at least another hour or so chatting and answering endless questions about our music. Despite overwhelming fatigue and desperately wanting nothing more than to collapse on the bed below us, I got a chance to know the two ladies quite well.

Jen, a slender reddish-brown haired lady, was a musician in her own right who wrote music and played with her own band at several local venues. Deb mentioned that she did some bartending at The Well, bearing witness to some of the finest touring bands around the world. After some length of time, she sauntered out of the room heading for the front porch to join Phoenix and converse with him. Randy had long since crashed out on the living room couch. Jen and I chatted until noticing it was now 5 a.m. Barely able to keep my eyes open for one second longer, I excused myself and wearily collapsed on the bed in our room.

Gary and I exchanged tired glances and he whispered, "Now, let's try to get some sleep."

"Yeah, right. Good luck with that!" I groggily answered knowing full well that sleep would be hard to come by for us both. Lying in bed and holding hands, with lucid images of all the day's events running rampant through our heads, Gary sleepily muttered, "Oh, by the way, we're playing The Well again tonight."

"That's nice... I sleepily muttered until startled awake by his comment. What??? I thought we were heading for home tomorrow or rather today?"

"I talked with Dusty after the show and he told me the opening band cancelled for Friday's show and I offered for us to be the openers."

"Really? OK, so we'd better try to get whatever sleep we can." Turning towards the window and noticing the first rays of light slowly peeking through the curtains, I groaned softly, *Today's going to be another long day...* and fell into a light and fitful slumber.

Friday night's show was not nearly as well attended or rowdy as that of the previous night, yet the crowd gave us a warm and welcoming Austin applause nonetheless. After the show, Dean met us outside as we loaded gear into our vehicles. He was staying to spend some quality time with his family. We bid him adieu and headed back to Deb's house to thank Deb and Jen for their hospitality. As we made our farewells, Deb promised to interview us for a filmed documentary she was planning to create. We hit the road somewhere before midnight, Randy and Phoenix in Randy's SUV and Gary and me in our crammed-to-the-max rental car, anticipating the long road back home to Colorado and another road trip to California later that summer.

CHAPTER 31
ALL THE WORLD'S A STUDIO
(and your Shingles are showing) (2015)

"We are made strong by the difficulties we face, not by those we evade."
— **Author unknown**

A few weeks after our Austin trip, while teaching my Monday evening yoga class, I noticed a persistent stabbing pain between my shoulders and tried to dismiss it, thinking I had pulled a muscle by getting too enthusiastic in a yoga pose. The next day I went to see a doctor and got one of the biggest surprises of my life when he informed me I had shingles. When in my thirties, I developed shingles after returning from the Honolulu Marathon and remembering the exquisite pain it produced, I shuddered. Back then it was relatively short-lived, lasting only about a month, yet this time it was here to stay for the duration.

Shingles is a reactivation of the herpes-zoster virus, the same virus that causes chickenpox. Once you recover from the first bout, the virus lies dormant in your nerve cells until another period of extreme stress and/or weakened immune system that causes the virus to reactivate. It typically affects a person only once in their lifetime, but can also reoccur a second and perhaps even third time. The best protection against shingles is getting the vaccine, which I discounted many times, thinking I was immune to the virus having already suffered through the first bout.

"Shouldn't I have a rash?" I questioned this doc.

After reassuring me I would, he advised I have an EKG just to make sure the pain wasn't related to my heart. The technician peered down at my wired for sound chest and pointed to a cluster of small red bumps she noticed. "It looks like you have a rash," she informed me.

"Great…" I sighed trying to prepare myself for the second go around of this hideous malady.

After months of feeling crappy with the flu and then being on the road, I was actually enjoying feeling well for a few weeks, Then suddenly I was back on the road less traveled and forced to switch gears. Isn't that the way life is?

Over the next several months, with shingles full blown, our band spent a tremendous amount of time recording the newest songs for our second album. Each session was like one wild roller coaster ride after another. Clutching my hot water bottle, "Big Pink," to my aching rib cage, I stumbled into the studio in a blaze of blisters and pain balm, while Gary and the guys bounced around the studio telling bad jokes and waiting for their turns to sing or record their instrumental parts. There were upbeat times such as playing a fancy Yamaha piano where I felt on top of the tracks, and times so low I could barely stand up, lying on the couch in one of the recording rooms in a heap of pain. Phoenix, who put in long hours at work, also took naps on the couch in the small break room near the back studio doorway. He and I would often try to beat each other to the couch. Every now and then, he would poke his tired head into the room to see if I was still alive, and utter the dreaded words, "You're up."

Moaning, I would gingerly slide my battered and polka-dotted body off the couch and stagger my way, like Lurch of "*The Adams Family*" fame, into the next room to pluck away on my keys as though the very act of plucking would strike a harmonious chord deep within, reawakening wellness. Playing and singing, although requiring enormous amounts of energy, were great distractions from the physical plague.

Big Pink has history. Mo sent it to me years prior as either a birthday or Christmas gift and after opening the wrapping, I thought it an odd gift at the time when still in relatively good health. Yet it was strangely comforting. The hot water bottle was tucked inside a fluffy, furry pink cover complete with fuzzy little dingle balls for the ultimate package. Little did I know then what a blessing it would be years later when soothing my accursed shingles-shattered nerve cells.

The next few months in the studio flew by in a flurry of furious guitar and keyboard riffs, shrill, shrieking vocals, crashing of drum cymbals, and lightning fast bass licks. While listening over and over again to our recordings, Brandon patiently took our suggestions, tweaking and somehow creating a great sounding album out of chaos. The album still needed to be mastered, the final step in recording and we didn't have a clue how long that would take. It was already heading into the heat of July. While we eagerly awaited the finished mastered CD to send to Todd at Ripple Music, we took a break to tour the west coast with our JOY friends.

CHAPTER 32

CHAPTER 32
CALIFORNIA ADVENTURES (2015)

*"Two roads diverged in a wood, and I — I took the one
less traveled by, and that has made all the difference."*
— Robert Frost, Poet

Zach had a plan! He contacted us sometime in early spring to ask if we could join them on tour. He informed us that we had a plethora of fans in California and would be well received. Remembering our Austin show, we doubted it could get much rowdier than that, yet we were in for a big surprise.

Our tour schedule started on Fri., July 3rd, in San Diego at a club called, Til-Two, then head for San Francisco on July 4th to play at the Amnesia Club. We would then do a show in Sacramento on the 5th at the Starlight Lounge, followed by a well-needed day of rest on the 6th, then on to our last show in Arcata on the 7th.

Although excited about doing another tour with JOY, I was still in a lot of pain from shingles, and the thought of being on the road again, lugging heavy equipment was about as exciting as being poked in the eye with a sharp stick. After doing last minute shopping and packing for the trip, we half-heartedly dropped off our beloved canine companion, Toby, at the house of our neighbor Tim. It did our hearts good to see Toby and Griz, Tim's dog, cavorting around like a bunch of wild monkeys. We headed up to stay the night at Dean's, knowing Toby was in good hands.

We got up early the next morning to start our trip, wondering if Phoenix would make the 70-mile trip from his home in Platteville to Dean's house in Conifer in time for our early 8 a.m. departure. Surprisingly enough, he did. While waiting for Phoenix to arrive, Leonore took pictures of the band standing around shivering and shaking in the early morning mountain air.

Somewhere around 8:30 a.m., with all equipment packed and loaded into Dean's trailer, we hitched the trailer to Randy's rig—aka: the "gnatmobile,"—and hit the road.

A few months prior to our trip, Randy bounded downstairs to our basement where we rehearsed, excitedly regaling us with news of the RV he bought to cart us out to California. "It's a beauty!" he exclaimed, his face beaming. Thinking it was a brand new vehicle and we would ride in style, we were buoyed by the news.

"I'm fixing it up to get it ready for the road," he proudly announced. It should be ready by July for sure." Upon hearing his last comment, my heart sank. Maybe we wouldn't be going anywhere, especially if an old fixer-upper RV broke down somewhere along the dusty trail heading out west.

"Randy, how old is the RV?" I asked.

"It's a mid-eighties model but it should get us out to California with no problems. I have to paint it, do some engine work, and figure out a few gas smells and then we'll be good to go."

I had some reservations about traveling in an older vehicle, which is why I didn't volunteer to drive my '98 Ford Ranger, yet figured Randy, a car mechanic, would make it roadworthy. As the saying goes, never assume anything.

A week before our tour, he drove it over to our house for us to inspect. It was a bit cramped for five people, yet looked in fairly good repair. Randy told us it was newly painted and soon thereafter a bunch of gnats flew right into the wet paint adding a bit of unwanted texture to the mix, justifying our nickname of gnatmobile. The smell of fresh gas permeated the air and when questioning Randy about it he shrugged it off, saying he was "still working on it."

He did work on it and we started our road trip sans gas odors. The problem was it didn't have a working generator. But we took in the sights heading west out of Colorado into Arizona, with Randy at the wheel, Dean, Gary, and me sitting in the back, and Phoenix, sitting up front riding shotgun next to Randy in his favorite captain's chair. The morning started out chilly, but grew stifling hot as we headed towards our first destination, Camp Verde, in the vast Painted Desert. It was a very long 13-hour ride without either working A/C or refrigeration due to the nonworking generator. Wiped out from the road heat we crashed early for the night—Phoenix in his chair, Gary in his sleeping bag on the floor, me on a hide-a-bed underneath the kitchen table, and Randy and Dean sharing the only bed in the back of the RV. They probably got the best sleep that night.

After another restless night, I awoke early, took a shower, and felt revived and ready for the day. Randy, Gary, and I headed over to Denny's for a nice, quiet breakfast until Dean and Phoenix joined us. So much for the quiet breakfast! Behind our table, sat a group of middle-age ladies minding their own business, until Phoenix announced that our band was heading out to California on tour and it wasn't long until the whole restaurant knew about it. The ladies were fawning over us and Phoenix was basking in the spotlight.

Hitting the road again around 10 a.m., we were soon being fried from the 110-degree desert heat as we limped along minus A/C and a working refrigerator. Randy pulled the RV over at a rest stop and I voiced my displeasure about being without a working generator in a potentially dangerous situation. After a heated discussion, he apologized and we got back on the road. Heading once more for San Diego, we chugged our way up some fairly steep hills barely doing 20 MPH! We literally willed that RV up those wicked steep hills, praying the whole way.

We finally reached San Diego around 6 p.m. with just enough time to find our club, Til Two and load in. We met up again with the JOY boys inside the club and it was good seeing their smiling faces. After chatting with them, we headed back to the gnatmobile to get ready for the show. Gathering my stage clothes, I felt the eyes of Randy, Phoenix, Dean, and Gary studying me intently as they were ready for a show of their own. I had to remind them that, much to their chagrin, there would be no private shows that night and they left the cramped RV to give me some privacy.

Slow Season played their set first followed by Loom, and both tore the place up with their raucous and rowdy musical renditions of Led Zeppelin. Looking around, I was surprised to see a brief glimpse of Kam and Grady before they disappeared into the increasing throngs of people milling around the stage and club. I remembered that sometime before our tour Grady had moved to California and Kam, his ever-present companion, was apparently paying him (and us) a visit.

By the time Medusa took the stage, the audience had filled the place to maximum capacity with their adoration and great fanfare. Todd, from Ripple, mentioned in an email that he would be there to meet us, although he never showed. We were a bit disappointed. It would have been nice to meet in person with the record label owner who was interested in releasing our second album and for him to see our live show. But the fans consoled us with their lavish praise for our music, engaging conversations, and requests for autographs. The owner of Til-Two remarked to Gary that our show was the best to date at the club. One young lad approached Gary and me after our set, engaged us in lengthy discussion about our music and asked for an autograph. We both grabbed some magic markers and wrote our names on the front of his white t-shirt while his face (and chest) burst at the seams with adulation and euphoria. "Wow, man, this is fuck'n great!"

we heard him repeatedly exclaim. JOY closed the show, showering the exuberant audience with their mind-blowing music and undulating amoebic light show.

Sometime during JOY's set into the wee morning hours, Dean approached Gary and me reminding us that we still had a long drive to get to his son Chris's house, where we would be staying that night. We hopped in the RV with Randy with Phoenix following behind us and drove for two hours to Lawndale, where his son lived. It was 5:30 a.m. by the time we arrived, and the first rays of daylight were already breaking on the horizon. Randy and Phoenix crashed in the RV parked down the street from where Chris lived. Gary and I followed Dean into the house and were introduced to Chris while they chatted for the better part of the morning. Gary and I hit Chris's couch by 6 a.m. to catch a few hours of much needed sleep. I soon fell into an exhausted and dreamless slumber, anticipating unknown adventures that awaited us down the road.

Saturday, 4th of July, 2015

After catching a few hours of sleep, quick showers, and a bite to eat, we were back on the road heading for San Francisco. We had another grueling trip having to endure more soaring heat temps of 100-degree heat as we traveled through the California countryside without A/C or refrigeration, forcing us to stop many times at rest stops to cool us ourselves down by pouring bottled water over our heads. Zach called Gary while we were still en route to Amnesia, our club for the night to let us know we were playing third on band line-up schedule. We finally arrived around 8 p.m. tired and irritable after another long, hot road slog.

The stage was very small, undoubtedly the smallest stage we had performed on to date. Dean's drums took up most of the space in the middle of the stage, leaving Phoenix up against the wall and the rest of us crammed in between like sardines! Despite a rough start of a malfunctioning tuning peg of Gary's guitar causing him to leave the stage, and my misplaced keyboard cable, we managed to get underway. We played "Strangulation," our opening number in front of another enthusiastic crowd of perhaps 100 people without our lead guitarist and still the crowd yelled their ardent approval. I found out later from Gary that he left the stage to find Zach and get a backup guitar to play.

Gary rejoined us onstage for the next song with Zach's spare Stratocaster guitar and we were once again a force to be reckoned with! During our set, I recall looking up from my keyboards, focusing beyond the crowd packing the room to the scene occurring outside. People were watching us outside the club dancing to the beat of our music and I marveled at the sight.

Sometime in the middle of "Transient Amplitudes," an instrumental song, Gary had a power failure in his amp. While he tried to fix the problem, the band played on without missing a beat. It's always a bit disconcerting to have your lead guitarist flummoxed by power outages, yet we band members learn to take it in stride and know that the show must go on. Once again, the fans barely took notice. One fan even wrote on Instagram that of countless shows he's seen over some 30 years, he had never previously born witness to a band so "killer" that it knocked out the power.

After playing our set, we were once again mobbed by the crowd, and it never ceased to amaze me. Mingling with our fans, I met a lady named Laura, who was a writer for a local magazine and wrote an article about us and even booked our show at Amnesia. During our lengthy conversation, she extended an invitation to return to San Francisco anytime and to contact her to book another show. If there were any fireworks going on outside, I never heard or saw them, immersed in the fireworks we created that night.

Arriving back at the RV sometime around 2 a.m., we headed for Denny's, our favorite stomping grounds to grab some food and discuss where we would crash that night. We decided to find a rest stop to park the RV and get some sleep. But Randy had a different plan and drove through the night to Sacramento where we would be playing the next night. Dean and Phoenix also took turns driving and dozing. Between the adrenaline rush of the gig we had just played and the overwhelming fatigue of being in almost constant motion, sleep was catch as catch can. We ended up parking in a Wal-Mart lot and by the time we got done shopping, we finally hit the sack at 5:30 a.m. After all, you can't just park at Wal-Mart without shopping!

Sunday, July 5, 2015

Looking forward to our day off on Monday, we pulled into an RV resort called "Flag City" and spent the day swimming in the pool and soaking our weary bones in the hot tub. Feeling revived after our spa day, followed by a hearty breakfast and lunch, we got dressed in our stage attire and headed down to our next gig at Starlight Lounge in downtown Sacramento.

Prior to the show, we met a silver-haired guy with a long pony-tail who ran the psychedelic light show. We had an interesting chat with him during which he told us that he didn't much care for "revival bands." I thought it a strange statement coming from a guy straight out of the same era our music was created!

Black Magic Acid was first up to play. I met Cheryl, the bassist, and enjoyed chatting and getting to know her. I enjoyed their music, yet was not a fan of their loud, growling vocals, reminiscent of many bands of the day.

JOY played before us and tore the place up, as they had a habit of doing wherever they played. After sneaking outside to take a few band photos outside the RV, we got back just as JOY finished their set. We took the stage and wearily gazed out towards the audience. I was a bit disappointed to see a small gathering of people. Nonetheless, we rocked the house and got great reception from those brave souls who stayed to the end of our 45-minute set. One fan approached me as I feverishly tried to untangle the chaos of twisted keyboard cables in the fast and furious minutes between tearing down equipment and the next band, Lecherous Gaze, setting up. "You guys baked it, man!" she exclaimed, instantly grabbing my hand and attention. Staring at her for a few seconds, the sensations of overwhelming fatigue and throbbing sinuses washing over me like tidal waves, I finally came to my senses. The impact our music had on fans across the country suddenly hit me over the head like a sledgehammer. Momentarily forgetting the chaotic cables and congestion, I thanked her and appreciated the welcome respite from the previous frenzied task at hand. "Hope you guys come back again…" We chatted briefly and I watched her disappear into the dark shadows of the bar room.

"Coming through!" my trance suddenly interrupted by Dean's gruff voice as he lugged sections of his drum kit off the stage. I jumped back out of his way, staring absently after him, then threw the mess of cables into my keyboard cases and wearily dragged them offstage.

After loading more equipment into our vehicle, I came back into the club and noticed Gary chatting with the light show guy and shaking his hand. Approaching where they stood, I overheard faint strains of their conversation.

"Great show, man! Great show!" Mr. Silver Pony Tail exclaimed excitedly pumping Gary's hand. *Not bad for a "revival" band, I thought biting my tongue.* Shaking my hand and wearing a huge grin Silver added, "You guys really rocked it tonight! Surprised the heck outta me!"

"No surprise to us," I smiled back at him.

After a lengthy conversation with Silver about the glory days of rock n' roll, we reconnected with Dean, Randy, and Phoenix and walked down the street to a nearby Subway to grab a bite to eat. Although it was late and I preferred to be heading back to the RV to crash, I thought some food might perk me up. We ordered sandwiches and sat down to eat at a table by the window. As we ate and chatted about the show, I thought about how far we had come on our musical journey and the enormity of our notoriety hit me like a ton of bricks. Several fans passed by waving at us and we waved back. I suddenly noticed a young lady approaching the window and she was waving at us. I started to wave back and in a flash noticed she had lifted up her blouse and was flashing us! This moment took us all by surprise as I gazed around at the stunned expressions on the faces of our band members. Just as suddenly as she appeared, she soon disappeared from sight.

We all exchanged glances and for a moment nothing was said. Sensing the tension between us, Randy chuckled and broke the silence with some playful humor.

"Hey Phoenix, I think she was trying to get your attention!" Randy teased.

"No man, I think she wanted YOU!"

Randy and Phoenix's lighthearted banter provided welcome comic relief and we laughed at the absurdity of the situation. Continuing our previous band-related conversations, we watched people passing by our window of the world.

Monday, July 6, 2015—Day Off or Off Day?

Despite our best intentions, Gary and I caught only a few hours of sleep and awoke sometime around 8 a.m. Randy and Dean, on the other hand, slept until 11 a.m. and we sat outside the RV waiting for them to awaken from their beauty rest. Getting tired of waiting and feeling pretty hungry, we headed over to Denny's to eat some breakfast. I was feeling run down from an impending cold and felt very low energy despite eating a hearty breakfast. The rigors of constant touring and getting very little sleep were taking its toll.

By the time we got back to the RV, Dean and Randy were awake and ready to hit the road. We started the long five-hour journey to our next gig in Arcata, not knowing what adventures lay ahead. Dean used his laptop to gather information on various campgrounds along the way. He picked one near Clear Lake and since he was the designated navigator, we thought he would also be making a reservation. But when we got there we were in for quite the surprise. We stopped in a local supermarket for supper fixings of pizza, burgers and buns and even picked up a few breakfast sandwiches for the next morning. Picking the perfect camping spot near the outhouse of course, we began settling in for the night. We were about an hour or so drive away from Arcata and enjoyed the scenic vistas of the surrounding mountains and lake. Gary had been in contact with Zach and let him know our whereabouts. They soon joined us, and the guys' spirits were all high. Famished from the four-hour drive to get to the campground, we started looking around for hookups for the gnatmobile to start preparing our food. To our dismay, we discovered that in a National Forest campground there are none to be found.

So, there we were without a working generator, no refrigeration, running water or microwave. Luckily the stove still worked! Sitting outside the RV and munching on charbroiled pizza that tasted more like burnt cardboard, we discussed our situation. With our dwindling finances, my being sick, and facing another two-hour drive to reach Arcata, we reluctantly decided to head for home the next day rather than play the last gig. The decision was a difficult one as a few band members still wanted to play Arcata regardless. I suggested that the guys could still play and I would rest, yet that idea fell on deaf ears. This situation wrought yet another round of resentment and uneasiness amongst the band.

Shortly thereafter, the JOY boys brought a gallon of Mad Dog 20/20 and saved the day. We sat around a blazing bonfire, they guys passing the gallon around, having a great time chatting about music, gigs yet to play in Arcata and laughing their asses off. Feeling so weak I could hardly stand from shingles pain and fatigue, I retired early to the RV telling the group they would have to play Arcata without me. Wearily glancing around the circle one last time, I saw the disappointed expressions on the guys' faces, yet felt I didn't have the strength to utter one more word. Zach followed me back to the RV, gave me a hug and tried a last attempt to talk me back into playing Arcata.

"If it's a money thing, I could make it up to you in merch," he offered intending to sell our t-shirts with theirs, giving us a cut of the sales.

"It's not that, Zach. I'm not feeling up to playing another gig," I replied laying it on the line.

"No worries," he smiled and hugged me. Thanking him and mumbling one last apology, I hurried into the RV and began searching for bottles of echinacea and pain relief meds in my backpack.

Gary came into the RV after a time in the midst of my futile attempts to find some bottles of homeopathic tinctures I used to relieve shingles relentless jolts, jabs and electric shocks of neuralgic rib and breastbone agony.

"What are you looking for?" he asked impatiently.

"I can't find the tinctures." After searching our bags and still coming up empty handed, we both became frustrated and didn't speak for a while. Gary finally broke the silence.

"So, you're not wanting to play Arcata?" he asked incredulously.

"Gary, I'm feeling like shit and don't want to argue!"

"We can't just back out! We've come this far, so you might as well just buck up and play this last gig tomorrow with us and then we can go back home and you can rest."

"You guys can play without me, and besides, Zach told me they're only expecting a small crowd anyway!"

"We're not playing without you! If you're not playing then the band won't play and the damn gig is cancelled!" Gary got up from the floor, slammed the door behind him, and stormed out into the dark, chilly night, wearing only a light fleece jacket and jeans.

Running out the door after him and seeing Randy and Phoenix sitting outside the RV watching the whole event going down, I yelled, "Gary, please wait. Damn it, don't do this!!!"

Realizing my attempts to stop him were futile, I dejectedly went back inside the RV, sat down at the table holding my head in utter despair, tears falling furiously from my eyes and dripping down my arms. I sat there for the longest time thinking he would be back soon after a short jaunt around the campground to cool off, as was his usual habit after we had an argument. Minutes turned to hours and he still had not returned. Looking at my watch, I noticed it was well after midnight and started getting worried.

Sometime around 1 a.m., the door opened and in walked Dean. With a quick glance in my direction, he wordlessly headed to the back bedroom to hit the sack.

"Did you see Gary anywhere out there?" I asked him. Continuing towards his bed, he casually shot back over his shoulder, "No."

Wearily walking outside the RV, I saw Randy and Phoenix still sitting there talking, casting furtive glances in my direction and suddenly becoming silent as I approached them. "Any sight of Gary?" I queried hoping perhaps they had seen him skulking around in the dark somewhere.

"No, we haven't," replied Phoenix as they both stared bewilderedly back at me. Sensing my despair, Phoenix tried his best to offer words of encouragement. "I'm sure he'll be back sometime soon." He wasn't.

Lying wide awake in bed for hours worrying about Gary, I wondered where he could be. I knew camping out in the wilderness was not his forte, and was concerned for his safety. I wished I could be with him and felt bad that we had such a stupid argument that lead to this pointless turn of events. Walking a short distance outside the RV, I met up with Phoenix and had a long conversation with him. He tried his best to comfort me, yet I was inconsolable.

After a sleepless night, I got out of bed the next morning, got dressed and headed outside to search for Gary on my own. Little did I know that Dean and Phoenix were also out looking for him in the area where the JOY boys were camped a short distance across the lake from our campsite. Randy was still sleeping in the RV. Taking a walk on a scenic little path that circled the lake, I missed Gary tremendously and wished he were walking next to me. My tired eyes darted back and forth, searching for my wayward, wayfaring husband. I bumped into Dean and Phoenix somewhere in the woods between our camps hoping to hear good news or see Gary strolling along with them, yet it was not in the cards. My heart sank as I stumbled back to the RV, finding Randy sitting in the driver's seat staring out through the windshield. Casting a sidelong glance at me and seeing my somber, tearful expression, he suggested calling the Ranger's station. Feeling the lowest I can ever recall, I slumped down in the seat next to him once again holding my head in my hands.

Gazing up to glance out the window for the umpteenth time, I noticed in my peripheral vision a bedraggled, tall, thin figure slowly making his way towards the RV. I practically flew out the door to meet him, flinging my arms around his neck and bear-hugging him. After sobbing uncontrollably for a long time, I peeled myself away, brushed back the tears with my sleeve and gazed intently at him. "Where in hell were you?"

He told me he had wandered around from bathroom to bathroom trying to keep warm and catch a few zzz's in the shower rooms occupied by myriads of spiders.

Staring at him standing before me, disheveled and in disarray, I felt relieved beyond description to see him safe and sound. Once again, I flung my arms around him and we embraced.

"I'm sorry," I mumbled, my head buried in his twig and leaf strewn fleece jacket.

"Yeah, me too."

Arm in arm we headed back to the RV. "Hey, man, glad you're OK!" said Randy as Gary walked in the door. They greeted each other, embracing and shaking hands. Dean and Phoenix followed in behind Gary and after more hugs and high fivers, we were soon ready to hit the road. After a quick stop for a breakfast snack, we were once again on our way, driving the next two days on the long road from California through Nevada, Utah, and Wyoming, to the Rocky Mountains we called home. It's said that we develop strength through adversity. But I could tell that the slender threads that bound us together were slowly beginning to unravel.

CHAPTER 33

BAND BLUES AND MOVING ON (2015-2016)

"New beginnings are often disguised as painful endings."
— Lao Tzu

Randy dropped us off at Dean's house in Conifer, Colorado, after our short California tour then bolted off in his camouflage truck as though it were on fire, shouting words barely audible, leaving a trail of flying dirt and gravel in its wake. "See you guys… gotta get to school…" He was finishing the last semester of his Master's Degree in Car Mechanics and neither hell nor high water would stop him! Phoenix was right behind him driving off on two wheels heading for home. Dean waved to us and began sauntering down the driveway to his home.

A light misty twilight rain was falling as we boarded my truck. Although not looking forward to another long drive to get to Broomfield, we anticipated finally getting home and resting. The ignition had other ideas and wouldn't even make a sound as I turned the key.

"Damn… it won't start!"

"It's dead?" Gary and I exchanged disappointed glances.

"Deader than a doornail," I sighed pounding my fist in exasperation on the steering wheel. Gary ran out of the truck after Dean who had already gone inside his house. About an hour or so later, a tow truck plowed up the gravel road to our stranded truck, then towed it and two bedraggled passengers back to Broomfield. Motor Club to the rescue! We finally arrived home late with just enough time to eat a few bites of dinner and drag ourselves off to bed.

There were other signs of discontentment among band members along the way that we should have heeded, yet were not aware of at the time. I developed a whopping sinus infection and started taking antibiotics and wondered if I would ever be well again. The rigors of being in constant motion were taking their toll, and we still had to finish recording our second album that would extend into September.

Prior to our tour, the album had gone through final mixing and mastering. After it was finished in mid-September, we reconnected with Todd Severin from Ripple and sent him a CD to listen to. We were anxious to have him hear our finally finished labor of love and extend us an offer to release this album. All communication with him during this time period was extremely positive, reinforcing how he couldn't wait to hear it after a year in the making, and telling us to take our time to perfect our craft.

His reply came one day hitting us like a ton of bricks. He informed us that despite the music being good, he couldn't take on yet another project, and suggested we produce it ourselves. Of course, we were shell-shocked and extremely disappointed to be turned down by someone whom we thought was one of the biggest supporters of our music. After some discussion of the situation, we decided not to let one label's rejection deter us from sharing a remarkable achievement with the world. As the saying goes, when one door closes, another one opens, and we were soon to discover a number of surprises right around the corner.

Prior to joining Medusa, Randy was in another band called Fear Of God, and had a manager that he kept in contact with. As we were looking for a manager at the time, Randy had recommended we make contact with him as a possible candidate. We set up a meeting time and date, had all band members present at our house where we rehearsed and anxiously awaited his call. The call never came and we were fairly disappointed, yet rescheduled the call with him for later in the week. Once again we sat around waiting for his call. After a few hours, just as we were about to give up on him, the phone finally rang. Apparently, he was at a tribute band concert and that took precedence over calling us. We all took turns talking with him through teleconference and discussed our situation with him. He gave little feedback regarding being our manager but instead made promises of numerous gigs that he would get us to play that never came to fruition.

During a third conversation our would-be manager mentioned the possibility of his booking us for both east and west Coast tours. Dean was hesitant and told him that we would have to discuss this matter before committing to the tours. Although I wasn't entirely certain as to his reasoning, I assumed his reluctance to do more touring was due to increasing demands from his job.

Prior to the manager's last phone call, Dean had informed us that he had accepted a position in upper management and was enthusiastically looking forward to stepping into that role. He was also playing cover music with another band

and wanted to spend more time with his wife, Leonore, who was recovering from surgery. Randy also had many commitments, playing with another band, working on his master's degree, and being a single father caring for his young son, Brandon. Phoenix was working at a hot dog stand and playing in the same band as Randy. Despite the fact that Gary and I knew full well that the band members had other side projects, we still hoped that we could somehow work out our differences. When we played together, it was with an unrivaled passion and magnitude that defies description! The cohesiveness of any group effort is only as strong as its members' commitment to its combined purpose. As with our band, when idle banter takes the place of honest dialog, especially on crucial issues, it eventually disrupts the very glue that binds them together.

The next few gigs we played during this time gave Gary and me glimpses of our bands' eventual demise. Despite overcast, cloudy skies at a barbecue gig in a small mountain town, we were smoking hot that night. There was a small crowd in attendance, but they were getting into our music. None of us knew about a noise ordinance that literally pulled the plug on us halfway through our set. Around 8 p.m. the sound guy jumped on stage waving his arms and yelling to us to "turn it down!" Shortly after following his orders, all we could hear was dead silence and jeers of the crowd also not understanding why the music had come to a screeching halt. There we stood dumbfounded and without any sound on stage wondering what had happened.

Wordlessly we tore down our gear and packed it all back into our vehicles. We found out only after the fact about the noise ordinance. The sound guy told us that neighbors of the small mountain community were complaining about the music being too loud. Other Country bands playing before us were even louder, yet they got to play their full set. Dejectedly, we drove away trying to put the gig and the night behind us, yet bad memories lingered.

On September 24, 2015, we had an interview on Radio 1190AM set up by Doug Gaddy, and perhaps this was the gig that sealed the band's fate. The station was located on the campus of University of Boulder, or more commonly known as CU. In addition to running his record store, Doug had his own radio show on 1190 a few nights a week. Prior to the interview, Gary and I stopped by the record store and met with James Calvet, an employee of Doug's and fellow DJ who would be interviewing all band members on his show. The interview would take place after we played a 20 minute set, and we told Randy, Phoenix, and Dean about it.

We played with the same heart pounding intensity of previous shows and really rocked the house. There were even several staff members and friends of ours including Doug and Henry Moffly, a fan, CU student and editor of a local publication called Freelance, standing around the room digging our music.

After the show, James, Doug, and fans showered us with accolades about our music and by the time we tore down our equipment and loaded it in our vehicles it was time for the interview. In a weird turn of events, James told us we had somehow missed his show, yet Doug was waiting to interview us. Gary and I tried rounding up Randy, Phoenix, and Dean, yet they told us they were planning on heading home. I reminded them about the interview, yet they said they had other plans. I thought that was strange at the time, as they knew prior to the gig about the interview. "We'll be listening to you, so break a leg," Randy told us as he and Phoenix were rushing out the door as per their usual routine post gig. Dean had already left not really saying much to anyone. Puzzled about the band's mass exit, Gary and I followed Doug down the hall to do the interview.

With headphones on, Doug soon began firing questions at us.

"So, we're here in the studio today with the original members of Medusa 1975, Gary and Donna Brown, and you'll be hearing more of their music. Can you tell us a bit of history about how the band got started?"

For the next few minutes, Gary regaled Doug and listeners about the band's formation in the early '70s and gave a bit of background on the two remaining original members, Pete and Lee. "Pete was our singer, Lee was our drummer, and you could not have found any better musicians than them at that point of time. Kim was also an excellent bass player, yet unfortunately had a heart attack and passed away some years ago. We got together in my garage…" and then suddenly Doug was off on a different topic.

"How did you manage to find the other guys for the current band?"

"It started with Arlo and then we got Kam, our youngest member at the time, and then we found Dean, and…" As Gary began introducing the current band members, Doug once again steered the conversation in a different direction in attempt to get as much information as he could in a relatively short time allotted for the interview. He asked for our descriptions of the songs on *First Step Beyond*, to introduce the songs he wanted to then play for his listeners. I was able to get in a few words about the songs I wrote, "Black Wizard" and melody for "Temptress," but Gary dominated much of the conversation.

The interview progressed in this fashion for half an hour, but there was much more we didn't get the opportunity to mention. Most importantly, we wanted to give recognition to Randy, Dean, and Phoenix for their significant roles in re-forming the band and helping us create our second album, yet time went by so fast and the interviewer's questions led us away from that. Suddenly, the interview was over. Thanking Doug, we then headed out for a bite to eat unaware of the repercussions that awaited us.

Gary's cell rang with its familiar southern twang ring tone, "answer the phone or I'm kicking your ass…" interrupting our meal. It was Randy calling to kick our asses. "So, we're just the other guys huh? That's all we are to you?" his rage audible through the phone.

"What do you mean?" Gary tried to explain and apologize for not getting a chance to mention their names during the interview, yet Randy wasn't having it. The final nail was already pounded into the coffin, sealing Medusa's fate and setting into motion the series of events that would lead to the band's breakup.

After their brief, futile conversation, Gary wearily put down his cell on the table. We stared at each for a few moments, in shock and disbelief that an unintentional omission would cause such an angry backlash from Randy. Not since the Wake and Bake Festival debacle did we ever hear Randy so angry. Unable to salvage the rest of our meal, we left the restaurant feeling confused and upset about the negative turn of events of that evening. After arriving back home, Gary called Randy again offering apologies for the misunderstanding. We still thought reconciliation was possible.

That same evening we received an email from Dean and reading it confirmed the worst. "Medusa team, I'm done…" without further discussion, cut and dry, to the point, end of story. I knew it was just a matter of time, yet can honestly say I didn't think it would end so quickly. Even the best musicians disagree about one thing or another, and some are able to resolve their differences while others feel the best way to settle disagreements is to go their separate ways. Unfortunately, our band members chose the latter.

Thinking back to when Dean first joined the band, I recalled a conversation we had. After his audition, when complimenting his style of drumming and asking about his future musical plans, he smiled, declaring he was just trying to "keep his chops up." Right then, it was apparent to me that his job came first and it would be a matter of time before he would be leaving.

Dean's timing was impeccable. We had just finished recording and mastering our second album and had spent a considerable amount of time in the recording studio listening again and again to the recordings and fine tuning its sound with Brandon our engineer. There were perhaps other mistakes we made, like deciding that wind sound effects should go into the final mixes when Dean thought there should be sounds of fire instead. On the other side of the coin, he was adamant about wanting his drums to be as close to perfection as possible and put in hours of extra time working with Brandon to achieve that goal. In that regard, mission accomplished! Listening to the final mastered mixes, we knew another masterpiece was created, yet the accomplishment was bitter sweet as we had lost our drummer in the process with other losses soon to follow.

Morale was at an all-time low amongst the remaining band members since

Dean's hasty exit. Try as we may, we were still unable to find another drummer. During this time, we received a few surprises to lift our flagging spirits. The first came in the form of a picture that was given to Gary as he wandered into his favorite hot dog stand in Boulder one cold November day. We were searching for ideas for a design or photo to place on our album cover and had decided on one photo of a headless woman warrior with a spirit rising from her torso drawn by Richard Luong, an artist from Austin, Texas. Gary had already paid Richard for the use of this photo for what was supposed to be our album cover, when he was handed a pencil drawing by John, one of the counter workers at Mustard's Last Stand that cold and dreary day in November.

Tommy Molecule, a homeless man, asked John to give the picture of his artwork to Gary for consideration for our cover art. I was sitting in our truck waiting for Gary to get his dog and join our picnic in the truck, our usual weekend routine. When he returned to the truck, he showed me the picture of a woman's face that resembled the mythological creature known as Medusa with snakes for her hair. The picture was quite a work of art and we instantly knew this picture was destined to be the cover of our new album.

John also gave Gary Tommy's phone number and Gary called him almost immediately. As fate would have it, Tommy was in the Boulder library, right next door to where our truck was parked! We met him at Mustard's and talked for a few hours while viewing his artwork. He told us he was also working on some artwork for The Syn, a band popular in the '60s whose members eventually formed the world renowned band Yes. He previously created the artwork for their first and second albums, Rosfest and Trustworks. We were so impressed with his considerable artistic talent despite his being legally blind in one eye and having a cataract in the other. Discovering he was homeless and in need of a place to stay to continue creating his artwork, we invited him to use our computer in the basement of our house. He also stayed overnight several times to complete the cover artwork and have a warm place to stay other than a shelter during the winter. This whole process was indeed labor intensive for Tommy, traveling between the library, Fedex, and our house throughout the course of several months. The process began as a business relationship, and developed into an enduring friendship.

We received another surprise in the form of an invitation to do a show at Summit Music Hall from Jason Chavez of Soda Jerk Presents, a promoter booking shows at this and other popular venues in downtown Denver. After several unsuccessful attempts to connect with Jason, I was finally able to establish a rapport with him and gain his interest in booking us for a few shows at Summit, a large and popular venue for both local and nationally known musicians.

Around this same time, a band from Pittsburgh, Carousel, invited us to play a show with them when they planned to come to Denver in December. When we learned they were in contact with JOY, we promptly agreed. They needed a venue to play in Denver and asked if we could find a place. After talking with Jason about booking a show at Summit with Carousel, he asked me for a contact name and number as he wanted to connect with them and said he would call me back. Later that same day, Jason called to confirm December 15th as the date he booked for our show. He said we would be playing with Cloud Catcher and Space In Time who would be the headliners as they had the biggest fan following. We were excited to play this show and knew the show would be killer! Dean had even agreed to play this gig with us for one last hurrah, yet without any offers for a re-placement drummer, we knew the band was done. During this time, Randy was also telling Gary that he was considering moving out of state for a better job offer.

As the date got closer, we looked forward to meeting the band members of Carousel, yet unfortunately, Mother Nature and the winds of fate intervened blowing a huge snowstorm in Denver's direction. Jason called to inform us the show was cancelled. We later heard from Carousel that they were stranded in Wyoming due to all the snow and wouldn't have been able to make it anyway. We were bummed that we would never get to meet them and that the show was cancelled. Nonetheless, a consolation prize was right around the corner.

A few days after the cancelled show, Jason called to book another show on January 16th at Summit and our spirits were lifted once again. Dean said he was on board, yet we knew this would be our very last show. We were booked with several other bands—Yawning, Mammyth, and Indigenous Robot—with whom we had a chance encounter a few months prior in Boulder.

Gary and I went to Bart's Record Shack to appease Gary's insatiable appetite for new vinyl and CD's to purchase and it just so happened that Indigenous was doing an impromptu concert outside the store that day. We decided to check out the show and were pleasantly surprised by their music. Their style was a combi-nation of folk and rock, and the band members reminded us of hippies from back in the '60s, wearing bell-bottoms and sporting long hair and beards, except for a female keyboard player. We sat through their whole show, presented from their touring vehicle which bore a striking resemblance to a VW microbus parked out-side the store. We had a lengthy conversation with the members afterwards, de-veloping a great rapport and receiving an invitation to play with them in the near future. When Jason fortuitously asked if we knew other bands interested in play-ing the January show, they immediately came to mind.

Shortly after confirming this show with Jason, we received a very curious email from a far off place. Svart Records, a Finnish label founded in 2009 by Jarkko

Pietarinen and Tomi Pulkki, is a company specializing in re-releasing underground music in both vinyl and CD formats. The email was sent from Jarkko, the "chief executioner" as he called himself, or rather head honcho of Svart, stating his "possible interest" in releasing our new album. This news came as a total surprise and was hard to believe: We were being handed an offer we couldn't refuse from a record label we had never heard of! Having previously sent promo packages containing band photos, bios and music reviews of First Step Beyond to several labels without response, we excitedly sent him demos of our music and awaited his reply. He was definitely interested and contacted us within a matter of weeks after his initial email. We corresponded for months thereafter, discussing everything from format to album cover design. He realized our music was hot and took his time in preparing the entire package to appear and sound as pleasing to the eye as to the ear.

In the interim, we played our last gig in the Moon Room at Summit Music Hall. We had asked a friend of ours, Basil Emmanuel, who works at Absolute Vinyl, a popular record store in Boulder, to be our roadie and it felt good to have help carrying all our heavy equipment into the venue. Doug and Annie Gaddy, the owners of Absolute Vinyl and devout fans of our music, played and sold *First Step Beyond* at their store almost immediately after its release. In the midst of weekly visits to Absolute and long-winded conversations with them, we gained their friendship as well.

Medusa took the stage last and despite any previous bad blood amongst band members, played and sounded as tight as ever. The audience was small, yet enthusiastic and gave us a warm reception during and after our set. Kalee, a photographer and friend, was also at the gig and took pictures of the band during the show to use as marketing tools for upcoming gigs and press kits. Kalee who had never previously heard our music became an instant fan, showering us with praise and great action shots from the show.

Between the lows of Dean's exit and the highs of playing the last show at Summit, Gary and I felt like we were on an emotional roller coaster ride without an end in sight. One month after Summit, another crippling blow to the band was dealt, this time by Randy. He informed Gary in a phone call that he was accepting an offer by his company for a better paying job in Pennsylvania. On one hand, we understood his need to pursue a better salary to support himself and his teenage son. And, on the other hand, we knew his move would seal the band's fate and finalize the breakup. Imagine our shock and grief at the realization of the band's end after all the work and money we put into reforming, touring, and recording a new album!

The final blow came when Phoenix came over to pick up some of his equipment from our basement and the conversation with him was short and strained. After leaving and wishing us good luck, we never saw him again. Gary made several calls to Phoenix in attempt to keep in touch and converse with him, yet we never heard back.

In the months following the band's breakup, Gary and I fell into a deep depression. Band members had disappeared following their own aspirations, leaving us to pick up the pieces and try to make sense of what had gone down.

CHAPTER 34

DOMINO EFFECT (2016-2017)

"Life is a series of natural and spontaneous changes. Don't resist them-that only creates sorrow. Let reality be reality. Let things flow naturally forward in whatever way they like.
— Lao Tzu

There are times in your life when you feel stuck in a rut and you know you are, and you either do nothing or something about it. Sometimes making a change in the status quo is much like navigating stormy seas in a rowboat and trying to find the energy to proceed forward seems overwhelming. Such was our situation. With every attempt we made to find new band members thwarted, Gary and I became more frustrated with the Denver music scene. Our jobs were increasingly irritating, friends seemed to be more unavailable, and the once familiar life we thought we knew was suddenly unfamiliar. We had red lights flashing all around us signaling that changes were imminent, yet we pretended not to notice them.

Gary came home from work one day in October 2016 slamming the door behind him. It had been a very frustrating day for me as well, yet I managed to switch gears when he came in the door.

"What's up?" I asked.

"Well, I turned in my notice to Dave today," he replied in his usual matter-of-fact tone of voice. Gary had been working at Frederick Printing for 12 years and every time the topic of changing jobs came up in our conversations, he would counter with, … "There are no other printing jobs available," and that would be the end of our conversation about jobs. Whenever I would suggest he try a different type of work, he would get angry and resistant.

"You know I don't know how to do anything else!" End of topic.

"You really turned in your notice?" I stared at him in disbelief that Mr. Work-steady-as-a-rock was now crumbling right in front of me. Here was a man who gave his company twelve years of reliability, efficiency and dedication despite minimal pay increases and a ten percent decrease. Working as a nurse for many years, I knew a thing or two about burnout and Gary was now facing his own.

"Well, sort of…" he hesitated as if not sure how to proceed. "When I gave him my notice, he didn't accept it and told me to get back to work."

"Did you stick to your guns?" I already knew how it ended before he said another word. He solemnly shook his head.

"Well, you know me. I went back to work." Sensing my growing frustration, he followed up with, "I let Dave talk me into staying just until the end of the year." I chuckled to myself wondering if he would be able to tolerate another two months there, and decided to take a wait and see approach.

"OK, so let me know when that day comes so I can quit my job too." Both of us wanted to stop working, but we didn't quite know how to stop doing, much less give ourselves permission to retire.

Near the end of the year, I asked Gary if he was ready to retire yet.

"Well, Dave told me if I stick it out until my birthday in April, it would give Frederick time to find someone to replace me and allow me to collect more money in my paycheck before I take an early retirement." It sounded good in theory, yet I was ready to quit working years before, being a few years older than him. We had talked extensively about selling the house and moving away from Colorado, but we weren't sure if we wanted to buy another house or an RV. The previous summer, Gary had even started the process of remodeling the house by asking one of his co-workers, Jerry, a painter and handyman to do some work on the front porch. We had been preparing and looking forward to this change in our lives for the past few years. Inside I was a bundle of nerves about making the transition. The endless questions churned around and around in my mind, *What will I do when I retire?" Where will we live? Should we buy an RV? What if we don't like living in an RV? Will we have enough money to retire?* I'm sure Gary was plagued by these same questions perhaps even more so than I was. He wasn't one to jump from one job to another as I did throughout my entire working career. He had longevity in the companies he worked for, staying anywhere from six to twelve years. Despite making a meager salary, it was a steady income nonetheless. Now he was calculating and comparing pros and cons of collecting early Social Security.

Never in my wildest dreams did I ever think that selling a house would be so expensive or so demanding of time and energy. It was even more difficult since we were working, remodeling and trying to sell our house at the same time. Despite Gary's best efforts to leave his job, his last day at work wasn't until June 2.

I left my nursing contract job of assessing clients for long -term care insurance at Long Term Solutions on May 29th, a week before Gary. It didn't take long for the realization to set in that I really had nowhere to go, no more clients to put on the calendar, no more clients to see, no more redundant paperwork to do, no one to impress, and no one to answer to except myself. This realization was both freeing and frightening! I put my nervous energy once reserved for work into the tedious and time consuming process of packing, sorting, giving and throwing away my worldly possessions. This process was far easier when I finally quit working and had the time it took to prepare and put the house up for sale. I traded one job for another.

Putting the house on the market was the easy part. Leaving a house where I had spent 26 years of my life was another story. After months of replacing all the old carpeting, getting a new roof, adding new kitchen tiles, and remodeling the entire basement, the bathroom, and the front porch, we looked at the place with new eyes and almost wished we could stay. Our realtor, Steve, wanted to put the house on the market in April 2017, yet we couldn't meet that deadline. The summer was fast approaching and still the endless repairs continued. We eventually sold the house on June 15th, after only two days on the market and without having fixed up the front lawn. (We ran out of time and energy.) Finally empty in July after radon testing and mitigation, chimney sweeping and inspections, our house, built in 1974, looked almost brand new.

Amidst the chaos of moving, I was dealing with a bureaucratic health care system that rewarded me for turning 65 by taking away medications that balanced my hormones and helped me deal with tinnitus. In researching the reason for this new protocol, I discovered some guidelines for "potentially inappropriate medications" (aka: Beers Criteria)(27.), were now being enforced by insurance companies and endorsed by the American Geriatrics Society. Originally published in 1991 by Mark Beers, MD, with the intent of informing the medical profession of the inherent dangers of these medications, especially for the elderly population, it seems to me these guidelines are causing more harm than good by taking away medication they depend on to survive. This list includes every medication you can imagine from antihistamines, anti-seizure medication, estrogen, benzodiazepines such as Xanax®, to heart medication and even sliding scale insulin. Although this list has had several revisions, the most recent in 2015, it clearly doesn't address the special needs and extenuating circumstances of the population it claims to save from serious consequences! In several articles I read written about the Beers List, they all end with similar commentary. One pharmacist writes, "The criteria should not serve as a substitute for professional judgment nor should it dictate prescribing for specific patients. The information presented in the criteria should serve only as a guide, with care tailored to each patient's needs." (28.) A failing health care system forces people to find ways to be resourceful and work around the system, and I managed to do just that in our travels around the country.

Although it seemed like the dark clouds looming overhead would never leave, these obstacles only made us more determined to get through all the bureaucracy and actually start to enjoy our retirement. After the sale of the house, we planned to pick up our trailer and hit the road heading to Buena Vista, Colorado. Like the music we played, our resilience enabled us to face the challenges we encountered however harmonious or dissonant they were.

CHAPTER 35
HIGH EXPECTATIONS (2017)

"Don't blame people for disappointing you. Blame yourself for expecting too much from them."
— Author Unknown

The familiar twangy guitar strains of "Hootchie Cootchie Man" were blaring away on Gary's cell phone signaling an incoming text message. Gary looked up from his phone with a puzzled expression on his face. We were days away from moving out of our house into our trailer, and were planning on heading to Black Canyon of the Gunnison after camping in Buena Vista and Salida. The Canyon brought back fond memories of a past trip to that area of Colorado when one sunny and warm Memorial Day turned quickly to snow and cold the next. The campsite we had back then was a perfect one in every way—spacious, sparsely populated with spectacular vistas of the surrounding rocky canyon shaped by eons of wind and water erosion carved by the Gunnison River.

"Randy just wrote to me. He wants to promote the new album."

"How does he propose to do that?"

"Well, are you ready for this one? He wants us to come out to Pennsylvania to put the band back together again." Our eyes locked in unison.

"OK, so what about our travel plans?" I was set on traveling, yet had no intention of heading east until Randy threw his monkey wrench into the mix. Despite all that had gone down with the band breakup, we still felt a musical pulse coursing through our veins. "What about a bass player and drummer?"

"Well, Randy said he could get John, the drummer of Beyond Fallen, his current band, to play with us. Guess we could give it a try," he shrugged.

"What about a bass player?" I persisted pretending not to be interested in the remote possibility that we could somehow resurrect the band for a third go around.

"Randy said maybe Phoenix might be on board, or we could find another player."

"Do we know that for sure?" Remembering Phoenix's quick exit after picking up his mic when we last saw him, I doubted he would want to play with us again.

"No, not really."

"Where will we stay with our trailer?"

"Probably in Randy's back yard next to his RV." It was insane to me from the beginning, yet somehow it all made perfect sense in that moment. Why not travel across the country to pursue something you love? Svart Records had just released our new album, "Rising From the Ashes," a few months prior, yet we were disappointed to learn that it wasn't a big seller. As is often the case, once a band establishes a particular sound and style, it is pigeonholed into that category and often loses fans when creating a new album. This was our situation as well, and despite feeling dejected, we hoped reuniting with Randy and possibly touring with our new band would spark more interest in the album.

After closing on the house, we loaded what was left of our worldly possessions and musical equipment into our 23-foot-long trailer and Ford F150 truck and hit the road. We first headed to our campground in Buena Vista since it was already booked, and pulled into our site in a torrential rainstorm. As newcomers to RV living, we learned the hard way about backing into tight confined sites and pulling back muscles when releasing stabilizer bars that hold the trailer in place. Hastily setting up in a torrential downpour, we discovered leaks first day out of the gate. What a fiasco! We also learned that, despite being a highly desirable lifestyle for many retirees and others who want to go off the grid, RV's are mass produced, cheaply made, and in many instances, not covered by the companies that built them.

We had to cut our trip short and stay in a motel for three days while the leak in my clothes closet was repaired at the dealership where we bought the trailer. Before we could get reimbursed for our motel stay, the work had to be "authorized" by the dealership. And although the repair work was done, it was not "authorized." So, we didn't really get reimbursed per se. The dealership paid for less than half of the motel stay. Good thing we bought the extended warranty that stated leaks aren't covered. Live and learn.

On the road again, we left Colorado and traveled through five states—Nebraska, Iowa, Illinois, Indiana and Ohio—in less than two weeks to reach East Stroudsburg, Pennsylvania. When finally pulling into East Stroudsburg in mid-

August, we made a wrong turn and ended up on a dead end road that we had to back out of, one of many opportunities for growth and learning! After several attempts, one almost backing into someone's front yard, we managed to learn the fine art of backing up a 23-foot trailer.

Meeting Randy and his son, Brandon, in a Wal-mart parking lot brought back some fond memories. Randy looked the same, but Brandon was much taller than I recalled from just a year and a half prior, and his hair was a darker brown. We followed them to their house in our trailer. This time, Gary had to back into a small space in Randy's back yard. Although he barely missed hitting a tree in the middle of Randy's yard, he kept the truck, trailer and side view mirrors intact. It was strange being in Randy's yard with our trailer, yet we kept reminding ourselves of our goal to put the band together again. We wondered when we could meet Randy's friend, John, who played drums in Beyond Fallen and when we could finally rehearse. Randy finally explained that he and John both worked full time, and John was only available to rehearse on Tuesdays.

Gary and I had a lot of time on our hands and the first week was spent sitting in our trailer or on the front porch waiting for Tuesday to come around. We got to rehearse twice and sounded fairly decent despite not having played with anyone since the band split. Our spirits were lifted when we finally played together. We knew it was only temporary, as work took precedence for Randy and John. Randy also informed us his band was in the process of recording a new album and touring later in the summer. Although John was willing to learn our songs and did his best to match Dean's drum licks, his work schedule was not very flexible and caused him to miss one rehearsal. It became increasingly apparent to Gary and me that we needed more time and commitment from Randy and John than they were able to give.

Bored with sitting around waiting for Randy to come home, we spent time hiking at various state parks in Pennsylvania, New Jersey and Maryland. We also visited historical places such as Gettysburg and sat beneath breathtaking waterfalls. These excursions reaffirmed our passion for traveling and seeing the world while we still can. In that moment we decided to hit the road again. Randy took the news in stride, and after thanking him in friendly conversation, we left him and his back yard far behind.

CHAPTER 36

DOWN ON THE FARM (2017)

"In the end you always go back to the people that were there in the beginning."
— Author unknown

Breaking free from Randy's back yard, the world was our oyster! Inundated with possibilities of places to visit and people to see, we had a difficult time deciding what to see and do when. Anxious to take in the Adirondacks in New York, and return to Austin, Texas, to visit with musician friends we met two years prior at South By Southwest, we knew we couldn't leave without reconnecting with my cousin Becky in her home state of Pennsylvania. After a five-day stay with her and brief tour of the East Coast, we headed west to Austin.

Gary had been communicating with several folks, including Sam Bryant from Crypt Trip, Aryn Jonathan Black, Dusty Brooks, and Deb Dangerfield while still en route to Austin, in hopes of spending time with them. Sam had invited us to jam with Crypt Trip and we were super excited to have musicians to play with!

We no sooner got settled in our campground when Gary received a text message from Aryn inquiring if we had arrived. As fate would have it, we were able to meet with Aryn that very evening at a small bar and grill called Yellow Jacket. It was good seeing and getting to know him better. We shared a mutual admiration and appreciation of our music genres and followed each other's musical excursions across the country with great interest, never realizing we would actually meet someday in person. Engaged in conversation for hours with Aryn and his friend, Ralph, we shared our triumphs and woes throughout our musical careers. The hours flew by and we finally embraced and parted ways.

Over the next several days, we hiked around the hills of Austin, enjoying and exploring a few state parks and waterfalls and meandering along the Pedernales River with our Sheltie companion, Toby.

Reconnecting with Sam at a small club, Barracuda, we finally saw his band, Crypt Trip, play along with another band, White Dog. We really enjoyed both bands and considered them incredibly talented musicians. We also were able to connect with Deb and Dusty from The Lost Well, the venue we played at SXSW. Deb, who rolled out the red carpet for us when we last visited Austin two years prior. This visit was no exception. We enjoyed walking along the lakefront trails with Deb and catching up with her and Dusty at The Well. Spending time with them again, especially reliving old memories of playing at The Well, cheered us tremendously.

Sauntering over to the stage, I lingered there lost in memories of when Medusa had played here two years prior. While I stood inside in front of the stage chatting with Deb, Gary was outside talking with Sam and I thought he was confirming plans for our jam session.

Walking outside The Well, I noticed Gary was hurriedly approaching like he had a secret to tell and was bursting at the seams to spill it!

"Well, we aren't jamming with Sam on Sat. as planned," he declared trying to keep a straight face. My heart sank, yet I felt the tone of his voice belied what his message conveyed.

"Sam just asked us to play a gig with them on Saturday at Swan Dive!" the excitement on his face now apparent.

"No way! I yelled and letting out a fearsome "Yes!" waved my fist wildly above my head. The realization of our purpose for traveling across the country was finally clear, and becoming a reality!

"Where and when are we rehearsing?" I asked.

"Sam said we could stay with him and Crypt Trip on their farm in San Marcos and rehearse tomorrow before the show." At the time, we wondered what adventures awaited us on the vast expanse of open acreage on Sam's farm.

Arriving at the farm, we parked our trailer next to Sam's in a field near a farmhouse where several band members and their girlfriends lived. The appearance and atmosphere of the farm was reminiscent of a hippie commune from the '60s with wind chimes on the front porch, walls of the house covered with posters of music legends such as Hendrix and Elvis, and guitars, amps and drums in practically every room. The ambience was welcoming, homey and super laid back—the antithesis of our modern day society's dictated run-yourself-into-the-ground rat race!

The farm was owned by one of the family's relatives, and the young folks we were about to meet cared for the horses and livestock and maintained the grounds to earn their keep. We sat on the porch meeting and getting acquainted with band members and friends. The "family" consists of members of Crypt Trip, their girlfriends and friends. Sam bassist extraordinaire, accomplished musician, photographer, and one of the most genuine, down-to-earth people you would ever want to meet; Ryan, accomplished guitarist, and vocalist; and Kam, somewhat shy, yet a monster drummer.

Their girlfriends are Nell, Brittany, and Quincy. Nell is very outgoing and down to earth like Sam. Brittany, Ryan's girlfriend, is a teacher, keyboards player of Astral Blue band and all around sweet person. We connected on keyboards with her showing and teaching me about her electric piano. Quincy, Kam's girlfriend, was jovial and full of life, expecting their first baby.

Oscar, talented guitarist of Astral Blue, is very outgoing, always smiling and a great conversationalist. I first saw him run by our trailer door wearing only his one-piece long underwear (aka: "Union suit"), chasing a few horses. Andrea is Oscar's girlfriend and was more reserved and quiet at first, yet another sweetheart. Rex, talented guitarist of Astral Blue and White Dog, is very outgoing and has quite the diverse record collection. Brooke, Rex's girlfriend was a bit quiet and shy until I got to talk with her about hiking in Big Bend National Park where we were traveling next. She was very helpful in recommending several hikes and other attractions in the park. Clay, another accomplished guitarist of White Dog, asked us many questions about our musical career. Clay and Gary got into a great blues jam one night. Steven, probably the youngest of the bunch, is another great guitarist and music historian well beyond his years! Gary and I enjoyed spending time with and getting to know all of these engaging, intelligent, young, "old souls."

After our meet and greet, we got right into rehearsing for our show that evening. Sam requested we play Black Wizard with them and we rehearsed the song perhaps five times before they had it down. During rehearsal, Sam mentioned to Gary the possibility of playing another show at SXSW with Crypt Trip as our back-up band and Gary heartily agreed. When he shared this news with me, we were both super stoked about getting to play this popular festival again!

Traveling an hour to get from San Marcos to downtown Austin and our venue, Swan Dive, we had to park our vehicles in an alley around the corner from the club. A huge Halloween celebration was in progress and throngs of ghouls, goblins, vampires, alien space creatures and even a few Santa's flooded the streets of downtown Austin, creating a parking nightmare! We had to carry all our heavy musical equipment from the alley, making several trips through the crowds to and from the club and repeating the whole tedious process in reverse after the show. Finding places to park our vehicles was also a challenge, forcing us to park by and feed meters several blocks from the club.

When finally inside and settled, we excitedly awaited our turn to take the stage.

We shared the stage with three other bands, Bridge Farmers, the show openers, Wo-Fat, and Duel, the headliners. After Bridge Farmers, ended their thrash metal set, Crypt Trip took the stage. Gary and I heard their live music that evening for the second time and were blown away by their heavy, psych rock sound and the level of incredible musicianship of the band members despite their young twenty-something years.

After playing their set for half an hour, Ryan stepped up to the mic and spoke the words we were nervously anticipating, introducing us to the crowd gathered in the club.

"We have a few special guests in the audience, Gary and Donna Brown from Medusa, and we would like to have them join us onstage." Taking the stage amidst appreciative yells and cheers brought back fond memories. Acknowledging the audience response, we broke into our rendition of Black Wizard learned for the first time by Crypt Trip a matter of hours before. Playing at fever pitch and intensity for a steady 10-to-15 minutes, we hardly noticed the passage of time. As always during a show, I scanned the audience looking for familiar faces and noticed Brittany and Nell standing below intently watching our show.

Rather than listening to what I was playing on keys, I was instead immersed and transfixed on the overall sound of the band. We sounded so tight playing with Crypt Trip despite only five rehearsals! The audience yelled their raucous approval and we were soon tearing down equipment and exiting the stage before the next band was up.

Making my way through the crowd holding two keyboard carrying cases in my hands, I was approached by Brittany and Nell who both showered me with compliments on our show. After chatting with them, a tall, muscular guy came up to me gregariously shaking my hand and greeting me. "You're from Medusa right?" Before I had a chance to respond, he added, "I really dig your guys' music!" Thanking him, we continued our conversation and he introduced himself as the singer in the first band to play, Bridge Farmers. The guitarist from this same band approached me as did several friends of Sam and Ryan. All were offering congratulatory sentiments about our show.

Realizing I hadn't eaten dinner, I walked outside and found Gary talking with some fans in front of Swan Dive. We headed back across the street, and sat together in front of a food stand, munching on huge slices of pizza in the chilly Austin night. Watching all the Halloween festivities and constant stream of costumed characters rushing by our table, we then noticed another character approaching us and discovered it was Sam. After having another lengthy conversation with him, it was well after midnight, and we headed back to the farm to get some sleep. Sam told us he was staying to watch the other bands and wait for his reimbursement from the club owner.

We reached the Farm and parked our vehicle in a fenced in area to keep the horses that surrounded us from nibbling at the truck's fenders for an after-midnight snack. Heading toward our trailer, we soon noticed a few horses slowly following behind us. Somewhat afraid of horses, I stood face to face with one white horse and shivered uncontrollably in the cold, starlit early morning air. Somewhat timidly, I reached out to stroke the horse's snout, and sensing my fear it lowered its head, playfully poking at my jacket pocket searching for food. I tried to look ferocious and chase the horse away, yet it stood its ground, persistently poking and chewing at my pocket. Seeing I was busy with my newly found equine friend, Gary sneaked into the trailer and I eventually joined him. We weren't inside for more than a few seconds when suddenly the trailer began shaking and shimmying back and forth. We both looked at each other in shock and waited to see what would happen next. After another round of violent trailer quakes, Gary rushed outside to deal with the cantankerous horse who was demanding our attention. After a few minutes, he returned informing me that he had shooed the horses away by yelling and waving his hands at them. We slept soundly for what was left of the night, without any further incidence of equine driven earthquakes.

The next morning, Gary told me another animal tale after his walk with our pup, Toby. Walking along the road next to a herd of cows, he noticed the cows stood along the side of the road staring intently at him and Toby as they passed by. Toby paused and pondered the strange creatures pondering him and after a few minutes walked away making it clear he wanted no part of the cows. Hearing Gary's story, I found it interesting that a Sheltie, a herding breed, would cower away from some cows.

We stayed at the farm for three of the most wondrous days of our cross-country adventure thus far. Soon we were bidding Sam and the family a fond farewell. It was difficult leaving them, yet new adventures at Big Bend National Park along the Rio Grande awaited us. We also knew we would be seeing them again in the near future especially if Sam's idea to play SXSW were to become a reality.

A few days after our show at Swan Dive, Gary had sent an email to Dusty informing him about Sam's idea to play SXSW with us in March of 2018. Dusty responded with a hale and hearty "Hell, yeah!" and extended a confirming invitation to play again at The Well. Gary then called Sam and confirmed they were still on board to do the show with us. Things were finally falling into place and we felt like we were back in the musical saddle once more.

CHAPTER 37
BIG BEND AND BEYOND (2017)

"We travel not to escape life, but for life not to escape us."
— **Author unknown**

Leaving Austin and its memorable, magical music scene was difficult, yet we looked forward to new adventures along the road as we made our way southwest to the Texas/Mexico border. We started our travel journey hoping to connect with musicians across the country, yet the more country we traveled through the more our journey took on a different perspective. We decided to visit as many national parks as possible and Gary was especially keen on visiting Big Bend from pictures he saw online. I wondered what the big attraction was about cacti and hot, desert terrain, but I decided to suspend my imagination.

What we found there was nothing like we had expected. Despite extremely hot days, often reaching the mid-nineties, the park offered some great hikes (i.e. The Window, Lost Mine Trail, and Emory Peak) and breathtaking panoramic vistas of mountains, rock and cacti formations. We spent two weeks exploring Big Bend and met some wonderful people at the campground where we stayed.

Wanting to connect with more musical friends on the West Coast, we decided to head towards California. We made several stops along the way in hopes of seeing friends in Las Cruces, New Mexico, and traveled through Arizona towards Las Vegas to visit with Mo and my niece, Emily, for Thanksgiving.

Gary was sending emails back and forth to our old friend, Zach, from JOY, and hoping to reconnect with him we traveled to San Diego where he lives. Zach informed us of his work schedule and we planned our arrival on Sun. December 3rd hoping to see him either that day or the next. Gary sent Zach another email letting him know we had arrived and then didn't hear from him. We spent our time at the Carlsbad beach enjoying the ocean waves lapping on the shore and

watching flocks of seagulls flying their aerial acrobatics above our heads and landing next to us in the sand. We also did a short hike up to the observation tower
on Palomar Mountain, took in the scenery and talked with a volunteer ranger
and wildfire watcher.

It had been several days since in our arrival in sunny California, and still no
word from Zach. We felt quite disappointed, since we had made the trip primarily
to see him. Then just as suddenly as he disappeared, he reappeared and we had a
great time spending a day with him and Kayla, his girlfriend.

Over the two years since our last west coast tour, when Medusa was still together, we kept in contact with several other bands and band members. One day,
I remembered that Donna DiBenedetto, the mother of Tommy, the drummer of
JOY, had extended an invitation to Gary and me to give her a call anytime we were
in the area. I wrote her an email wondering if she would be available, and, surprisingly enough, she wrote back, once again opening up her house to us. Gary also
called Tommy and received an invite to meet up with him the next day at Pannikin,
a small café in Encinitas. We had only seen Tommy during a short visit to Denver
a few years back when he played drums with Sacri Monti, a psychedelic hard rock
band from San Diego, and were looking forward to seeing him again.

Tommy was sitting at a table outside of Pannikin when we arrived. With
dark brown curly hair past his shoulders and tall, thin stature, he is a dead
ringer of Frank Zappa, or perhaps could have been his younger brother. Exchanging hugs and handshakes, we chatted for hours between trips to the
beach and getting a bite to eat. We asked Tommy if he was down to jam and
no sooner said than done. He made a phone call to one of his bands, Color,
which was rehearsing at a recording studio, to let them know we would be
jamming with them. After meeting the Color band members—Brenden, guitarist, and Dominic, bassist—we played for a few hours and had a great session. Later that evening, Tommy informed us they were playing a gig on
Saturday, December 16th, and suggested they learn a few of our songs so that
we could play the gig together. Once again we were super stoked to get another chance to play a live show with more great musicians. They learned the
songs in three additional rehearsals.

In between rehearsals, Donna opened her house to us to jam and we got a
chance to know her better. Donna is a teacher, and all around warm and wonderful person. We sat around immersed in conversation and great food for hours
on end. Although never getting to jam with Donna, we enjoyed spending quality
time with her, as well as with Tommy, his sister, Vanessa, and his girlfriend, Sara,
whom we had met during our previous west coast tour.

On the night of our gig, we followed Brenden, to the club, The Pourhouse in

Oceanside, unloaded our equipment, and set it down near the stage. Feeling hungry, we got seated at a table to eat some dinner. Brenden signaled to one of the waitresses, Macarena (aka: Mac), who greeted us and took our orders. While waiting for our dinners to arrive, we listened to a country band onstage and thought it curious that we would be following a band playing country music. It was interesting to see that the audience was comprised of only a handful of people.

During dinner, we chatted with Brenden and Sara, and a friend of Sara's. Mac came to chat with us on short breaks from her waitress duties and we enjoyed her friendly personality and great service. Noticing our camp hosts, Dawn and Marc, seated at a nearby table, we joined them for more pre-show chatter until the country band ended their set and Color started setting up their equipment. Gary and I headed towards the stage to talk with the band members to find out when we would be playing. Color was going to first play their set first and we would join them onstage mid-set. Monarch, Tommy's other band, would be up last.

As Color took the stage, passionately laying down their hard rock licks, I noticed the number of people in the audience had increased and were digging it. They played a half hour or so, then introduced Gary and me. Setting up our equipment amidst a flutter and flurry of yells and cheers from the audience, we were ready to play! Gazing out into a sea of faces and packed house, I was once again reminded of our show at The Lost Well. Breaking into "Strangulation," the crowd went nuts! They were there for us! After a few seconds, I listened for Brenden's vocals and guitar, yet only heard his vocals. Glancing to my left, I saw him kneeling down onstage, bent over his guitar, feverishly trying to replace a broken string. We played most of the song without his guitar sound and still the audience roared their approval as the song ended.

"Temptress," our next song, also received tremendous applause, the likes of which exceeded that of SXSW and our wildest expectations. "Black Wizard," the last song we played, turned into a 15-minute jam to beat all jams! Towards the middle of the song as Gary finished his guitar solo, Brenden and I traded off on solos, each of us playing with wild abandon. During my solo, I didn't notice Gary at first standing close to me, watching as I played. It was uncustomary for him to glance away from his guitar while playing. But when I felt him lightly touch my arm signaling for me to wind up my solo, I brought my keyboard volume down and turned my head toward him. I observed him pointing to Dominic, motioning for him to solo on bass. Dominic looked puzzled, as this was not what we rehearsed. He took the cue, though, and played some heavy bass runs, prompting the audience to respond with more appreciative yells and cheers. After he finished, the focus shifted to Tommy, who stole the show, pounding away on his drums like a madman in a frenzied blur of cymbals, snares and toms. The audience loved every minute of his madness!

Back into full swing of the song, we jammed it to a momentary dead silence amidst deafening roar of the crowd. Gary suddenly started the familiar lead back into the beginning of the song and we hammered it home. The house now in an uproar, the air was charged with electricity, filled with whoops, screams and thunderous applause.

Standing on stage amid the hoopla, I was barely able to believe the scenario. Glancing around, I saw mirrored on the faces in the audience and my fellow band members expressions of ecstasy and absolute jubilation. With arms locked around each other, we stood onstage acknowledging the crowd and taking in the wild fanfare. The spectacle before me was similar to that of previous shows, yet this one stood out above all others. I fulfilled a lifelong dream of playing music and it was now coming full circle back to its inception. Bowing my head and savoring the moment, I envisioned the baby bird spreading her wings and taking flight.

EPILOGUE

March 16, 2018—Austin, Texas
Sitting on a picnic bench on the front patio of The Lost Well, I was lost in thought. Memories came to mind of just three years prior, hanging out in the same front patio shooting the breeze with Randy and Phoenix, waiting hours for our time to finally hit the stage. That day was a scorcher as we whiled away the time, waiting for Dean to arrive from the airport. Back to present time every now and then, I caught bits and pieces of Gary and Deb catching up on the latest and greatest happenings in their lives. Then I faded out again recalling the events that led up to this moment.

Nearly three months earlier, Gary and I hobbled along the last few miles of our eight-mile hike through Bear Canyon in Tucson, Arizona, with dusk fast approaching. We were admiring an incredibly beautiful orange and peach color sunset in the distance when Gary got a message from Sam. Stopping dead in his tracks staring intently at his phone, Gary pondered the message. A few months prior, Sam had confirmed that Crypt Trip would be the backup band for our 2018 show at SXSW. Although we still had no singer, Sam said he would work on finding us one. But it was the end of December, less than three months before our show. We wondered if we could even pull this show off.

Gary looked up from his phone and turned to me smiling. "Guess who Sam found to be our singer?"

From out of nowhere an image of a tall, gangly guy wearing a stunning Stetson came into my mind, and I excitedly blurted out his name. "Aryn Jonathan Black from Scorpion Child?" Gary nodded.

"NO WAY!!!" Despite being pretty wiped from our long hike, we slapped each other high fivers, and bantered ecstatically about the prospect of collaboration with such talented musicians as Aryn and Crypt Trip. By hike's end, we had our plans all made for when we would travel to Austin and where we would stay. We could hardly contain our excitement and were exuberantly anticipating playing again at The Lost Well. I wondered if we would be playing to a full house as we did back in 2015.

As planned, Gary and I left our campground in Tucson at the end of February to allow sufficient time for rehearsal with Crypt Trip and Aryn. Arriving in Austin, we had several band rehearsals, and learned all seven songs off our premier album, *First Step Beyond*. Aryn was only able to make two rehearsals and I wondered how he would handle reciting all the lyrics. He tried reassuring me, yet was none too convincing.

Suddenly Dusty rushed up to greet us, interrupting my reverie. He welcomed us back to Austin with hugs, smiles and brief conversation before rushing away into the depths of The Well to greet other bands and guests. On the bill for the night were several bands, including Crypt Trip, Voidstrider, Doomstress and Josephus, a Houston-based band who got their start in the late '60s. I especially looked forward to meeting the members of the last two bands, as we were in communication with Alexis, the bass player from Doomstress prior to our show. Alexis also plays bass with Josephus. I learned that Pete and Dave, the original two members of Josephus, were older then Gary and me at 68 and 71, and wondered how they withstood the rigors of the road.

While waiting for our set to start around midnight, I talked with a few fans, the most memorable of whom I will call the Three Amigos: Sebastian, Chris, and Luis. They traveled eight hours from El Paso to Austin, about 580 miles, just to see our show. While they rushed toward us, we recognized them from our previous show in 2015. After chatting with them for a time, Gary left to visit with other friends and fans. The Three Amigos asked me questions about what it was like to see The Beatles, Hendrix, and Led Zeppelin, and our conversation would have extended well into the wee morning hours had I not excused myself to get ready to play our show. Chris exclaimed, "I quit my job for you!" Feeling their excitement and watching their beaming faces took me right back to the adulation I felt when seeing The Beatles.

After watching Crypt Trip's stellar set, I met and chatted with Alexis, thanking her for getting us a radio interview with her DJ friend while we traveled across country heading for Austin. "Can't wait to hear you guys play," she exclaimed. "This should be one hell of a show especially with bands of the same era playing on the same bill!" Before their set, I enjoyed a brief meet and chat with Pete and Dave from Josephus. I also enjoyed hearing the heavy Sabbath-like music of Doomstress before our show and checking out Josephus afterwards.

Then it came, this moment we had anticipated for months. We took the stage and suddenly 45 minutes flew by in a blur of crashing drum cymbals, Hammond organ overtures, ripping guitar riffs, and Aryn's passionate vocals penetrating the small, yet jam-packed dimly lit barroom. Our music spewed forth like red hot molten lava, pouring full force over the audience. Memories were flooding my mind like slide show images in perfect staccato rhythm of the rabid, moshing crowd engulfing the stage, finding Medusa.

ACKNOWLEDGMENTS

So many people were instrumental in the course of writing this book, it is indeed difficult to remember them all. Yet I did my best to acknowledge everyone who came to mind. My deepest apologies and sincere thanks go out to those who aren't listed, for serving their own special purpose throughout this book writing process.

First and foremost, I would like to thank Ma and Dad for introducing me to and influencing my love of the outdoors, running, cross-country skiing, hiking, climbing, art, and especially music.

A huge thanks goes out to all our fans worldwide who believed in our music and made us feel like rock stars.

I would also like to express my sincerest thanks and appreciation to Rob Sevier of Numero Group Records in Chicago, Illinois, for putting us back on the map and having a vision of where to place us in musical history.

Sincerest thanks to Jarkko Pietarinen of Svart Records in Finland for making our second album, Rising From The Ashes, a reality.

Heartfelt thanks goes out to original Medusa band members, Peter Basaraba—vocals, Lee Teuber—drums, Kim Gudaniec—bass, Gary Brown—lead guitar. Together we created and played some of the best original music of that era, carving out our own unique niche in musical history.

Thanks also to Randy Bobzien—vocals and guitar, Dean McCal—drums, Phoenix Johnson—bass, and Kameron Wentworth—guitar for bringing Medusa back to life after nearly forty years.

Thanks also to Dan Schlosser for being in the right place at the right time to retrieve a piece of musical history from a dusty bin of obscurity, dusting it off, and presenting it to the right person for all the world to bear witness to.

I would also like to thank The Beatles for their music that helped me get through some rough times and inspired me to pursue my musical passions and dreams. Thanks especially to Sir Paul McCartney for giving me a taste of my first teenage crush and granting me permission to use one of his quotes in this book. I am an eternal fan.

Thanks also to the following people for granting me permission to use their quotes for this book:

- Bruce Barcott, an American editor, environmental journalist and author of a number of books including, The Measure of a Mountain: Beauty and Terror on Mount Rainier (1997). I read this book and found your experience and background on this beautiful and deadly mountain to be very helpful in preparing for my own climbs on Rainier and Hood.
- Gregg Goldston, founder of The Goldston and Johnson School for Mime Theatre, granted permission to use a quote from Marcel Marceau.
- Christina Rasmussen, Crisis Intervention Counselor and Author
- Steve Maraboli, Keynote Speaker, Life Coach and Best Selling Author of several books
- Craig D. Lounsbrough, M. Div., LPC and Author
- Greg Plitt, Actor, Entrepreneur and Motivational Speaker
- Rawsi Williams, JD, BSN, RN

Thanks to Jan Townsend and Sue Wolcott for accompanying me to many of the best live concerts ever played in Chicago at the Kinetic Playground.

Thanks to Katy Thach, Cindy Davis and Dee Moore, my dearest hut buddy friends, for the gift of her friendship and companionship on numerous back country ski trips, hikes, and outdoor adventures too numerous to recount. A heartfelt thanks especially goes out to Katy, my partner on numerous climbs, hikes and llama treks for taking me under her wings and sharing her climbing and outdoor expertise with me. Another heartfelt thanks to Cindy Davis, who recently lost her battle with ALS, yet during the living years was truly an inspiration and taught me the true meaning of grace under pressure and strength through adversity.

Thanks to Tommy DiBenedetto, drums, Brenden Dellar, guitar, Dominic Denholm, bass, the members of Color and Monarch, for inviting us to play a gig with them in Oceanside, California, and to Sam Bryant, bass, Ryan Lee, guitar, and Kam Martin, drums, the members of Crypt Trip, for their invites to play at Swan Dive and SXSW Fest in Austin, Texas.

Thanks also to the members of JOY, Zachary Oakley, vocals and guitar, Justin Hulson, bass, and Tommy DiBenedetto, drums, the members of JOY, for inviting us to tour with them on our first and third tours through the Midwest and West Coast.

Thanks to Dusty Brooks for inviting us to play at SXSW Fest in 2015 and 2018, and to Deb Dangerfield for putting us up at her house and for putting up with us in general. Also, thanks to Sasha and Marcello, owners of The Lost Well, for believing in and being fans of our music.

Thanks also to Aryn Jonathan Black of Scorpion Child for taking time out of his busy music and filming schedule to add his great vocals to our songs at SXSW in 2018.

Special thanks goes to Barbara Garber for her professional editing expertise in the editing of this book. Your guidance helped me stay on task, challenged me where I needed it, and helped me convey my words with more clarity. Barb Garber has a degree in business and management and is a health writer and editor by trade. Most notably, she was Editor of Tinnitus Today and served as Director of Education and Communication for the American Tinnitus Association for many years. In 2001, Barb (as Barbara Tabachnick Sanders) co-authored Tinnitus: Questions and Answers with her dear mentor Jack Vernon, PhD. She is a wife, mother, sister, auntie, and grandmother to a spectacular granddaughter, and is also a songwriter, jewelry designer, watercolorist, contra dancer, and special friend of mine.

I also would like to acknowledge and thank Donna Fazio DiBenedetto, Bachelor's and Master's Degree in Literature and Writing Studies from California State University, San Marcos, for help with editing this book. She was the first person to read my story and I deeply appreciate her time and honest feedback, and professional guidance on how to make my story more concise and write with clarity.

Thanks also to my mime teachers, especially Gregg Goldston, Nick Johnson, Marcel Marceau, and Tony Montanaro for helping me come into my own as an entertainer.

Thanks to John Fedak, wherever he is, for believing in our music and for bringing Medusa's original band members together from the very beginning in Gary's garage. Also, thanks goes out to Tommy Molecule for all his labor -intensive work, numerous trips to libraries, book stores and Fedex to complete the exquisite artwork for our second album, *Rising From The Ashes*.

I would most of like to thank Gary Brown, my dearest husband, lover, and lifelong musical companion for continually showing me his undying love and support, and for sharing this incredible musical journey we've been on.

A heartfelt thanks to Rick Wamer for all the time devoted to helping me through the publishing process, and the rest of the A3D Impressions' team, Donn Poll and Dina Delaney.

And a special shout out to Crave Coffee Bar in Tucson, as our official meeting place for the countless hours spent there working on the completion of my book.

References

1. Mescaline –Wikepedia
2. Wikipedia – The Free Encyclopedia, The Auditorium Theatre of Roosevelt University
3. Lyndon Johnson's "Great Society" ushistory.org
4. Sources: "Miami and the Siege of Chicago" by Norman Mailer, Facts on File, CQ's Guide to U.S. Elections)
5. http://makemyday.free.fr/whitepanthers.htm
6. http://www.historylearningsite.co.uk
7. www.history.com/this-day-in-history/police-kill-two-members-of-the-black-panther-party 8.www.wbez.org -April 30, 2013, Robert Loerzel
9. https://en.wikipedia.org/wiki/Kilauea
10. www.historynet.com/pearl-harbor
11. www.gohawaii.com/…/leahi-diamondhead
12. & 13. www.history.com/news/ask-history-why-is-a-marathon-26.2-miles
14. www.nyrr.org/about-us/nyrr-hall-of-fame/alberto-salazar
15. Northglenn-Thornton Sentinel Feb. 6, 2013 (newspaper article)
16. https://vimeo.com/goldmime
17. webs.wichita.edu/
18. Tony Montanaro – Wikipedia -The Free Encyclopedia
19. www.mime.info./encyclopedia/marceau.html
20. www.ata.org/undersandingfacts
21. article, Dr. Jack Vernon: A Life in Hearing Research by Joe Rojas-Burke, The Oregonian on Dec. 18, 2010
22. No Mountain Too High: A Triumph Over Breast Cancer (Adventura Books) by Andrea Gabbard, Seal Press, July 2, 1998
23. Business Wire article entitled, Military Veterans Suffer Dramatic Increase in Tinnitus, Other Hearing Damage from Wars in Iraq, Afghanistan
24. www.huts.org – the Official Website of the 10th Mountain Hut Association
25. numerogroup.com – Behind The Numbers & The Grammys and The Numero Group
26. SXSW announces performers for the 2015 Music Festival – axs.com
27. American Geriatrics Society – 2012 Beers Criteria article
28. Maria G. Tanzi, PharmD. Contributing writer, Pharmacy Today

Quotes resources

Paul McCartney's quote: https://www.rollingstone.com/music/music-features/paul-mccartney-looks-back-the-rolling-stone-interview-102797/

Jim Morrison's quote: https://www.goodreads.com/quotes/24149-the-most-important-kind-of- freedom-is-to-be-what

Walter Cronkite's quote:
    https://www.goodreads.com/author/quotes/30807.Walter_Cronkite

Marcel Marceau's quote: https://en.wikiquote.org/wiki/Marcel_Marceau

Donna in Lincoln Park with her
Ovation acoustic Summer of 1971.

Donna and Sam Bryant at the Casbah club San Diego, CA.

The original Medusa pre-Peter
in Lee's basement 1973.

Gary and Donna in Gar's
basement collaborating on
ideas for originals for
Medusa 1973.

Early Promo Pic.

Original band members in Gary's garage 1974.

Medusa 1973 - 1976
Live at The Glen Ellyn Civic Center 1974. (photos by Richard Jajko)

Medusa 1974 group shot left to right Gary, Kim, Lee, Donna and Peter.

Kim   Donna   Donna and Gary

Lee   Peter

Lee, Donna and Gary 2017. (right)

Kim 1973 Lee's Basement.

Jamming with Lee 2017.

Donna, Peter, and Gary meeting Rob Sevier at Numero Group. This was the moment that started it all musically 2013. (photo by Dawnn Basaraba)

Outside Permanent Records in Chicago 2013. (photo by Dawnn Basaraba)

Donna's Outdoor Adventures

Above, Donna taking a break before summiting Mt. Hood. At left, Donna on the summit of Mt. Rainier July 2007 and, at right, Katie and Donna, summit Mt. Hood July 2013.

Katie and Donna on a back country hut ski trip.

Donna and Barb Garber. Ecstatic after successful Hood Climb.

Cousin Becky with Donna on Mt. Wrightson in Southern AZ.

After a successful Rainier summit left to right Jeff, climbing guide, Katie and Donna.

Katie and Donna on Mt. Huron summit, a Colorado 14'er.

Medusa1975

Getting ready to tour with Joy from San Diego February 2015. Left to right: Back row: Magic Spiegel, Tyler Daughn, Thomas DiBenidetto, Dean McCall, Kameron Wentworth. Middle Row: Grady O'Donnell, Justin Hulson, Donna Brown, Randy Bobzien Front Row: Zachary Oakley and Gary Brown

Pictures from the Cobra Lounge In Chicago Feb 7, 2015 Last night of the tour that took us from Denver to Kansas City to St. Louis to Chicago.

(these four photos by Barbara Wagner)

Donna

Gary and Peter

Dean

Gary and Randy

Peter, left, and below with the crowd at the Cobra.

Kameron Wentworth

(top five photos photos by Barbara Wagner)

Gary, Donna, Fred(Medusa's sound and pyrotechnics guy from the '70s) and Peter.

Group shot from all bands that played that night at the Cobra. Dead Feathers(Chicago) Joy(San Diego) and Medusa1975 with guest vocalist Peter Basaraba from Original Medusa.

Crowd at the Well that night. The house was jam packed.

Medusa1975 from the Lost Well in Austin Texas SXSW 2015 with Tasha Murphy co-owner of the Lost Well.

Medusa1975 Farewell show at the Moonroom in Denver Jan. 16, 2016.

Randy   Phoenix   Donna

Gary

Dean

(all photos on this page by Kalee Sorenson)

Medusa1975 with tour bus for the California tour.

Group shot after Amnesia club in SF.

Medusa with Josefus 1969. Left to right: Alexis Hollada, Gary Brown, Dave Mitchell, Donna Brown, Pete Bailey and Aryn Jonathon Black

Medusa band at SXSW 2018. Left to right: Donna Brown keyboards, Gary Brown Lead Guitar, Cameron Martin Drums, Ryan Lee Lead Guitar, Aryn Jonathon Black Vocals and Sam Bryant Bass

Medusa band at the Pourhouse. Thomas DiBenedetto, Dominic Denholm, Brenden Dellar, Gary Brown and Donna Brown

Donna signing an album.

Donna and Thomas DiBenedetto.

Donna at the Pourhouse.

Donna and Gary caught in a gaze.

The Pourhouse Medusa Band left to right: Dominic Denholm Bass, Thomas DiBenedetto Drums, Donna Brown Keyboards, Gary Brown Lead Guitar and Brenden Dellar Rhythm and Lead Guitar and Vocals.
(all photos on this page by Tylor Stewart)

Gregg, Marceau, Nick after onstage
performance with Marcel Marceau.
(photo by Marilyn McKinley)

Nick Johnson, Michael Corrigan owner of the Cove,
Gregg Goldston.

Gregg Goldston and Nick Johnson the two
founding members of the Goldston-Johnson
School for Mimes - 20th Anniversary.
(photo by Marilyn McKinley)

Rick Wamer,
Publisher, and
Donna Brown,
Author - reuniting
after 20 years.

Donna on stage with Marcel Marceau.

About the author

Donna currently lives in Pearce, Arizona, with her husband, Gary, and her faithful Sheltie companion, Toby. They have been traveling around the country in their RV since last summer, after selling their house in Colorado where they lived for 26 years. During their travels, they have played several gigs, the most recent at South By Southwest Music Festival in Austin, TX. Donna and Gary always enjoy jamming with fellow musicians they meet along the road.

Contact Information

Donna F. Brown
1205 East Klassen Court
Pearce, AZ 85625

CPSIA information can be obtained
at www.ICGtesting.com
Printed in the USA
LVHW051227010419
612521LV00004B/170